INSTITUTES

OF

HINDU LAW

OR, THE

ORDINANCES OF MENU,

ACCORDING TO THE

GLOSS OF CULLÚCA

COMPRISING THE

INDIAN SYSTEM OF DUTIES,

RELIGIOUS AND CIVIL

WILLIAM JONES

GYAN

Published by

GYAN

Gyan Publishing House
5, Ansari Road
Daryaganj, New Delhi-110002
Phone: 011-47034999, 9811692060
E-mail: books@gyanbooks.com

Distribution Network
gyanbooks.com
India, USA, Canada, UK, Australia

ISBN: 978-93-6920-386-4 (HB)

First Published, 1794

2nd Impression 2025

Printed at: Gyan Press, Delhi.

INSTITUTES OF HINDU LAW
Translator: WILLIAM JONES

INSTITUTES

OF

HINDU LAW:

OR, THE

ORDINANCES OF MENU,

ACCORDING TO THE

GLOSS OF CULLÚCA.

COMPRISING THE

INDIAN SYSTEM OF DUTIES, RELIGIOUS AND CIVIL.

VERBALLY TRANSLATED FROM THE ORIGINAL SANSCRIT.

WITH A PREFACE,

BY SIR WILLIAM JONES.

CALCUTTA:

PRINTED BY ORDER OF THE GOVERNMENT.

LONDON:

REPRINTED FOR J. SEWELL, CORNHILL; AND J. DEBRETT, PICCADILLY. 1796.

THE PREFACE.

IT is a maxim in the ſcience of legiſlation and government, that *Laws are of no avail without manners*, or, to explain the ſentence more fully, that the beſt intended legiſlative proviſions would have no beneficial effect even at firſt, and none at all in a ſhort courſe of time, unleſs they were congenial to the diſpoſition and habits, to the religious prejudices, and approved immemorial uſages of the people for whom they were enacted; eſpecially if that people univerſally and ſincerely believed, that all their ancient uſages and eſtabliſhed rules of conduct had the ſanction of an actual revelation from heaven: the legiſlature of *Britain* having ſhown, in compliance with this maxim, an intention to leave the natives of theſe *Indian* provinces in poſſeſſion of their own Laws, at leaſt on the titles of *contracts* and *inheritances*, we may humbly preſume, that all future proviſions, for the adminiſtration of juſtice and government in *India*, will be conformable, as far as the natives are affected by them, to the manners and opinions of the natives themſelves; an object which cannot poſſibly be attained, until thoſe manners and opinions can be fully and accurately known. Theſe conſiderations, and a few others more immediately within my province, were my principal motives for wiſhing to know, and have induced me at length to publiſh, that ſyſtem of duties, religious and civil, and of law in all its branches, which the *Hindus* firmly believe to have been promulged in the beginning of time by MENU, ſon or grandſon of BRAHMA', or, in plain language, the firſt of created beings, and not the oldeſt only, but the holieſt of legiſlators; a ſyſtem ſo comprehenſive and ſo minutely exact, that it may be conſidered as the *Inſtitutes* of *Hindu* Law, preparatory to the copious *Digeſt*, which has lately been compiled by *Pandits* of eminent learning, and introductory perhaps to a *Code* which may ſupply the many natural defects in the old juriſprudence of this country, and, without any deviation from its principles, accommodate it juſtly to the improvements of a commercial age.

WE are loſt in an inextricable labyrinth of imaginary aſtronomical cycles, *Yugas*, *Maháyugas*, *Calpas*, and *Menwantaras*, in attempting to calculate the time, when the firſt MENU, according to the *Bráhmens*, governed this world, and became the progenitor of mankind, who from him are called *Mánaváh*; nor can we, ſo clouded are the old hiſtory and chronology of *India* with fables and allegories, aſcertain the preciſe age, when the work, now preſented to the Publick, was actually compoſed; but we are in poſſeſſion of ſome evidence, partly extrinſick and partly internal, that it is really one of the oldest compositions existing. From a text of PARA'SARA discovered by Mr. DAVIS, it appears, that the vernal equinox had gone back from the *tenth* degree of *Bharanì* to the *first* of *Aswinì*, or *twenty-three degrees and twenty minutes*, between the days of that *Indian* philosopher, and the year of our Lord 499, when it coincided with the origin of the *Hindu* ecliptick; so that PARA'SARA probably flourished near the close of the *twelfth* century before CHRIST; now PARA'SARA was the grandson of another sage, named VA'SISHT'HA, who is often mentioned in the laws of MENU, and once as contemporary with the divine BHRĬGU himself; but the character of BHRĬGU, and the whole dramatical arrangement of the book before us, are clearly fictitious and ornamental, with a design, too common among ancient lawgivers, of stamping authority on the work by the introduction of supernatural personages, though VA'SISHT'HA may have lived many generations before the actual writer of it, who names him, indeed, in one or two places as a philosopher in an earlier period. The style, however, and metre of this work (which there is not the smallest reason to think affectedly obsolete) are widely different from the language and metrical rules of CA'LIDA's, who unquestionably wrote before the beginning of our era; and the dialect of MENU is even observed, in many passages, to resemble that of the *Véda*, particularly in a departure from the more modern grammatical forms ; whence it muſt, at firſt view, ſeem very probable, that the laws, now brought to light, were conſiderably older than thoſe of SOLON or even of LYCURGUS, although the promulgation of them, before they were reduced to writing, might have been coeval with the firſt monarchies eſtabliſhed in *Egypt* or *Aſia:* but, having had the ſingular good fortune to procure ancient copies of eleven *Upaniſhads*, with a very perſpicuous comment, I am enabled to fix, with more exactneſs, the probable age of the work before us, and even to limit its higheſt poſſible age by a mode of reaſoning, which may be thought new, but will be found, I perſuade myſelf, ſatisfactory ; if the Publick ſhall, on this occaſion, give me credit for a few very curious facts, which, though capable of ſtrict proof, can at preſent be only aſſerted. The *Sanſcrit* of the three firſt *Védas*, (I need not here ſpeak of the fourth) that of the *Mánava Dherma Sáſtra*, and that of the *Purànas*, differ from each other in pretty exact proportion to the *Latin* of NUMA, from whoſe laws entire ſentences are preſerved, that of APPIUS, which we ſee in the fragments of the Twelve Tables, and that of CICERO, or of LUCRETIUS, where he has not affected an obſolete ſtyle : if the ſeveral changes, therefore, of *Sanſcrit* and *Latin* took place, as we may fairly aſſume, in times very nearly proportional, the *Védas* muſt have been written about 300 years before theſe Inſtitutes, and

about

about 600 before the *Puránas* and *Itihásas*, which, I am fully convinced, were not the productions of VYA'SA; so that, if the son of PARA'SARA committed the traditional *Védas* to writing in the *Sanscrit* of his father's time, the original of this book must have received its present form about 880 years before CHRIST's birth. If the texts, indeed, which VYA'SA collected, had been actually *written* in a much older dialect, by the sages preceding him, we must inquire into the greatest possible age of the *Védas* themselves: now one of the longest and finest *Upanishads* in the second *Véda* contains three lists, in a regular series upwards, of at most *forty-two* pupils and preceptors, who successively received and transmitted (probably by oral tradition) the doctrines contained in that *Upanishad*; and as the old *Indian* priests were students at *fifteen*, and instructors at *twenty-five*, we cannot allow more than *ten* years, on an average, for each interval between the respective traditions; whence, as there are *forty* such intervals, in two of the lists between VYA'SA, who arranged the whole work, and AYA'SYA, who is extolled at the beginning of it, and just as many, in the third list, between the compiler and YA'JNYAWALCYA, who makes the principal figure in it, we find the highest age of the *Y jur Véda* to be 1580 years before the birth of our Saviour, (which would make it older than the five books of MOSES) and that of our *Indian* law tract about

1280

1280 years before the ſame epoch. The former date, however, ſeems the more probable of the two, becauſe the *Hindu* ſages are ſaid to have delivered their knowledge orally, and the very word *Sruta*, which we often ſee uſed for the *Véda* itſelf, means *what was heard*; not to inſiſt that CULLU'CA expreſsly declares the ſenſe of the *Véda* to be conveyed in the *language* of VYA'SA. Whether MENU or MENUS in the nominative and MENO'S in an oblique caſe, was the ſame perſonage with MINOS, let others determine; but he muſt indubitably have been far older than the work, which contains his laws, and though perhaps he was never in *Crete*, yet ſome of his inſtitutions may well have been adopted in that iſland, whence LYCURGUS, a century or two afterwards, may have imported them to *Sparta*.

THERE is certainly a ſtrong reſemblance, though obſcured and faded by time, between our MENU with his divine Bull, whom he names as DHERMA himſelf, or the genius of abſtract juſtice, and the MNEUES of *Egypt* with his companion or ſymbol *Apis*; and, though we ſhould be conſtantly on our guard againſt the deluſion of etymological conjecture, yet we cannot but admit that MINOS and MNEUES, or *Mneuis*, have only *Greek* terminations, but that the crude noun is compoſed of the ſame radical letters both in *Greek* and in *Sanſcrit*. 'That APIS and MNEUIS,' ſays the Analyſt of ancient Mythology, 'were both repreſen-

'tations

'tations of ſome perſonage, appears from the 'teſtimony of LYCOPHRON and his ſcholiaſt; 'and that perſonage was the ſame, who in '*Crete* was ſtyled MINOS, and who was alſo 'repreſented under the emblem of the *Mino-* '*taur:* DIODORUS, who confines him to *Egypt*, 'ſpeaks of him by the title of the bull *Mneuis*, 'as the firſt lawgiver, and ſays, "That he lived "after the age of the gods and heroes, when "a change was made in the manner of life "among men; that he was a man of a moſt "exalted ſoul, and a great promoter of civil "ſociety, which he benefited by his laws; "that thoſe laws were unwritten, and receiv- "ed by him from the chief *Egyptian* deity "HERMES, who conferred them on the world "as a gift of the higheſt importance." He 'was the ſame, adds my learned friend, with 'MENES, whom the *Egyptians* repreſented as 'their firſt king and principal benefactor, who 'firſt ſacrificed to the gods, and brought about 'a great change in diet.' If MINOS, the ſon of JUPITER, whom the *Cretans*, from national vanity, might have made a native of their own iſland, was really the ſame perſon with MENU, the ſon of BRAHMA', we have the good fortune to reſtore, by means of *Indian* literature, the moſt celebrated ſyſtem of heathen juriſprudence, and this work might have been entitled *The Laws of* MINOS; but the paradox is too ſingular to be confidently aſſerted, and the geographical part of the book, with moſt of the

the allusions to natural history, must indubitably have been written after the *Hindu* race had settled to the south of *Himálaya*. We cannot but remark that the word MENU has no relation whatever to the *Moon*; and that it was the *seventh*, not the *first* of that name, whom the *Bráhmens* believe to have been preserved in an ark from the general deluge: him they call the *Child of the Sun*, to distinguish him from our legislator; but they assign to his brother YAMA *the office* (which the *Greeks* were pleased to confer on MINOS) *of Judge in the shades below*.

THE name of MENU is clearly derived (like *menes*, *mens*, and *mind*) from the root *men* to *understand*; and it signifies, as all the *Pandits* agree, *intelligent*, particularly in the doctrines of the *Véda*, which the composer of our *Dherma Sástra* must have studied very diligently; since great numbers of its texts, changed only in a few syllables for the sake of the measure, are interspersed through the work, and cited at length in the commentaries: the Publick may, therefore, assure themselves, that they now possess a considerable part of the *Hindu* scripture, without the dullness of its profane ritual or much of its mystical jargon. DA'RA SHUCU'H was persuaded, and not without sound reason, that the first MENU of the *Bráhmens* could be no other person than the progenitor of mankind, to whom *Jews*, *Christians*, and *Muselmáns*, unite in giving the name of ADAM; but, who-

whoever he might have been he is highly honoured by name in the *Véda* itſelf, where it is declared, that 'whatever MENU pronounced, 'was a medicine for the ſoul,' and the ſage VRIHASPATI, now ſuppoſed to preſide over the planet *Jupiter*, ſays in his own law tract, that 'ME'NU held the firſt rank among legiſla-'tors, becauſe he had expreſſed in his code the 'whole ſenſe of the *Véda*; that no code was 'approved, which contradicted MENU; that 'other *Sáſtras*, and treatiſes on grammar or lo-'gick, retained ſplendour ſo long only, as 'MENU, who taught the way to juſt wealth, to 'virtue and to final happineſs, was not ſeen in 'competition with them:' VYA'SA too, the ſon of PARA'SARA before mentioned, has decided, that 'the *Véda* with its *Angas*, or the 'ſix compoſitions deduced from it, the reveal-'ed ſyſtem of medicine, the *Puránas*, or ſa-'cred hiſtories, and the code of MENU were 'four works of ſupreme authority, which 'ought never to be ſhaken by arguments 'merely human.'

IT is the general opinion of *Pandits*, that BRAHMA' taught his laws to MENU in a *hundred thouſand verſes*, which MENU explained to the primitive world, in the very words of the book now tranſlated, where he names himſelf, after the manner of ancient ſages, in the third perſon, but in a ſhort preface to the law tract of NA'RED, it is aſſerted, that 'MENU, 'having written the laws of BRAHMA' in a

'hundred

'hundred thousand *slócas* or couplets, arranged under *twenty-four* heads in a thousand chapters, delivered the work to NA'RED, the sage among gods, who abridged it, for the use of mankind, in *twelve thousand* verses, and gave them to a son of BHRĬGU, named SUMATI, who, for greater ease to the human race, reduced them to *four thousand*; that mortals read only the second abridgement by SUMATI, while the gods of the lower heaven, and the band of celestial musicians, are engaged in studying the primary code, beginning with the fifth verse, a little varied, of the work now extant on earth; but that nothing remains of NA'RED's abridgement, except an elegant epitome of the *ninth* original title *on the administration of justice*.' Now, since these institutes consist only of *two thousand six hundred* and *eighty five* verses, they cannot be the whole work ascribed to SUMATI, which is probably distinguished by the name of the *Vrĭddha*, or ancient *Mánava*, and cannot be found entire; though several passages from it, which have been preserved by tradition, are occasionally cited in the new digest.

A NUMBER of glosses or comments on MENU were composed by the *Munis*, or old philosophers, whose treatises, together with that before us, constitute the *Dhermasástra*, in a collective sense, or *Body of Law*; among the more modern commentaries, that called *Médhátit'hi*, *bátit'hi*, that by GO'VINDARA'JA, and that by DHARANI'-DHERA, were once in the greateſt repute; but the firſt was reckoned prolix and unequal; the ſecond conciſe but obſcure; and the third often erroneous. At length appeared CULLU'CA BHATTA; who, after a painful courſe of ſtudy and the collation of numerous manuſcripts, produced a work, of which it may, perhaps, be ſaid very truly, that it is the ſhorteſt, yet the moſt luminous, the leaſt oſtentatious, yet the moſt learned, the deepeſt, yet the moſt agreeable, commentary ever compoſed on any author ancient or modern, *European* or *Aſiatick*. The *Pandits* care ſo little for genuine chronology, that none of them can tell me the age of CULLU'CA, whom they always name with applauſe; but he informs us himſelf, that he was a *Bráhmen* of the *Váréndra* tribe, whoſe family had been long ſettled in *Gaur* or *Bengal*, but that he had choſen his reſidence among the learned, on the banks of the holy river at *Cáſi*. His text and interpretation I have almoſt implicitly followed, though I had myſelf collated many copies of MENU, and among them a manuſcript of a very ancient date: his gloſs is here printed in *Italicks*; and any reader, who may chooſe to paſs it over as if unprinted, will have in *Roman* letters an exact verſion of the original, and may form ſome idea of its character and ſtructure, as well as of the *Sanſcrit* idiom which muſt neceſſarily be preſerved in a verbal tranſlation; and a tranſla-

tion,

tion, not ſcrupulouſly verbal, would have been highly improper in a work on ſo delicate and momentous a ſubject as private and criminal juriſprudence.

SHOULD a ſeries of *Bráhmens* omit, for three generations, the reading of MENU, their ſacerdotal claſs, as all the *Pandits* aſſure me, would in ſtrictneſs be forfeited; but they muſt explain it only to their pupils of the three higheſt claſſes; and the *Bráhmen*, who read it with me, requeſted moſt earneſtly, that his name might be concealed; nor would he have read it for any conſideration on a forbidden day of the moon, or without the ceremonies preſcribed in the ſecond and fourth chapters for a lecture on the VE'DA: ſo great, indeed, is the idea of ſanctity annexed to this book, that, when the chief native magiſtrate at *Banares* endeavoured, at my requeſt, to procure a *Perſian* tranſlation of it, before I had a hope of being at any time able to underſtand the original, the *Pandits* of his court unanimouſly and poſitively refuſed to aſſiſt in the work; nor ſhould I have procured it at all, if a wealthy *Hindu* at *Gayà* had not cauſed the verſion to be made by ſome of his dependants, at the deſire of my friend Mr. LAW. The *Perſian* tranſlation of MENU, like all others from the *Sanſcrit* into that language, is a rude intermixture of the text, looſely rendered, with ſome old or new comment, and often with the crude notions of the tranſlator; and though it expreſſes the general ſenſe of the original, yet it ſwarms with errours, imputable partly

partly to haſte, and partly to ignorance: thus where MENU ſays, *that emiſſaries are the eyes of a prince*, the *Perſian* phraſe makes him aſcribe *four eyes* to the perſon of a king; for the word *chár*, which means *an emiſſary* in *Sanſcrit*, ſignifies *four* in the popular dialect.

THE work, now preſented to the *European* world, contains abundance of curious matter extremely intereſting both to ſpeculative lawyers and antiquaries, with many beauties which need not be pointed out, and with many blemiſhes which cannot be juſtified or palliated. It is a ſyſtem of deſpotiſm and prieſtcraft, both indeed limited by law, but artfully conſpiring to give mutual ſupport, though with mutual checks; it is filled with ſtrange conceits in metaphyſicks and natural philoſophy, with idle ſuperſtitions, and with a ſcheme of theology moſt obſcurely figurative, and conſequently liable to dangerous miſconception; it abounds with minute and childiſh formalities, with ceremonies generally abſurd and often ridiculous; the puniſhments are partial and fanciful; for ſome crimes, dreadfully cruel, for others, reprehenſibly ſlight; and the very morals, though rigid enough on the whole, are in one or two inſtances (as in the caſe of light oaths and of pious perjury) unaccountably relaxed: neverthelеſs, a ſpirit of ſublime devotion, of benevolence to mankind, and of amiable tenderneſs to all ſentient creatures, pervades the whole work; the ſtyle of it has a certain auſtere majeſty, that ſounds like the language of legiſlation, and extorts a reſpectful awe; the ſentiments of independence on all beings but GOD, and the harſh admonitions, even to kings, are truly noble; and the many panegyricks on the *Gáyatrì*, the *Mother* as it is called, of the *Véda*, prove the author to have *adored* (not the viſible material *ſun*, but) *that divine and incomparably greater light*, to uſe the words of the moſt venerable text in the *Indian* ſcripture, *which illumines all, delights all, from which all proceed, to which all muſt return, and which alone can irradiate* (not our viſual organs merely, but our ſouls and) *our intellects*. Whatever opinion in ſhort may be formed of MENU and his laws, in a country happily enlightened by ſound philoſophy and the only true revelation, it muſt be remembered, that thoſe laws are actually revered, as the word of the Moſt High, by nations of great importance to the political and commercial intereſts of *Europe*, and particularly by many millions of *Hindu* ſubjects, whoſe well directed induſtry would add largely to the wealth of *Britain*, and who aſk no more in return than protection for their perſons and places of abode, juſtice in their temporal concerns, indulgence to the prejudices of their old religion, and the benefit of thoſe laws, which they have been taught to believe ſacred, and which alone they can poſſibly comprehend.

W. JONES.

THE

LAWS OF MENU,

SON OF BRAHMÁ.

CHAPTER THE FIRST.

On the Creation; with a Summary of the Contents.

---

1. MENU *ſat* reclined, with his attention fixed on one object, *the Supreme* GOD; *when* the divine Sages approached *him, and,* after mutual ſalutations in due form, delivered the following addreſs:

2. 'Deign, ſovereign ruler, to apprize us of 'the ſacred laws in their order, as they muſt be 'followed by all the *four* claſſes, and by each of 'them, in their ſeveral degrees, together with 'the duties of every mixed claſs;

3. 'For thou, Lord, *and thou* only *among mortals,* knoweſt the true ſenſe, the firſt principle, '*and* the preſcribed ceremonies, of this univerſal, 'ſupernatural *Véda,* unlimited in extent and unequalled in authority.'

4. HE, whoſe powers were meaſureleſs, being thus requeſted by the great Sages, whoſe thoughts were profound, ſaluted them all with reverence, and gave them a comprehenſive anſwer, *ſaying:* 'Be it heard!

5. 'This *univerſe* exiſted only *in the firſt divine* '*idea yet unexpanded, as if involved* in darkneſs, 'imperceptible, undefinable, undiſcoverable *by*

'*reaſon, and* undiſcovered *by revelation,* as if it 'were wholly immerſed in ſleep:

6. 'Then the *ſole* ſelf-exiſting power, himſelf 'undiſcerned, but making this world diſcernible, 'with five elements and other principles *of nature,* 'appeared with undiminiſhed glory, *expanding* '*his idea, or* diſpelling the gloom.

7. 'He, whom the mind alone can perceive, 'whoſe eſſence eludes the external organs, who 'has no viſible parts, who exiſts from eternity, 'even HE, the ſoul of all beings, whom no being 'can comprehend, ſhone forth in perſon.

8. 'He, having willed to produce various 'beings from his own divine ſubſtance, firſt with 'a thought created the waters, and placed in 'them a productive ſeed:

9. 'The *ſeed* became an egg bright as gold, 'blazing like the luminary with a thouſand 'beams; and in that egg he was born himſelf, '*in the form of* Brahma', the great forefather of 'all ſpirits.

10. 'The waters are called *nárá,* becauſe they 'were the production of Nara, *or the ſpirit of* 'God; and, ſince they were his firſt *ayana,* or '*place of motion,* he thence is named Na'ra'yana, 'or *moving on the waters.*

11. 'From that which is, the firſt cauſe, 'not the object of ſenſe, exiſting *every where in* '*ſubſtance,* not exiſting *to our perception,* without 'beginning or end, was produced the divine male, 'famed in all worlds under the appellation of 'Brahma'.

12. 'In that egg the great power ſat inactive a 'whole year *of the Creator,* at the cloſe of which, 'by his thought alone, he cauſed the egg to divide 'itſelf;

13. 'And

13. ‘ And from its two diviſions he framed the ‘ heaven *above* and the earth *beneath:* in the midſt ‘ *he placed* the ſubtil ether, the eight regions, and ‘ the permanent receptacle of waters.

14. ‘ From the ſupreme ſoul he drew forth ‘ Mind, exiſting ſubſtantially though unperceived ‘ by ſenſe, immaterial; and *before mind, or the* ‘ *reaſoning power, he produced* conſciouſneſs, the ‘ internal monitor, the ruler;

15. ‘ And, *before them both,* he produced the ‘ great *principle of the ſoul, or firſt expanſion of the* ‘ *divine idea*; and all vital forms endued with the ‘ three qualities of *goodneſs, paſſion,* and *darkneſs*; ‘ and the *five* perceptions of ſenſe, and the five ‘ organs of ſenſation.

16. ‘ *Thus,* having at once pervaded, with ema- ‘ nations from the Supreme Spirit, the minuteſt ‘ portions of ſix principles immenſely operative, ‘ *conſciouſneſs and the five perceptions,* He framed all ‘ creatures;

17. ‘ And ſince the minuteſt particles of viſible ‘ nature have a dependence on thoſe *ſix* emanations ‘ from GOD, the wiſe have accordingly given the ‘ name of *s'arira* or *depending on ſix, that is, the ten* ‘ *organs on conſciouſneſs, and the five elements on as* ‘ *many perceptions,* to His *image or* appearance in ‘ viſible nature:

18. ‘ Thence proceed the great elements, en- ‘ dued with peculiar powers, and Mind with ‘ operations infinitely ſubtil, the unperiſhable ‘ cauſe of all apparent forms.

19. ‘ This *univerſe,* therefore, is compacted ‘ from the minute portions of thoſe ſeven divine ‘ and active principles, *the great Soul, or firſt ema-* ‘ *nation, conſciouſneſs, and five perceptions*; *a* mutable ‘ *univerſe* from immutable *ideas.*

 20. ‘ Among

20. ' Among them each ſucceeding element ' acquires the quality of the preceding; and, in ' as many degrees as each of them is advanced, ' with ſo many properties is it ſaid to be endued.

21. ' He too firſt aſſigned to all creatures diſ- ' tinct names, diſtinct acts, and diſtinct occupa- ' tions; as they had been revealed in the pre- ' exiſting *Véda*.

22. ' He, the ſupreme Ruler, created an aſſem- ' blage of inferior Deities, with divine attributes ' and pure ſouls; and a number of Genii exqui- ' ſitely delicate; and he *preſcribed* the ſacrifice ' ordained from the beginning.

23. ' From fire, from air, and from the ſun ' he milked out, *as it were*, the three primordial ' *Védas*, named *Rĭch*, *Yajuſh*, and *Sáman*, for the ' due performance of the ſacrifice.

24. ' He gave being to time and the diviſions ' of time, to the ſtars alſo, and to the planets, to ' rivers, oceans, and mountains, to level plains, ' and uneven valleys.

25. ' To devotion, ſpeech, complacency, de- ' ſire, and wrath, and to the creation, which ſhall ' preſently be mentioned; for He willed the exiſ- ' tence of all thoſe created things.

26. ' For the ſake of diſtinguiſhing actions, ' He made a total difference between right and ' wrong, and enured theſe ſentient creatures to ' pleaſure and pain, *cold and heat*, and other oppo- ' ſite pairs.

27. ' With very minute transformable portions, ' called *mátrás*, of the five elements, all this ' perceptible world was compoſed in fit order;

28. ' And in whatever occupation the ſupreme ' Lord firſt employed any vital ſoul, to that occu- ' pation

'pation the ſame ſoul attaches itſelf ſpontaneouſly, 'when it receives a new body again and again:

29. 'Whatever quality, noxious or innocent, 'harſh or mild, unjuſt, or juſt, falſe or true, He 'conferred on any being at its creation, the ſame 'quality enters it of courſe *on its future births*;

30. 'As the *ſix* ſeaſons of the year attain 'reſpectively their peculiar marks in due time 'and of their own accord, even ſo the ſeveral 'acts of each embodied ſpirit *atten*: *it n*:*u*-'*rally*.

31. 'That the human race might be multi-'plied, He cauſed the *Brahmen*, the *Cſhatriya*, 'the *Vaiſya*, and the *Súdra* (ſo named from the '*ſcripture*, *protection*, *wealth*, and *labour*) to pro-'ceed from his mouth, his arm, his thigh and his 'foot.

32. 'Having divided his own ſubſtance, the 'mighty Power became half male, half female, '*or nature active and paſſive*; and from that fe-'male he produced VIRA'J:

33. 'Know Me, O moſt excellent of *Br'hmens*, 'to be that perſon, whom the male *power* VIRA'J, 'having performed auſtere devotion, produced 'by himſelf; Me, the *ſecondary* framer of all this '*viſible world*.

34. 'It was I, who, deſirous of giving birth 'to a race of men, performed very difficult reli-'gious duties, and firſt produced ten Lords of 'created beings, eminent in holineſs,

35. 'MARI'CHI, ATRI, ANGERAS, PULASTYA, 'PULAHA, CRATU, PRACHE'TAS, or DACSHA, 'VASISHT'HA, BHRĬGU, and NARADA:

36. 'They, abundant in glory, produced 'ſeven other *Menus*, together with deities, and

'the mansions of deities, and *Maharshis*, or great 'Sages, unlimited in power;

37. 'Benevolent genii, and fierce giants, blood-'thirsty savages, heavenly quiristers, nymphs and 'demons, huge serpents and snakes of smaller 'size, birds of mighty wing, and separate com-'panies of *Pitris*, or progenitors of mankind;

38. 'Lightnings and thunder-bolts, clouds and 'coloured bows of *Indra*, falling meteors, earth-'rending vapours, comets, and luminaries of va-'rious degrees;

39. 'Horse-faced sylvans, apes, fish, and a 'variety of birds, tame cattle, deer, men, and 'ravenous beasts with two rows of teeth;

40. 'Small and large reptiles, moths, lice, 'fleas, and common flies, with every biting gnat, 'and immoveable substances of distinct sorts.

41. 'Thus was this whole assemblage of sta-'tionary and moveable bodies framed by those 'high-minded beings, through the force of their 'own devotion, and at my command, with sepa-'rate actions allotted to each.

42. 'Whatever act is ordained for each of 'those creatures here below, *that* I will now de-'clare to you, together with their order in respect 'to birth.

43. 'Cattle and deer, and wild beasts with two 'rows of teeth, giants, and blood-thirsty savages, 'and the race of men, are born from a secundine:

44. 'Birds are hatched from eggs, *so are* 'snakes, crocodiles, fish *without shells*, and tor-'toises, with other animal kinds, terrestrial, *as* '*chamelions*, and aquatick, *as shell-fish*:

45. 'From hot moisture are born biting gnats, 'lice, fleas, and common flies; these, and what-'ever is of the same class, are produced by heat.

46. ' All vegetables, propagated by ſeed or by ' ſlips grow from ſhoots: ſome herbs, abounding ' in flowers and fruits, periſh when the fruit is ' mature;

47. ' Other plants, called lords of the foreſt, ' have no flowers, but produce fruit; and, whe- ' ther they have flowers alſo, or fruit only, *large* ' *woody plants* of both ſorts are named trees.

48. ' There are ſhrubs with many ſtalks from ' the root upwards, and reeds with ſingle roots ' but united ſtems, all of different kinds, and ' graſſes, and *vines or* climbers, and creepers, ' which ſpring from a ſeed or from a ſlip.

49. ' Theſe *animals and vegetables*, encircled ' with multiform darkneſs, by reaſon of paſt ac- ' tions, have internal conſcience, and are ſenſible ' of pleaſure and pain.

50. ' All tranſmigrations, recorded *in ſacred* ' *books*, from the ſtate of BRAHMÁ, to that of ' plants, happen continually in this tremendous ' world of beings; a world *always* tending to ' decay.

51. ' HE, whoſe powers are incomprehenſible, ' having thus created both me and this univerſe, ' was again abſorbed in the ſupreme Spirit, chang- ' ing *the* time *of energy* for *the* time *of repoſe*.

52. ' When that Power awakes, *(for, though* ' *ſlumber be not predicable of the ſole eternal Mind,* ' *infinitely wiſe and infinitely benevolent, yet it is pre-* ' *dicated of* BRAHMÁ, *figuratively, as a general pro-* ' *perty of life)* then has this world its full expanſion; ' but, when he ſlumbers with a tranquil ſpirit, ' then the whole ſyſtem fades away;

53. ' For, while he repoſes, *as it were*, in calm ' ſleep, embodied ſpirits, endued with principles

'of action, depart from their several acts, and the 'mind itself becomes inert;

54. 'And when they once are absorbed in that 'supreme essence, then the divine soul of all 'beings withdraws his energy, and placidly slum-'bers;

55. 'Then too this vital soul *of created bodies*, 'with all the organs of sense and of action, re-'mains long immersed *in the first idea or in* dark-'ness, and performs not its natural functions, but 'migrates from its corporeal frame:

56. 'When, being *again* composed of minute 'elementary principles, it enters at once into 'vegetable or animal seed, it then assumes a '*new* form.

57. 'Thus that immutable Power, by waking 'and reposing alternately, revivifies and destroys 'in eternal succession, this whole assemblage of 'locomotive and immoveable creatures.

58. 'HE, having enacted this code of laws, 'himself taught it fully to me in the beginning: 'afterwards I taught it MARICHI and the *nine* 'other holy sages.

59. 'This *my son* BHRIGU will repeat the divine 'code to you without omission; for that sage 'learned from me to recite the whole of it.'

60. BHRĬGU, great and wise, having thus been appointed by MENU to promulge his laws, addressed all the *Rĭshis* with an affectionate mind, saying: 'Hear!

61. 'FROM this MENU named SWA'YAMBHUVA, 'or *Sprung from the self-existing*, came six des-'cendants, other MENUS, *or perfectly understanding* '*the scripture*, each giving birth to a race of his 'own, all exalted in dignity, eminent in power;

62. 'SWARO'CHISHA, AUTTAMI, TA'MASA, RAIVATA

'RAIVATA likewiſe and CHA'CSHUSHA, beaming 'with glory, and VAIVASWATA, child of the ſun.

63. 'The ſeven MENUS, (or *thoſe firſt created, 'who are to be followed by ſeven more*) of whom 'SWA'YAMBHUVA is the chief, have produced and 'ſupported this world of moving and ſtationary 'beings, each in his own *antara*, or *the period of 'his reign*.

64. 'Eighteen *nimeſhas*, or *twinklings of an eye*, 'are one *cáſht'há*; thirty *cáſht'hás*, one *calá*; 'thirty *calás*, one *muhúrta*: and juſt ſo many '*muhúrtas* let mankind conſider as the duration 'of their day and night.

65. 'The ſun cauſes the diſtribution of day and 'night, both divine and human; night being '*intended* for the repoſe of *various* beings, and day 'for their exertion.

66. 'A month *of mortals* is a day and a night 'of the *Pitris* or *patriarchs inhabiting the moon*; 'and the diviſion *of a month* being into equal 'halves, the half beginning from the full moon is 'their day for actions; and that beginning from 'the new moon is their night for ſlumber:

67. 'A year *of mortals* is a day and a night of 'the Gods, or *regents of the univerſe ſeated round 'the north pole*; and again their diviſion is this, 'their day is the northern, and their night the 'ſouthern courſe of the ſun.

68. 'Learn now the duration of a day and a 'night of BRAHMA', and of the ſeveral ages 'which ſhall be mentioned in order ſuccinctly.

69. 'Sages have given the name of *Crĭta* to an 'age containing four thouſand years of the Gods; 'the twilight preceding it conſiſts of as many 'hundreds, and the twilight following it, of the 'ſame number;

70. 'In

70. 'In the other three *ages*, with their twilights
'preceding and following, are thousands and
'hundreds diminished by one.

71. 'The divine years, in the four *human* ages
'just enumerated, being added together, their
'sum, *or* twelve thousand, is called the age of the
'Gods:

72. 'And, by reckoning a thousand such divine
'ages, a day of BRAHMA' may be known: his
'night also has an equal duration:

73. 'Those persons best know the divisions of
'the days and nights, who understand that the
'day of BRAHMA, which endures to the end of a
'thousand such ages, gives rise to virtuous ex-
'ertions; and that his night endures as long as
'his day.

74. 'At the close of his night, having long
'reposed, he awakes, and awaking, exerts in-
'tellect, *or reproduces the great principle of anima-*
'*tion*, whose property it is to exist unperceived by
'sense:

75. 'Intellect, called into action by his will
'to create worlds, performs *again* the work of
'creation; and thence *first* emerges the subtil
'ether, to which philosophers ascribe the quality
'of conveying sound;

76. 'From ether, effecting a transmutation
'in form, springs the pure and potent air, a ve-
'hicle of all scents; and air is held endued with
'the quality of touch:

77. 'Then from air, operating a change, rises
'light *or fire*, making objects visible, dispelling
'gloom, spreading bright rays; and it is declared
'to have the quality of figure;

78. 'But from light, a change being effected,
'comes water with the quality of taste; and from
'water

'water *is deposited* earth with the quality of smell:
'such were they created in the beginning.

79. 'The before-mentioned age of the Gods, 'or twelve thousand *of their* years, being multiplied by seventy-one, *constitutes what* is here 'named a *Menwantara, or the reign of a* MENU.

80. 'There are numberless *Menwantaras*; 'creations also and destructions of worlds, *innumerable*: the Being supremely exalted performs all this, *with as much ease* as if in sport; 'again and again, *for the sake of conferring happiness*.

81. 'In the *Crĭta* age *the Genius of* truth and 'right, *in the form of a Bull*, stands firm on his 'four feet; nor does any advantage accrue to 'men from iniquity;

82. 'But in the following ages, by reason of 'unjust gains, he is deprived successively of one 'foot; and even just emoluments, through the 'prevalence of theft, falsehood, and fraud, are '*gradually* diminished by a fourth part.

83. 'Men, free from disease, attain all sorts of 'prosperity, and live four hundred years in the '*Crĭta* age; but, in the *Trétà* and the succeeding 'ages, their life is lessened gradually by one 'quarter.

84. 'The life of mortals, which is mentioned 'in the *Véda*, the rewards of good works, and the 'powers of embodied spirits, are fruits proportioned among men to the order of the *four* 'ages.

85. 'Some duties are performed by *good* men 'in the *Crĭta* age; others, in the *Trétà*; some, 'in the *Dwápara*; others, in the *Cali*; in proportion as those ages decrease in length.

86. 'In the *Crĭta* the prevailing virtue is declared

'clared to be in devotion; in the *Trétà*, divine 'knowledge; in the *Dwâpara*, holy ſages call 'ſacrifice the duty chiefly performed; in the '*Cali*, liberality alone.

87. 'For the ſake of preſerving this univerſe, 'the Being, ſupremely glorious, allotted ſeparate 'duties to thoſe who ſprang reſpectively from his 'mouth, his arm, his thigh, and his foot.

88. 'To *Bráhmens* he aſſigned the duties of 'reading the *Véda*, of teaching it, of ſacrificing, 'of aſſiſting others to ſacrifice, of giving alms, '*if they be rich*, and, *if indigent*, of receiving 'gifts:

89. 'To defend the people, to give alms, to 'ſacrifice, to read the *Véda*, to ſhun the allure-'ments of ſenſual gratification, are, in a few 'words, the duties of a *Chatriya:*

90. 'To keep herds of cattle, to beſtow lar-'geſſes, to ſacrifice, to read the ſcripture, to carry 'on trade, to lend at intereſt, and to cultivate 'land are preſcribed *or permitted* to a *Vaiſya:*

91. 'One principal duty the ſupreme Ruler 'aſſigns to a *Súdra*; namely, to ſerve the be-'fore-mentioned claſſes, without depreciating 'their worth.

92. 'Man is declared purer above the navel; 'but the ſelf-creating Power declared the pureſt 'part of him to be his mouth.

93. 'Since the *Bráhmen* ſprang from the moſt 'excellent part, ſince he was the firſt born, and 'ſince he poſſeſſes the *Véda*, he is by right the 'chief of this whole creation.

94. 'Him, the Being, who exiſts of himſelf, 'produced in the beginning from his own mouth, 'that, having performed holy rites, he might 'preſent clarified butter to the Gods, and cakes

'of

'of rice to the progenitors of mankind, for the 'preservation of this world:

95. 'What created being then can surpass 'Him, with whose mouth the Gods of the firmament continually feast on clarified butter, and 'the manes of ancestors, on hallowed cakes?

96. 'Of created things, the most excellent are 'those which are animated; of the animated, 'those which subsist by intelligence; of the intelligent, mankind; and of men, the sacerdotal 'class;

97. 'Of priests, those eminent in learning; 'of the learned, those who know their duty; of 'those who know it, such as perform it virtuously; 'and of the virtuous, those who seek beatitude 'from a perfect acquaintance with scriptural doctrine.

98. 'The very birth of *Brâhmens* is a constant 'incarnation of DHERMA, *God of Justice*; for the '*Brâhmen* is born to promote justice, and to procure ultimate happiness.

99. 'When a *Brâhmen* springs to light, he is 'born above the world, the chief of all creatures, 'assigned to guard the treasury of duties, religious 'and civil.

100. 'Whatever exists in the universe, is all 'in effect, *though not in form*, the wealth of 'the *Brâhmen*; since the *Brâhmen* is entitled 'to it all by his primogeniture and eminence 'of birth:

101. 'The *Brâhmen* eats but his own food; 'wears but his own apparel; and bestows but his 'own in alms: through the benevolence of the '*Brâhmen*, indeed, other mortals enjoy life.

102. 'To declare the sacerdotal duties, and 'those of the other classes in due order, the sage

'Menu, ſprung from the ſelf-exiſting, promulged 'this code of laws:

103. 'A code which muſt be ſtudied with extreme eaſe by every learned *Bráhmen*, and fully 'explained to his diſciples, but *muſt be taught* by 'no other man *of an inferior claſs*.

104. 'The *Bráhmen* who ſtudies this book, 'having performed ſacred rites, is perpetually 'free from offence in thought, in word, and in 'deed;

105. 'He confers purity on his living family, 'on his anceſtors, and on his deſcendants, as far 'as the ſeventh perſon; and He alone deſerves 'to poſſeſs this whole earth.

106. 'This moſt excellent code produces every'thing auſpicious; this code increaſes under'ſtanding; this code procures fame and long life; 'this code leads to ſupreme bliſs.

107. 'In this book appears the ſyſtem of law 'in its full extent, with the good and bad pro'perties of human actions, and the immemorial 'cuſtoms of the four claſſes.

108. 'Immemorial cuſtom is tranſcendent law, 'approved in the ſacred ſcripture, and in the 'codes of divine legiſlators: let every man, there'fore, of the three principal claſſes, who has a due 'reverence for the *ſupreme* ſpirit *which dwells in* '*him*, diligently and conſtantly obſerve imme'morial cuſtom:

109. 'A man of the prieſtly, military, or 'commercial claſs, who deviates from imme'morial uſage, taſtes not the fruit of the *Véda*; 'but, by an exact obſervance of it, he gathers 'that fruit in perfection.

110. 'Thus have holy ſages, well knowing 'that law is grounded on immemorial cuſtom, embraced,

'embraced, as the root of all piety, good usages 'long established.

111. 'The creation of this universe, the forms 'of institution and education, with the observances 'and behaviour of a student in theology; the best 'rules for the ceremony on his return from the 'mansion of his preceptor;

112. 'The law of marriage in general, and 'of nuptials in different forms; the regulations 'for the great sacraments, and the manner, 'primevally settled, of performing obsequies;

113. 'The modes of gaining subsistence, and 'the rules to be observed by the master of a 'family; the allowance and prohibition of diet, 'with the purification of men and utensils;

114. 'Laws concerning women, the devotion 'of hermits, and of anchorets wholly intent on 'final beatitude, the whole duty of a king, and 'the judicial decision of controversies,

115. 'With the law of evidence and examina-'tion; laws concerning husband and wife, canons 'of inheritance; the prohibition of gaming, and 'the punishments of criminals;

116. 'Rules ordained for the mercantile and 'servile classes, with the origin of those that are 'mixed; the duties and rights of all the classes in 'time of distress for subsistence; and the penances 'for expiating sins;

117. 'The several transmigrations in this uni-'verse, caused by offences of three kinds, with 'the ultimate bliss attending good actions, on the 'full trial of vice and virtue;

118. 'All these titles of law, promulgated 'by Menu, and *occasionally* the customs of dif-'ferent countries, different tribes, and different

 'families,

'families, with rules concerning hereticks and 'companies of traders, are discuſſed in this 'code.

119. 'Even as MENU, at my requeſt, formerly 'revealed this divine *Sáſtra*, hear it now from 'me without any diminution or addition.

CHAPTER THE SECOND.

On Education; or on the Sacerdotal Clafs, and The Firft Order.

1. ‘ Know that fyftem of duties, which is revered by fuch as are learned in the *Védas*, and impreffed, *as the means of attaining beatitude*, on the hearts of the juft, who are ever exempt from hatred and inordinate affection.

2. ‘ Self-love is no laudable motive, yet an exemption from felf-love is not *to be found* in this world: on felf-love is grounded the ftudy of fcripture, and the practice of actions recommended in it.

3. ‘ Eager defire *to act* has its root in expectation of fome advantage; and with fuch expectation are facrifices performed; the rules of religious aufterity and abftinence from fins are all known to arife from hope of remuneration.

4. ‘ Not a fingle act here below appears ever to be done by a man free from felf-love; whatever he performed, it is wrought from his defire of a reward.

5. ‘ He, indeed, who fhould perfift in *difcharging* thefe duties without any view to their fruit, would attain hereafter the ftate of the immortals, and even in this life, would enjoy all the virtuous gratifications, that his fancy could fuggeft.

6. 'The roots of law are the whole *Véda*, 'the ordinances and moral practices of ſuch as 'perfectly underſtand it, the immemorial cuſtoms 'of good men, and, *in caſes quite indifferent*, ſelf-'ſatisfaction.

7. 'Whatever law has been ordained for any 'perſon by MENU, that law is fully declared in 'the *Véda:* for He was perfect in divine know-'ledge:

8. 'A man of true learning, who has viewed 'this complete ſyſtem with the eye of ſacred 'wiſdom, cannot fail to perform all thoſe duties, 'which are ordained on the authority of the *Véda*.

9. 'No doubt, that man who ſhall follow the 'rules preſcribed in the *Sruti* and in the *Smrĭti*, 'will acquire fame in this life, and, in the next, 'inexpreſſible happineſs:

10. 'By *Sruti*, or *what was heard from above*, 'is meant the *Véda*; and by *Smrĭti*, or *what was* '*remembered from the beginning*, the body of law: 'thoſe two muſt not be oppugned by heterodox 'arguments; ſince from thoſe two, proceeds the 'whole ſyſtem of duties.

11. 'Whatever man of the three higheſt claſſes, 'having addicted himſelf to heretical books, ſhall 'treat with contempt thoſe two roots of law, he 'muſt be driven, as an Atheiſt and a ſcorner of 'revelation, from the company of the virtuous.

12. 'The ſcripture, the codes of law, ap-'proved uſage, and, *in all indifferent caſes*, ſelf-'ſatisfaction, the wiſe have openly declared to 'be the quadruple deſcription of the juridical 'ſyſtem.

13. 'A knowledge of right is a ſufficient in-'centive for men unattached to wealth or to ſen-'ſuality; and to thoſe who ſeek a knowledge of

'right,

'right, the ſupreme authority is divine revela-
'tion;

14. 'But, when there are two ſacred texts, *apparently inconſiſtent*, both are held to be law; for 'both are pronounced by the wiſe to be valid 'and reconcileable;

15. 'Thus in the *Véda* are theſe texts: "let 'the ſacrifice be when the ſun has ariſen," and, "before it has riſen," and, "when neither ſun 'nor ſtars can be ſeen:" the ſacrifice, therefore, 'may be performed at any or all of thoſe times.

16. 'He, whoſe life is regulated by holy texts, 'from his conception even to his funeral pile, 'has a decided right to ſtudy this code; but no 'other man whatſoever.

17. 'BETWEEN the two divine rivers *Saraſwatí* 'and *Driſhadwatí*, lies the tract of land, which 'the ſages have named *Brahmáverta*, becauſe it 'was frequented by Gods:

18. 'The cuſtom preſerved by immemorial 'tradition in that country, among the four *pure* 'claſſes, and among thoſe which are mixed, is 'called approved uſage.

19. '*Curucſhétra*, *Matſya*, *Panchála*, or *Cányacubja*, and *Súraſéna*, or *Mat'hurà*, form the re-'gion called *Brahmarſhi*, diſtinguiſhed from *Brahmáverta*:

20. 'From a *Bráhmen* who was born in that 'country, let all men on earth learn their ſeveral 'uſages.

21. 'That country which lies between *Himawat* and *Vindhya*, to the eaſt of *Vinas'ana*, and to 'the weſt of *Prayága*, is celebrated by the title of '*Medhya-dés'a*, or *the central region*.

22. 'As far as the eaſtern, and as far as the 'weſtern oceans, between the two mountains juſt

'mentioned, lies the tract which the wise have 'named *Ariáverta*, or *inhabited by respectable men.*

23. 'That land, on which the black antelope 'naturally grazes, is held fit for the performance 'of sacrifices; but the land of *Mléch'has*, or *those 'who speak barbarously,* differs widely from it.

24. 'Let the three first classes invariably dwell 'in those before-mentioned countries; but a *Sú'dra*, distressed for subsistence, may sojourn 'wherever he chuses.

25. 'Thus has the origin of law been succinct'ly declared to you, together with the formation 'of this universe: now learn the laws of the 'several classes.

26. 'With auspicious acts prescribed by the '*Véda*, must ceremonies on conception, and so 'forth, be duly performed, which purify the 'bodies of the three classes in this life, and *qualify 'them* for the next.

27. 'By oblations to fire during the mother's 'pregnancy, by holy rites on the birth of the 'child, by the tonsure of his head with a lock of 'hair left on it, by the ligation of the sacrificial 'cord, are the seminal and uterine taints of the 'three classes wholly removed:

28. 'By studying the *Véda*, by religious ob'servances, by oblations to fire, by the ceremony 'of *Traividia*, by offering to the Gods and Manes, 'by the procreation of children, by the five great 'sacraments, and by solemn sacrifices, this human 'body is rendered fit for a divine state.

29. 'Before the section of the navel string a 'ceremony is ordained on the birth of a male: 'he must be made, while sacred texts are pro'nounced, to taste a little honey and clarified 'butter from a golden spoon.

30. 'Let

30. ‘ Let the father *perform or, if absent*, cause
‘ to be performed, on the tenth or twelfth day
‘ *after the birth*, the ceremony of giving a name;
‘ or on some fortunate day of the moon, at a
‘ lucky hour, and under the influence of a star
‘ with good qualities.

31. ‘ The first part of a *Bráhmen's* compound
‘ name should indicate holiness; of a *Cshatriya's*,
‘ power; of a *Vaisya's*, wealth; and of a *Súdra's*
‘ contempt:

32. ‘ Let the second part of the priest's name
‘ imply prosperity; of the soldier's, preservation;
‘ of the merchant's, nourishment; of the servant's,
‘ humble attendance.

33. ‘ The names of women should be agreeable,
‘ soft, clear, captivating the fancy, auspicious,
‘ ending in long vowels, resembling words of
‘ benediction.

34. ‘ In the fourth month the child should be
‘ carried out of the house *to see the sun:* in the
‘ sixth month, he should be fed with rice; or
‘ that *may be done*, which, by the custom of the
‘ family, is thought most propitious.

35. ‘ By the command of the *Véda*, the cere-
‘ mony of tonsure should be legally performed
‘ by the three *first* classes in the first or third
‘ year *after birth*.

36. ‘ In the eighth year from the conception
‘ of a *Bráhmen*, in the eleventh from that of a
‘ *Cshatriya*, and in the twelfth from that of a
‘ *Vaisya*, let the father invest the child with the
‘ mark of his class:

37. ‘ Should a *Bráhmen*, or *his father for him*,
‘ be desirous of his advancement in sacred know-
‘ ledge; a *Cshatriya*, of extending his power; *or* a
‘ *Vaisya* of engaging in mercantile business; the

 ‘ in-

'investiture may be made in the fifth, sixth, or 'eighth years respectively.

38. 'The ceremony of investiture hallowed by 'the *gáyatrí* must not be delayed, in the case of a 'priest, beyond the sixteenth year; nor in that 'of a soldier, beyond the twenty-second; nor in 'that of a merchant, beyond the twenty-fourth.

39. 'After that *all youths* of these three classes, 'who have not been invested at the proper time, 'become *vrátyas*, or outcasts, degraded from the '*gáyatrí*, and contemned by the virtuous:

40. 'With such impure men, let no *Bráhmen*, 'even in distress for subsistence, ever form a con-'nexion in law, either by the study of the *Véda*, 'or by affinity.

41. 'Let students in theology wear *for their* '*mantles*, the hides of black antelopes, of common 'deer, or of goats, with *lower vests of* woven *s'ana*, 'of *cshumà*, and of wool, in the direct order of their 'classes.

42. 'The girdle of a priest must be made of '*munja*, in a triple cord, smooth and soft; that 'of a warrior must be a bow string of *múrvá*; 'that of a merchant, a triple thread of *s'ana*.

43 'If the *munja* be not procurable, their zones 'must be formed *respectively* of the grasses *cusa* '*asmántaca*, *valvaja*, in triple strings with one, three, 'or five knots, *according to the family custom*.

44, 'The sacrificial thread of a *Bráhmen* must 'be made of cotton, so as to be put on over his 'head, in three strings; that of a *Cshatriya*, of '*s'ana* thread only; that of a *Vais'ya* of woollen 'thread.

45. 'A priest ought by law to carry a staff of '*Bilva* or *Palása*; a soldier, of *Bata* or *C'hadira*; 'a merchant of *Vénu* or *Udumbara*:

46. 'The

46. ‘ The ſtaff of a prieſt muſt be of ſuch length ‘ as to reach his hair; that of a ſoldier, to reach ‘ his forehead; and that of a merchant, to reach ‘ his noſe.

47. ‘ Let all the ſtaves be ſtraight, without ‘ fracture, of a handſome appearance, not likely ‘ to terrify men, with their bark perfect, unhurt ‘ by fire.

48. ‘ Having taken a legal ſtaff to his liking, ‘ and ſtanding oppoſite to the ſun, let the ſtudent ‘ thrice walk round the fire from left to right, and ‘ perform, according to law, the ceremony of aſk- ‘ ing food:

49. ‘ The moſt excellent of the three claſſes, ‘ being girt with the ſacrificial thread, muſt aſk ‘ food with the reſpectful word *bhavati*, at the ‘ beginning of the phraſe; thoſe of the ſecond ‘ claſs, with that word in the middle; and thoſe ‘ of the third, with that word at the end.

50. ‘ Let him firſt beg food of his mother, or ‘ of his ſiſter, or of his mother's whole ſiſter; then ‘ of ſome other female who will not diſgrace him.

51. ‘ Having collected as much of the deſired ‘ food as he has occaſion for, and having preſented ‘ it without guile to his preceptor, let him eat ‘ ſome of it, being duly purified, with his face to ‘ the eaſt:

52. ‘ If he ſeek long life, he ſhould eat with his ‘ face to the eaſt, if exalted fame to the ſouth; if ‘ proſperity to the weſt; if truth *and its reward* to ‘ the north.

53. ‘ Let the ſtudent, having performed his ‘ ablution, always eat his food without diſtraction ‘ of mind; and, having eaten, let him *thrice* waſh ‘ his mouth completely, ſprinkling with water the

'*six* hollow parts of his head, *or his eyes, ears, and* '*nostrils.*

54. 'Let him honour all his food, and eat it 'without contempt; when he sees it, let him 'rejoice and be calm, and pray, that he may 'always obtain it.

55. 'Food, eaten constantly with respect, gives 'muscular force and generative power; but, eaten 'irreverently, destroys them both.

56. 'He must beware of giving any man what 'he leaves; and of eating any thing between '*morning and evening:* he must also beware of 'eating too much, and of going any whither with 'a remnant of his food unswallowed.

57. 'Excessive eating is prejudicial to health, 'to fame, and to future bliss in Heaven; it is 'injurious to virtue, and odious among men: 'he must, for these reasons, by all means avoid it.

58. 'Let a *Bráhmen* at all times perform the 'ablution with the pure part of his hand denomi-'nated from the *Véda*, or with the part sacred to 'the Lord of creatures, or with that dedicated to 'the Gods; but never with the part named from 'the *Pitrĭs:*

59. 'The pure part under the root of the 'thumb is called *Bráhma*, that at the root of the 'little finger, *Cáya*; that at the tips of the fingers, '*Daiva*; and the part between the thumb and 'index *Pitrya.*

60. 'Let him first sip water thrice; then twice 'wipe his mouth; and lastly touch with water 'the *six before mentioned* cavities, his breast, 'and his head.

61. 'He who knows the law and seeks purity 'will ever perform his ablution with the pure part 'of his hand, and with water neither hot nor

'frothy

'frothy, ſtanding in a lonely place, and turning
'to the eaſt or the north.

62. 'A *Bráhmen* is purified by water that 'reaches his boſom; a *Chatriya*, by water deſcending to his throat; a *Vaiſya*, by water barely 'taken into his mouth; a *Súdra* by water touched 'with the extremity of his lips.

63. 'A youth of the three higheſt claſſes is 'named *upavíti*, when his right hand is extended '*for the cord to paſs over his head and be fixed on his left ſhoulder*; when his left hand is extended, '*that the thread may be placed on his right ſhoulder*, 'he is called *práchínávíti*; and *nivíti*, when it is 'faſtened on his neck.

64. 'His girdle, his leathern mantle, his ſtaff, 'his ſacrificial cord, and his ewer, he muſt throw 'into the water, when they are worn out or 'broken, and receive others hallowed by myſtical 'texts.

65. 'The ceremony of *céſánta*, or *cutting off the hair*, is ordained for a prieſt in the ſixteenth year 'from conception; for a ſoldier, in the twenty-ſecond; for a merchant, two years later than 'that.

66. 'The ſame ceremonies, *except that of the ſacrificial thread*, muſt be duly performed for 'women at the ſame age and in the ſame order, 'that the body may be made perfect; but without any text from the *Véda*:

67. 'The nuptial ceremony is conſidered as 'the complete inſtitution of women, ordained for 'them in the *Véda*, together with reverence to 'their huſbands, dwelling firſt in their father's 'family, the buſineſs of the houſe, and attention 'to ſacred fire.

68. ‘ Such is the real law of inſtitution for the ‘ twice born; an inſtitution in which their ſecond ‘ birth clearly conſiſts, and which cauſes their ad‘ vancement in holineſs: now learn to what du‘ ties they muſt afterwards apply themſelves.

69. ‘ The venerable preceptor, having girt his ‘ pupil with the thread, muſt firſt inſtruct him ‘ in purification, in good cuſtoms, in the manage‘ ment of the conſecrated fire, and in the holy ‘ rites of morning, noon, and evening.

70. ‘ When the ſtudent is going to read the ‘ *Véda*, he muſt perform an ablution, as the law ‘ ordains, with his face to the north, and, having ‘ paid ſcriptural homage, he muſt receive inſtruc‘ tion, wearing a clean veſt, his members being ‘ duly compoſed:

71. ‘ At the beginning and end of the lecture, ‘ he muſt always claſp both the feet of his precep‘ tor; and he muſt read with both his hands ‘ cloſed: (this is called ſcripture homage.)

72. ‘ With croſſed hands let him claſp the feet ‘ of his tutor, touching the left foot with his left, ‘ and the right with his right hand.

73. ‘ When he is prepared for the lecture, the ‘ preceptor, conſtantly attentive, muſt ſay: “hoa! ‘ read;” and at the cloſe of the leſſon he muſt ‘ ſay: “take reſt.”

74. ‘ A *Bráhmen*, beginning and ending a ‘ lecture on the *Véda*, muſt always pronounce to ‘ himſelf the ſyllable *óm*; for, unleſs the ſyllable ‘ *óm* precede, his learning will ſlip away from him; ‘ and, unleſs it follow, nothing will be long ‘ retained.

75. ‘ If he have ſitten on culms of *cus'a* with ‘ their points toward the eaſt, and be purified ‘ by *rubbing* that holy graſs on both his hands,

‘ and

'and be further prepared by three ſuppreſſions of 'breath *each equal in time to five ſhort vowels*, he 'then may fitly pronounce *óm*.

76. 'BRAHMA' milked out, *as it were*, from the 'three *Védas*, the letter A, the letter U, and 'the letter M, *which form by their coalition the trilite-'ral monoſyllable*, together with three myſterious 'words, *bhur*, *bhuvah*, *ſwer*, or *earth*, *ſky*, *heaven*:

77. 'From the three *Védas*, alſo, the Lord of 'creatures, incomprehenſibly exalted, ſucceſſively 'milked out the three meaſures of that ineffable 'text, beginning with the word *tad*, and entitled '*ſávitrí* or *gáyatrí*.

78. 'A prieſt who ſhall know the *Véda*, and ſhall 'pronounce to himſelf, both morning and even-'ing, that ſyllable, and that holy text preceded 'by the three words, ſhall attain the ſanctity 'which the *Véda* confers;

79. 'And a twice born man, who ſhall a thou-'ſand times repeat thoſe three (or *óm*, the *vyáhrĭtis*, 'and the *gayatrí*,) apart *from the multitude*, ſhall be 'releaſed in a month even from a great offence, 'as a ſnake from his ſlough.

80. 'The prieſt, the ſoldier, and the merchant, 'who ſhall neglect this myſterious text, and fail 'to perform in due ſeaſon his peculiar acts of 'piety, ſhall meet with contempt among the 'virtuous.

81. 'The three great immutable words, pre-'ceded by the triliteral ſyllable, and *followed by* 'the *gáyatrí* which conſiſts of three meaſures, muſt 'be conſidered as the mouth, or *principal part* 'of the *Véda*:

82. 'Whoever ſhall repeat, day by day, for 'three years, without negligence, that ſacred 'text, ſhall *hereafter* approach the divine eſſence,

'move as freely as air, and assume an ethereal 'form.

83. 'The triliteral monosyllable is *an emblem of* 'the supreme, the suppressions of breath *with a* '*mind fixed on* God are the highest devotion; but 'nothing is more exalted than the *gáyatrí: a de-*'*claration of* truth is more excellent than silence.

84. 'All rites ordained in the *Véda*, oblations to 'fire, and solemn sacrifices pass away; but that 'which passes not away, is declared to be the 'syllable *óm*, thence called *acshara*; since it is a '*symbol of* God, the Lord of created beings.

85. 'The act of repeating his Holy Name is 'ten times better than the appointed sacrifice; 'an hundred times better when it is heard by no 'man; and a thousand times better when it is 'purely mental:

86. 'The four domestic sacraments which are 'accompanied with the appointed sacrifice, are not 'equal, though all be united, to a sixteenth part 'of the sacrifice performed by a repetition of the '*gáyatrí*:

87. 'By the sole repetition of the *gáyatrí*, a 'priest may indubitably attain beatitude, let him 'perform, or not perform, any other religious 'act; if he be *Maitra*, or a *friend to all creatures*, 'he is *justly* named *Bráhmena*, or *united to the Great* '*One*.

88. 'In restraining the organs which run wild 'among ravishing sensualities, a wise man will 'apply diligent care, like a charioteer in ma-'naging restive horses.

89. 'Those eleven organs, to which the first 'sages gave names, I will comprehensively enu-'merate as the law considers them in due order.

90. 'The

90. 'The nose is the fifth after the ears, the 'skin, the eyes, and the tongue; and the organs 'of speech are reckoned the tenth, after those 'of excretion and generation, and the hands and 'feet:

91. 'Five of them, the ear and the rest in succession, learned men have called organs of sense; 'and the others, organs of action:

92. 'The heart must be considered as the 'eleventh; which, by its natural property, comprises both sense and action; and which being 'subdued, the two other sets, with five in each, 'are also controled.

93. 'A man, by the attachment of his organs 'to sensual pleasure incurs certain guilt; but, 'having wholly subdued them, he thence attains 'heavenly bliss.

94. 'Desire is never satisfied with the enjoyment 'of desired objects; as the fire is not appeased 'with clarified butter; it only blazes more vehemently.

95. 'Whatever man may obtain all those gratifications, or whatever man may resign them 'completely, the resignation of all pleasures is far 'better than the attainment of them.

96. 'The organs being strongly attached to 'sensual delights cannot so effectually be restrained 'by avoiding incentives to pleasure, as by a constant pursuit of divine knowledge.

97. 'To a man contaminated by sensuality 'neither the *Védas*, nor liberality, nor sacrifices, 'nor strict observances, nor pious austerities, ever 'procure felicity.

98. 'He must be considered as really triumphant over his organs, who, on hearing and touching, on seeing and tasting and smelling, *what*

'*may*

' *may please or offend the senses*, neither greatly re-
' joices nor greatly repines:

99. ' But, when one among all his organs fails,
' by that single failure his knowledge of God
' passes away, as water flows through one hole in
' a leathern bottle.

100. ' Having kept all his members *of sense*
' *and action* under control, and obtained also com-
' mand over his heart, he will enjoy every ad-
' vantage, even though he reduce not his body
' by religious austerities.

101. ' At the morning twilight let him stand
' repeating the *gáyatrí* until he see the sun; and
' at evening twilight, let him repeat it sitting,
' until the stars distinctly appear:

102. ' He who stands repeating it at the morn-
' ing twilight, removes *all unknown* nocturnal sin;
' and he who repeats it sitting at evening twilight,
' disperses the taint, that has *unknowingly* been
' contracted in the day;

103. ' But he who stands not repeating it in
' the morning, and sits not repeating it in the
' evening, must be precluded, like a *Súdra*, from
' every sacred observance of the twice born
' classes.

104. ' Near pure water, with his organs holden
' under control, *and* retiring from circumspection
' to some unfrequented place, let him pronounce
' the *gáyatrí*, performing daily ceremonies.

105. ' In reading the *Védángas*, or *grammar*,
' *prosody*, *mathematicks*, *and so forth*, or even such
' parts of the *Véda* as ought constantly to be read,
' there is no prohibition on particular days; nor
' in pronouncing the texts appointed for oblations
' to fire:

106. ' Of

106. 'Of that, which muſt conſtantly be read, 'and is therefore called *Bráhmaſatra*, there can 'be no ſuch prohibition; and the oblation to 'fire, according to the *Véda*, produces good fruit, 'though accompanied with the text *vaſhat'*, which '*on other occaſions* muſt be intermitted on cer-'tain days.

107. 'For him, who ſhall perſiſt a whole year 'in reading the *Véda*, his organs being kept in 'ſubjection, and his body pure, there will always 'riſe good fruit from his *offerings of* milk and 'curds, *of* clarified butter and honey.

108. 'LET the twice born youth, who has 'been girt with the ſacrificial cord, collect wood 'for the holy fire, beg food of his relations, ſleep 'on a low bed, and perform ſuch offices as may 'pleaſe his preceptor, until his return to the 'houſe of his natural father.

109. 'Ten perſons may legally be inſtructed 'in the *Véda*; the ſon of a ſpiritual teacher; 'a boy who is aſſiduous; one who can impart 'other knowledge; one who is juſt; one who 'is pure; one who is friendly; one who is 'powerful; one who can beſtow wealth; one 'who is honeſt; and one who is related by 'blood.

110. 'Let not a ſenſible teacher tell any *other* 'what he is not aſked, nor what he is aſked im-'properly; but let him however intelligent, act 'in the multitude as if he were dumb:

111. 'Of the two perſons, him, who illegally 'aſks, and him, who illegally anſwers, one will 'die, or incur odium.

112. 'Where virtue, and wealth *ſufficient to ſe-'cure it*, are not found, or diligent attention, *at 'leaſt* proportioned *to the holineſs of the ſubject*, in

'that

'that ſoil divine inſtruction muſt not be ſown: it 'would periſh like fine ſeed in barren land.

113. 'A teacher of the *Véda* ſhould rather die 'with his learning, than ſow it in ſterile ſoil, even 'though he be in grevious diſtreſs for ſubſiſtence.

114. 'Sacred Learning, having approached a '*Bráhmen*, ſaid to him: "I am thy precious 'gem; preſerve me with care; deliver me not to 'a ſcorner; (ſo *preſerved* I ſhall become ſupremely 'ſtrong.)

115. 'But communicate me, as to a vigilent de-'poſitory of thy gem, to that ſtudent, whom thou 'ſhalt know to be pure, to have ſubdued his 'paſſions, to perform the duties of his order."

116. 'He who ſhall acquire *knowledge of* the '*Véda* without the aſſent of his preceptor, incurs 'the guilt of ſtealing the ſcripture, and ſhall ſink 'to the region of torment.

117. 'From whatever teacher a ſtudent has 'received inſtruction, either popular, ceremonial, 'or ſacred, let him firſt ſalute his inſtructor, when 'they meet.

118. 'A *Bráhmen*, who completely governs his 'paſſions, though he know the *gáyatrí* only, is 'more honourable than he, who governs not his 'paſſions, who eats all *ſorts of food*, and ſells all '*ſorts of commodities*, even though he know the 'three *Védas*.

119. 'When a ſuperior ſits on a couch or 'bench, let not an inferior ſit on it with him; 'and, if an inferior be ſitting on a couch, let him 'riſe to ſalute a ſuperior.

120. 'The vital ſpirits of a young man mount 'upwards *to depart from him*, when an elder ap-'proaches; but by riſing and ſalutation he reco-'vers them.

121. 'A

121. ‘ A youth who habitually greets and con-
‘ ſtantly reveres the aged, obtains an increaſe of
‘ four things ; life, knowledge, fame, ſtrength.

122. ‘ After the word of ſalutation, a *Bráhmen*
‘ muſt addreſs an elder ; ſaying, “ I am ſuch an
‘ one,” pronouncing his own name.

123. ‘ If any perſons, *through ignorance of the*
‘ Sanſcrit *language*, underſtand not the import of
‘ his name, to them ſhould a learned man ſay,
“ It is I ;” and in that manner he ſhould addreſs
‘ all *claſſes of* women.

124. ‘ In the ſalutation he ſhould pronounce,
‘ after his own name, the vocative particle *bhós* ;
‘ for the particle *bhós* is held by the wiſe to have
‘ the ſame property with names *fully expreſſed*.

125. ‘ A *Bráhmen* ſhould thus be ſaluted in re-
‘ turn : “ May’ſt thou live long, excellent man !”
‘ and at the end of his name, the vowel and pre-
‘ ceding conſonant ſhould be lengthened, *with an*
‘ *acute accent*, to three ſyllabick moments *or ſhort*
‘ *vowels*.

126. ‘ That *Bráhmen*, who knows not the form
‘ of returning a ſalutation, muſt not be ſaluted by
‘ a man of learning : as a *Súdra*, even ſo is he.

127. ‘ Let a learned man aſk a prieſt, when he
‘ meets him, if his devotion proſpers ; a warriour,
‘ if he is unhurt ; a merchant, if his wealth is
‘ ſecure ; and one of the ſervile claſs, if he enjoys
‘ good health ; *uſing reſpectively the words*, cus’alam,
‘ anámayam, cſhémam, *and* árógyam.

128. ‘ He, who has juſt performed a ſolemn
‘ ſacrifice and ablution, muſt not be addreſſed by
‘ his name, even though he be a younger man ;
‘ but he, who knows the law, ſhould accoſt him
‘ with the vocative particle, or with *bhavat*, the
‘ the pronoun of reſpect.

D 129. ‘ To

129. ‘ To the wife of another, and to any wo-
‘ man not related by blood, he muſt ſay, “ *bhavati*,
‘ and amiable ſiſter.”

130. ‘ To his uncles paternal and maternal, to
‘ his wife's father, to performers of the ſacrifice,
‘ and to ſpiritual teachers; he muſt ſay, “ I am
‘ ſuch an one”—riſing up to ſalute them, even
‘ though younger than himſelf.

131. ‘ The ſiſter of his mother, the wife of his
‘ maternal uncle, his own wife's mother, and the
‘ ſiſter of his father, muſt be ſaluted like the wife
‘ of his father or preceptor: they are equal to his
‘ father's or his preceptor's wife.

132. ‘ The wife of his brother, if ſhe be of the
‘ ſame claſs, muſt be ſaluted every day; but his
‘ paternal and maternal kinſwomen need only be
‘ greeted on his return from a journey.

133. ‘ With the ſiſter of his father and of his
‘ mother, and with his own elder ſiſter, let him
‘ demean himſelf as with his mother; though his
‘ mother be more venerable than they.

134. ‘ Fellow citizens are equal for ten years;
‘ dancers and ſingers, for five; learned theolo-
‘ gians, for leſs than three; but perſons related by
‘ blood, for a ſhort time: *that is, a greater difference*
‘ *of age deſtroys their equality.*

135. ‘ The ſtudent muſt conſider a *Bráhmen*,
‘ though but ten years old, and a *Cſhatriya*, though
‘ aged a hundred years, as father and ſon; as
‘ between thoſe two, the young *Bráhmen* is *to be*
‘ *reſpected as* the father.

136. ‘ Wealth, kindred, age, moral conduct,
‘ and, fifthly, divine knowledge, entitle men to
‘ reſpect; but that which is laſt mentioned in
‘ order, is the moſt reſpectable.

137. ‘ Whatever man of the three *highest* classes ‘ possesses the most of those five, both in number ‘ and degree, that man is entitled to most respect; ‘ even a *Súdra*, if he have entered the tenth decad ‘ of his age.

138. ‘ Way must be made for a man in a ‘ wheeled carriage, or above ninety years old, or ‘ afflicted with disease, or carrying a burthen; for ‘ a woman; for a priest just returned from the ‘ mansion of his preceptor; for a prince, and for ‘ a bridegroom:

139. ‘ Among all those, if they be met at one ‘ time, the priest just returned home and the ‘ prince are most to be honoured; and of those ‘ two, the priest just returned, should be treated ‘ with more respect than the prince.

140 ‘ That priest who girds his pupil with the ‘ sacrificial cord, and afterwards instructs him in ‘ the whole *Véda*, with the law of sacrifice and ‘ the sacred *Upanishads*, holy sages call an *áchárya*:

141. ‘ But, he, who for his livelihood, gives ‘ instruction in a part only of the *Véda*, or in gram- ‘ mar, and in other *Védángas*, is called an *upádhyáya*, ‘ or sublecturer.

142. ‘ The father, who performs the ceremo- ‘ nies on conception and the like, according to ‘ law, and who nourishes the child with his first ‘ rice, has the epithet of *guru*, or venerable.

143. ‘ He, who receives a stipend for preparing ‘ the holy fire, for conducting the *páca* and ‘ *agnishtóma*, and for performing other sacrifices, ‘ is called in this code the *ritwij* of his employer.

144. ‘ He, who truly and faithfully fills both ‘ ears with the *Véda*, must be considered as equal ‘ to a mother; he must be revered as a father; ‘ him the pupil must never grieve.

145. 'A mere *ácbárya*, or *a teacher of the* gá-
'yatrí *only*, ſurpaſſes ten *upádbyáyas*; a father, a
'hundred ſuch *ácháryas*; and a mother, a thouſand
'natural fathers.

146. 'Of him, who gives natural birth, and
'him, who gives knowledge of the whole *Véda*,
'the giver of ſacred knowledge is the more ve-
'nerable father; ſince the *ſecond or* divine birth
'enſures life to the twice born both in this world
'and hereafter eternally.

147. 'Let a man conſider that as a mere
'human birth, which his parents gave him for
'their mutual gratification, and which he receives
'after lying in the womb;

148. 'But that birth, which his principal
'*ácbárya*, who knows the whole *Véda*, procures for
'him by *his divine mother* the *gáyatrí*, is a true
'birth: that birth is exempt from age and from
'death.

149. 'Him, who confers on a man the benefit
'of ſacred learning, whether it be little or much,
'let him know to be here named *guru*, or *ve-
'nerable father*, in conſequence of that heavenly
'benefit.

150. 'A *Brábmen*, who is the giver of ſpiritual
'birth, the teacher of preſcribed duty, is by right
'*called* the father of an old man, though himſelf
'be a child.

151. 'CAVI, or *the learned*, child of ANGIRAS,
'taught his paternal uncles and couſins to read the
'*Véda*, and, excelling them in divine knowledge,
'ſaid to them, "little ſons:"

152. 'They, moved with reſentment, aſked the
'Gods the meaning of that *expreſſion*; and the
'Gods, being aſſembled, anſwered them: "The
'child has addreſſed you properly;

153. 'For

152. ‘ For an unlearned man is in truth a ‘ child; and he who teaches him the *Véda*, is his ‘ father: holy ſages have always ſaid child to an ‘ ignorant man, and father to a teacher of ſcrip- ‘ ture.”

154. ‘ Greatneſs is not conferred by years, not ‘ by gray hairs, not by wealth, not by powerful ‘ kindred: the divine ſages have eſtabliſhed this ‘ rule; “ Whoever has read the *Védas* and their ‘ *Angas*, he among us is great.”

155. ‘ The ſeniority of prieſts is from ſacred ‘ learning; of warriours from valour; of mer- ‘ chants from abundance of grain; of the ſervile ‘ claſs only from priority of birth.

156. ‘ A man is not therefore aged, becauſe his ‘ head is gray: him, ſurely, the Gods conſidered ‘ as aged, who, though young in years, has read ‘ *and underſtands* the *Véda*.

157. ‘ As an elephant made of wood, as an ‘ antelope made of leather, ſuch is an unlearned ‘ *Bráhmen*: thoſe three have nothing but names.

158. ‘ As an eunuch is unproductive with wo- ‘ men, as cow with a cow is unprolifick, as libe- ‘ rality to a fool is fruitleſs, ſo is a *Bráhmen* uſeleſs, ‘ if he read not the holy texts.

159. ‘ Good inſtruction muſt be given without ‘ pain to the inſtructed; and ſweet gentle ſpeech ‘ muſt be uſed by a preceptor, who cheriſhes virtue.

160. ‘ He, whoſe diſcourſe and heart are pure, ‘ and ever perfectly guarded, attains all the fruit ‘ ariſing from his complete courſe of ſtudying the ‘ *Véda*.

161. ‘ Let not a man be querulous even ‘ though in pain; let him not injure another in ‘ deed or in thought; let him not even utter a word, ‘ by which his fellow creature may ſuffer uneaſi- ‘ neſs;

'ness; since that will obstruct his own progress to 'future beatitude.

162. 'A *Bráhmen* should constantly shun wordly 'honour, as he should shun poison; and rather 'constantly seek disrespect, as he would seek nectar;

163. 'For though scorned, he may sleep with 'pleasure; with pleasure may he awake; with 'pleasure may he pass through this life: but the 'scorner utterly perishes.

164. 'Let the twice born youth, whose soul 'has been formed by this regular succession of 'prescribed acts, collect by degrees, while he 'dwells with his preceptor, the devout habits 'proceeding from the study of scripture.

165. 'With various modes of devotion, and 'with austerities ordained by the law, must the 'whole *Véda* be read, and above all the sacred '*Upanishads*, by him, who has received a new birth.

166. 'Let the best of the twice born classes, 'intending to practise devotion, continually repeat 'the reading of scripture; since a repetition of 'reading the scripture is here styled the highest 'devotion of a *Bráhmen*.

167. Yes verily; that student in theology per- 'forms the highest act of devotion *with his whole* '*body*, to the extremities of his nails, even though 'he *be so far sensual as to* wear a chaplet of sweet 'flowers, who to the utmost of his ability daily 'reads the *Véda*.

168. 'A twice born man, who not having stu- 'died the *Véda*, applies diligent attention to a dif- 'ferent *and worldly* study, soon falls, even when 'living, to the condition of a *Súdra*; and his des- 'cendants after him.

169. 'The first birth is from a natural mother; 'the second, from the ligation of the zone; the

'third

'third from the due performance of the ſacrifice;
'ſuch are the births of him who is uſually called
'twice born, according to a text of the *Véda*:

170. 'Among them his divine birth is that, 'which is diſtinguiſhed by the ligation of the 'zone, *and ſacrificial cord*; and in that *birth* the '*Gáyatrí* is his mother, and the *Achárya*, his father.

171. 'Sages call the *Achárya* father, from his 'giving inſtruction in the *Véda*: nor can any holy 'rite be performed by a young man, before his 'inveſtiture.

172. '*Till he be inveſted with the ſigns of his claſs*, 'he muſt not pronounce any ſacred text, except 'what ought to be uſed in obſequies to an anceſtor; 'ſince he is on a level with a *Súdra* before his new 'birth from the revealed ſcripture:

173. 'From him, who has been duly inveſted, 'are required both the performance of devout acts 'and the ſtudy of the *Véda* in order, preceded by 'ſtated ceremonies.

174. 'Whatever ſort of leathern mantle, ſacri'ficial thread, and zone, whatever ſtaff, and what'ever under-apparel are ordained, *as before men'tioned*, for a youth of each claſs, the like muſt 'alſo be uſed in his religious acts.

175. 'Theſe *following* rules muſt a *Brahmachárí* 'or *ſtudent in theology*, obſerve, while he dwells 'with his preceptor; keeping all his members 'under control, for the ſake of increaſing his ha'bitual devotion.

176. 'Day by day, having bathed and being 'purified, let him offer freſh water to the Gods, 'the Sages, and the Manes; let him ſhow reſpect 'to the images of the deities, and bring wood for 'the oblation to fire.

177. 'Let him abstain from honey, from flesh 'meat, from perfumes, from chaplets of flowers, 'from sweet vegetable juices, from women, from 'all sweet substances turned acid, and from in-'jury to animated beings;

178. 'From unguents for his limbs, and from 'black powder for his eyes, from wearing san-'dals, and carrying an umbrella, from sensual 'desires, from wrath, from covetousness, from 'dancing, and from vocal and instrumental musick;

179. 'From gaming, from disputes, from de-'traction, and from falsehood, from embracing 'or wantonly looking at women, and from dis-'service to other men.

180. 'Let him constantly sleep alone: let him 'never waste his own manhood; for he, who vo-'luntarily wastes his manhood, violates the rule of 'his order, *and becomes an* avacírni:

181. 'A twice born youth, who has involun-'tarily wasted his manly strength during sleep, 'must repeat with reverence, having bathed and 'paid homage to the sun, this text of scripture: "*Again let my strength return to me.*"

182. 'Let him carry water pots, flowers, cow-'dung, fresh earth, and *cus'a*-grass, as much as 'may be useful to his preceptor; and let him per-'form every day the duty of a religious mendicant.

183. 'Each day must a *Bráhmen* student receive 'his food by begging, with due care, from the 'houses of persons renowned for discharging their 'duties, and not deficient in performing the sacri-'fices which the *Véda* ordains.

184. 'Let him not beg from the cousins of his 'preceptor; nor from his own cousins; nor from 'other kinsmen by the father's side, or by the 'mother's; but, if other houses be not accessible,

'let

'let him begin with the laſt of thoſe in order, 'avoiding the firſt;

185. 'Or, if none of thoſe *houſes* juſt mentioned 'can be found, let him go begging through the 'whole diſtrict, round the village, keeping his 'organs in ſubjection, and remaining ſilent; but 'let him turn away from ſuch as have committed 'any deadly ſin.

186. 'Having brought logs of wood from a 'diſtance, let him place them in the open air; and 'with them let him make an oblation to fire with'out remiſſneſs, both evening and morning.

187. 'He, who for ſeven ſucceſſive days omits 'the ceremony of begging food, and offers not wood 'to the ſacred fire, muſt perform the penance of 'an *avacírní*, unleſs he be afflicted with illneſs.

188. 'Let the ſtudent perſiſt conſtantly in ſuch 'begging, but let him not eat the food of one 'perſon only: the ſubſiſtence of a ſtudent by beg'ging is held equal to faſting *in religious merit.*

189. 'Yet, when he is aſked in a ſolemn act in 'honour of the Gods or the Manes, he may eat 'at his pleaſure the food of a ſingle perſon; ob'ſerving, however, the laws of abſtinence and the 'auſterity of an anchoret: thus the rule of his 'order is kept inviolate.

190. 'This duty of a mendicant is ordained by 'the wiſe for a *Bráhmen* only; but no ſuch act is 'appointed for a warriour, or for a merchant.

191. 'Let the ſcholar, when commanded by his 'preceptor, and even when he has received no 'command, always exert himſelf in reading, 'and in all acts uſeful to his teacher.

192. 'Keeping in due ſubjection his body, his 'ſpeech, his organs of ſenſe, and his heart, let him

'ſtand

'stand, with the palms of his hands joined, looking 'at the face of his preceptor.

193. 'Let him always keep his right arm uncovered, be always decently apparelled, and properly composed; and when his instructor says, "be seated," let him sit opposite to his venerable 'guide.

194. 'In the presence of his preceptor let him 'always eat less, and wear a coarser mantle with 'worse appendages; let him rise before, and go 'to rest after his tutor.

195. 'Let him not answer his teacher's orders, 'or converse with him, reclining on a bed; nor 'sitting, nor eating, nor standing, nor with an 'averted face:

196. 'But let him both *answer and converse*, if 'his preceptor sit, standing up; if he stand, advancing toward him; if he advance, meeting 'him; if he run, hastening after him;

197. 'If his face be averted, going round to 'front him, *from left to right*; if he be at a little 'distance, approaching him; if reclined, bending 'to him; and, if he stand ever so far off, running 'toward him.

198. 'When his teacher is nigh, let his couch 'or his bench be always placed low: when his 'preceptor's eye can observe him, let him not sit 'carelessly at ease.

199. 'Let him never pronounce the mere name 'of his tutor, even in his absence; nor ever mimick 'his gait, his speech, or his manner.

200. 'In whatever place, either true but censorious, or false and defamatory, discourse is held 'concerning his teacher, let him there cover his 'ears or remove to another place:

201. 'By censuring his preceptor, though justly, 'he will be born an ass; by falsely defaming him,

'a dog;

' a dog; by uſing his goods without leave, a ſmall
' worm; by envying his merit, a larger inſect
' or reptile.

202 ' He muſt not ſerve his tutor by the in-
' tervention of another, while himſelf ſtands aloof;
' nor muſt he attend him in a paſſion, nor when a
' woman is near; from a carriage or raiſed ſeat
' he muſt deſcend to ſalute his heavenly director.

203. ' Let him not ſit with his preceptor to the
' leeward, or to the windward of him; nor let
' him ſay any thing which the venerable man can-
' not hear.

204. ' He may ſit with his teacher in a carriage
' drawn by bulls, horſes, or camels; on a terrace,
' on a pavement of ſtones, or on a mat of woven
' graſs; on a rock, on a wooden bench, or in
' a boat.

205. ' When his tutor's tutor is near, let him
' demean himſelf as if his own were preſent; nor
' let him, unleſs ordered by his ſpiritual father,
' proſtrate himſelf *in his preſence* before his natural
' father, or paternal uncle.

206. ' This is likewiſe ordained as his conſtant
' behaviour toward his other inſtructors in ſcience;
' toward his elder paternal kinſmen; toward all
' who may reſtrain him from ſin, and all who
' give him ſalutary advice.

207. ' Toward men alſo, who are truly vir-
' tuous, let him always behave as toward his pre-
ceptor; and, in like manner, toward the ſons of
' his teacher, who are entitled to reſpect *as older
' men, and are not ſtudents*; and toward the paternal
' kinſmen of his venerable tutor.

208. ' The ſon of his preceptor, whether
' younger or of equal age, or a ſtudent, if he be
' capable of teaching the *Véda,* deſerves the ſame

' honour

'honour with the preceptor himſelf, *when he is* '*preſent* at any ſacrificial act:

209. 'But he muſt not perform for the ſon of 'his teacher, the duty of rubbing his limbs, or of 'bathing him, or of eating what he leaves, or of 'waſhing his feet.

210. 'The wives of his preceptor, if they be 'of the ſame claſs, muſt receive equal honour 'with their venerable huſband; but if they be of a 'different claſs, they muſt be honoured only by 'riſing and ſalutation.

211. 'For no wife of his teacher muſt he per-'form the offices of pouring ſcented oil on them, 'of attending them while they bathe, of rubbing 'their legs and arms, or of decking their hair;

212. Nor muſt a young wife of his preceptor 'be greeted even by the ceremony of touching her 'feet, if he have completed his twentieth year, or 'can diſtinguiſh virtue from vice.

213. 'It is the nature of women in this world 'to cauſe the ſeduction of men; for which reaſon 'the wiſe are never unguarded in the company of 'females:

214. 'A female indeed, is able to draw from 'the right path in this life not a fool only, but 'even a ſage, and can lead him in ſubjection to 'deſire or to wrath.

215. 'Let not a man, therefore, ſit in a ſequeſ-'tered place with his neareſt female relations: 'the aſſemblage of corporeal organs is powerful 'enough to ſnatch wiſdom from the wiſe.

216. 'A young ſtudent may, as the law directs, 'make proſtration at his pleaſure on the ground 'before a young wife of his tutor, ſaying, "I am 'ſuch an one;"

217. 'And

217. ‘ And on his return from a journey, he ‘ must once touch the feet of his preceptor’s *aged* ‘ wife, and salute her each day by prostration, ‘ calling to mind the practice of virtuous men.

218. ‘ As he who digs deep with a spade ‘ comes to a spring of water, so the student, who ‘ humbly serves his teacher, attains the knowledge ‘ which lies deep in his teacher’s mind.

219. ‘ WHETHER his head be shorn, or his hair ‘ long, or one lock be bound above in a knot, let ‘ not the sun ever set or rise while he lies asleep ‘ in the village.

220. ‘ If the sun should rise or set, while he ‘ sleeps through sensual indulgence, and knows it ‘ not, he must fast a whole day, repeating the ‘ *gáyatrí*:

221. ‘ He, who has been surprised asleep by the ‘ setting or by the rising sun, and performs not ‘ that penance, incurs great guilt.

222. ‘ Let him adore GOD both at sunrise ‘ and at sunset, as the law ordains, having made ‘ his ablution and keeping his organs controled; ‘ and, with fixed attention, let him repeat the ‘ text, which he ought to repeat, in a place free ‘ from impurity.

223. ‘ IF a woman or a *Súdra* perform any act ‘ leading to the chief temporal good, let the stu- ‘ dent be careful to emulate it; and he may do ‘ whatever gratifies his heart, unless it be for- ‘ bidden by law:

224. ‘ The chief temporal good is by some ‘ declared to consist in virtue and wealth; by ‘ some, in wealth and lawful pleasure; by some, ‘ in virtue alone; by others, in wealth alone; ‘ but the chief good here below is an assemblage ‘ of all three: this is a sure decision.

225. ‘ A

225. 'A TEACHER of the *Véda* is the image of 'GOD; a natural father, the image of BRAHMA': 'a mother, the image of the earth; an elder 'whole brother, the image of the soul:

226. 'Therefore a ſpiritual and a natural fa- 'ther, a mother, and an elder brother, are not to 'be treated with diſreſpect, eſpecially by a *Bráh- 'men*, though the ſtudent be grievouſly pro- 'voked.

227. 'That pain and care which a mother and 'father undergo in producing and rearing chil- 'dren, cannot be compenſated in an hundred 'years.

228. 'Let every man conſtantly do what may 'pleaſe his parents; and, on all occaſions, what 'may pleaſe his preceptor: when thoſe three are 'ſatisfied, his whole courſe of devotion is accom- 'pliſhed.

229. 'Due reverence to thoſe three is con- 'ſidered as the higheſt devotion; and without their 'approbation he muſt perform no other duty.

230. 'Since they alone are held equal to the 'three worlds; they alone, to the three principal 'orders; they alone, to the three *Védas*; they 'alone, to the three fires:

231. 'The natural father is conſidered as the '*gárbapatya*, or nuptial fire; the mother as the '*dacſhina*, or ceremonial; the ſpiritual guide, as 'the *áhavaniya* or ſacrificial: this triad of fires is 'moſt venerable.

232. 'He, who neglects not thoſe three, when 'he becomes a houſe-keeper, will ultimately ob- 'tain dominion over the three worlds; and his 'body being irradiated like a God, he will enjoy 'ſupreme bliſs in heaven.

233. 'By

233. 'By honouring his mother he gains this 'terrestrial world; by honouring his father, the 'intermediate, or *etherial*; and, by assiduous at'tention to his preceptor, even the *celestial* world 'of BRAHMA':

234. 'All duties are completely performed by 'that man, by whom those three are completely 'honoured; but to him by whom they are dis'honoured, all other acts of duty are fruitless.

235. 'As long as those three live, so long he 'must perform no other duty *for his own sake*; 'but delighting in what may conciliate their af'fections and gratify their wishes, he must from 'day to day assiduously wait on them:

236. 'Whatever duty he may perform in 'thought, word, or deed, with a view to the 'next world, without derogation from his respect 'to them; he must declare to them his entire 'performance of it.

237. 'By honouring those three, without more, 'a man effectually does whatever ought to be 'done: this is the highest duty, appearing before 'us like DHERMA himself, and every other act is 'an *upadherma*, or subordinate duty.

238. 'A believer in scripture may receive pure 'knowledge even from a *Súdra*; a lesson of the 'highest virtue, even from a *Chandála*; and a 'woman, bright as a gem, even from the basest 'family:

239. 'Even from poison may nectar be taken; 'even from a child, gentleness of speech; even 'from a foe, prudent conduct; and even from 'an impure substance, gold.

240. 'From every quarter, therefore, must be 'selected women bright as gems, knowledge,

'virtue,

‘ virtue, purity, gentle ſpeech, and various liberal
‘ arts.

241. ‘ In caſe of neceſſity, a ſtudent is required
‘ to learn the *Véda* from one who is not a *Bráh-*
‘ *men*, and, as long as that inſtruction continues, to
‘ honour his inſtructor with obſequious aſſiduity;

242. ‘ But a pupil who ſeeks the incomparable
‘ path to heaven, ſhould not live to the and of
‘ his days in the dwelling of a preceptor who is
‘ no *Bráhmen*, or who has not read all the *Védas*
‘ with their *Angas*.

243. ‘ If he anxiouſly deſire to paſs his whole
‘ life in the houſe of a ſacerdotal teacher, he muſt
‘ ſerve him with aſſiduous care, till he be releaſed
‘ from his mortal frame:

244. ‘ That *Bráhmen*, who has dutifully at-
‘ tended his preceptor, till the diſſolution of his
‘ body, paſſes directly to the eternal manſion of
‘ God.

245. ‘ Let not a ſtudent, who knows his duty,
‘ preſent any gift to his preceptor *before his return*
‘ *home*; but when, by his tutor's permiſſion, he
‘ is going to perform the ceremony on his return,
‘ let him give the venerable man ſome valuable
‘ thing to the beſt of his power;

246. ‘ A field, or gold, a jewel, a cow, or an
‘ horſe, an umbrella, a pair of ſandals, a ſtool,
‘ corn, cloths, or even any very excellent vege-
‘ table: thus will he gain the affectionate re-
‘ membrance of his inſtructor.

247. ‘ The ſtudent for life muſt, if his teacher
‘ die, attend on his virtuous ſon, or his widow,
‘ or on one of his paternal kinſmen, with the ſame
‘ reſpect which he ſhowed to the living:

248. ‘ Should none of thoſe be alive, he muſt
occupy

'occupy the ſtation of his preceptor, the ſeat, 'and the place of religious exerciſes; muſt con- 'tinually pay due attention to the fires, which he 'had conſecrated; and muſt prepare his own 'ſoul for heaven.

249. 'The twice born man, who ſhall thus 'without intermiſſion have paſſed the time of his 'ſtudentſhip, ſhall aſcend, after death, to the moſt 'exalted of regions, and no more again ſpring to 'birth in this lower world.

CHAPTER THE THIRD.

On Marriage; or on the Second Order.

1. ' The diſcipline of a ſtudent in the three ' *Védas* may be continued for thirty-ſix years, in ' the houſe of his preceptor; or for half that time, ' or for a quarter of it, or until he perfectly com- ' prehend them:

2. ' A ſtudent, whoſe rules have not been vio- ' lated, may aſſume the order of a married man, ' after he has read in ſucceſſion a *ſ'ác'há*, or branch ' from each of the three, or from two, or from ' any one of them.

3. ' Being juſtly applauded for the ſtrict per- ' formance of his duty, and having received from ' his *natural or ſpiritual* father the ſacred gift of the ' *Véda*, let him ſit on an elegant bed, decked with ' a garland of flowers, and let his father honour ' him before his nuptials, with a preſent of a cow.

4. ' Let the twice born man, having obtained ' the conſent of his venerable guide, and having ' performed his ablution with ſtated ceremonies, ' on his return home, as the law directs, eſpouſe a ' wife of the ſame claſs with himſelf and endued ' with the marks of excellence.

5. ' She, who is not deſcended from his *pater- ' nal or maternal* anceſtors, within the ſixth degree, ' and who is not *known by her family name to be* of ' the ſame primitive ſtock with his father *or mother*,

'is eligible by a twice born man for nuptials and
'holy union:

6. 'In connecting himself with a wife, let him 'studiously avoid the ten following families, be 'they ever so great, or ever so rich in kine, goats, 'sheep, gold and grain:

7. 'The family which has omitted pre'scribed acts of religion; that, which has pro'duced no male children; that, in which the *Véda* 'has not been read; that, which has thick hair 'on the body; and those, which have been sub'ject to hemorrhoids, to phthisis, to dispepsia, to 'epilepsy, to leprosy, and to elephantiasis.

8. 'Let him not marry a girl with reddish hair, 'nor with any deformed limb; nor one troubled 'with habitual sickness; nor one either with no 'hair or with too much; nor one immoderately 'talkative; nor one with inflamed eyes;

9. 'Nor one with the name of a constellation, 'of a tree or of a river, of a barbarous nation, or 'of a mountain, of a winged creature, a snake, or 'a slave; nor with any name raising an image of 'terrour.

10. 'Let him chuse for his wife a girl, whose 'form has no defect; who has an agreeable name; 'who walks *gracefully* like a phenicopteros, or like 'a young elephant; whose hair and teeth are 'moderate respectively in quantity and in size; 'whose body has exquisite softness.

11. 'Her, who has no brother, or whose father 'is not well known, let no sensible man espouse, 'through fear lest, *in the former case*, her father 'should take her first son as his own *to perform his 'obsequies*; or, *in the second case*, lest an illicit mar'riage should be contracted.

12. 'For

12. 'For the first marriage of the twice born 'classes, a woman of the same class is recommended; but for such as are impelled by inclination to marry again, women in the direct 'order of the classes are to be preferred:

13. 'A *Súdra* woman only must be the wife of 'a *Súdra*; she and a *Vaisyà*, of a *Vaisya*; they two 'and a *Cshatriyá*, of a *Cshatriya*; those two and a '*Brahmaní* of a *Bráhmen*.

14. 'A woman of the servile class is not mentioned, even in the recital of any ancient story, as 'the first wife of a *Bráhmen* or of a *Cshatriya*, though 'in the greatest difficulty to find a suitable match.

15. 'Men of the twice born classes, who through 'weakness of intellect, irregularly marry women 'of the lowest class, very soon degrade their families and progeny to the state of *Súdras*:

16. 'According to ATRI and to (GO'TAMA) 'the son of UTAT'HYA, he who *thus* marries a woman of the servile class, *if he be a priest*, is degraded instantly; according to SAUNACA, on 'the birth of a son, *if he be a warriour*; and, *if he* '*be a merchant*, on the bith of a son's son, according to (me) BHRĬGU.

17. 'A *Bráhmen*, if he take a *Súdra* to his bed, '*as his first wife*, sinks to the regions of torment; 'if he beget a child by her, he loses even his 'priestly rank:

18. 'His sacrifices to the Gods, his oblations 'to the Manes, and his hospitable attentions to 'strangers, must be supplied principally by her; 'but the Gods and Manes will not eat such offerings; nor can heaven be attained by such hospitality.

19. 'For the crime of him, who *thus illegally* 'drinks the moisture of a *Súdra's* lips, who is

 'tainted

'tainted by her breath, and who even begets a 'child on her body, the law declares no ex- 'piation.

20. 'Now learn compendiously the eight forms 'of the nuptial ceremony, used by the four classes, 'some good and some bad in this world, and in 'the next:

21. 'The ceremony of BRAHMA', of the *Dévas* 'of the *Rishis*, of the *Prajápatis*, of the *Asuras*, 'of the *Gandharvas*, and of the *Racshasas*; the 'eighth and basest is that of the *Pisáchas*.

22. 'Which of them is permitted by law to 'each class and what are the good and bad pro- 'perties of each ceremony, all this I will fully 'declare to you, together with the qualities, good 'and bad, of the offspring.

23. 'Let mankind know, that *the* six *first* in 'direct order are *by some held* valid in the case of 'a priest; the four last, in that of a warriour; and 'the same four, except the *Racshasa* marriage, in 'the cases of a merchant and a man of the servile 'class:

24. Some consider the four first only as ap- 'proved in the case of a priest; one, that of *Racshasas*, 'as peculiar to a soldier; and that of *Asuras*, to 'a mercantile and a servile man:

25. 'But in this code, three of *the* five *last* are 'held legal, and two illegal: the ceremonies of '*Pisáchas* and *Asuras* must never be performed.

26. 'For a military man the before mentioned 'marriages of *Gandharvas* and *Racshasas*, whether 'separate or mixed, *as when a girl is made captive* '*by her lover, after a victory over her kinsmen*, are 'permitted by law.

27. 'The gift of a daughter, clothed only with 'a single robe, to a man learned in the *Véda*,

'whom

'whom her father voluntarily invites, and re-'spectfully receives, is the nuptial right called 'Bráhma.

28. 'The rite which sages call *Daiva*, is the 'gift of a daughter, whom her father has decked 'in gay attire, when the sacrifice is already begun, 'to the officiating priest, who performs that act 'of religion.

29. 'When the father gives his daughter away, 'after having received from the bridegroom one 'pair of kine, or two pairs, for uses prescribed 'by law, that marriage is termed *Arsha*.

30. The nuptial rite called *Prájápatya*, is when 'the father gives away his daughter with due ho-'nour, saying distinctly, "May both of you 'perform together your civil and religious 'duties!"

31. 'When the bridegroom, having given as 'much wealth as he can afford to the father and 'paternal kinsmen, and to the damsel herself, 'takes her voluntarily as his bride, that marriage 'is named *Asura*.

32. 'The reciprocal connection of a youth and 'a damsel, with mutual desire, is the marriage 'denominated *Gandharva*, contracted for the 'purpose of amorous embraces, and proceeding 'from sensual inclination.

33. 'The seizure of a maiden by force from 'her house, while she weeps and calls for assist-'ance, after her kinsmen and friends have been 'slain in battle, or wounded, and their houses 'broken open, is the marriage styled *Racshasa*.

34. 'When the lover secretly embraces the 'damsel, either sleeping or flushed with strong 'liquor, or disordered in her intellect, that sinful

'marriage, called *Piſácha,* is the eighth and the 'baſeſt.

35. 'The gift of daughters in marriage by the 'ſacerdotal claſs, is moſt approved, when they 'previouſly have poured water into the hands of 'the bridegroom; but the ceremonies of the other 'claſſes may be performed according to their ſe-'veral fancies.

36. 'Among theſe nuptial rites, what quality is 'aſcribed by MENU to each, hear now ye '*Bráhmens,* hear it all from me, who fully de-'clare it!

37. 'The ſon of a *Bráhmì,* or wife by the firſt 'ceremony, redeems from ſin, if he perform vir-'tuous acts, ten anceſtors, ten deſcendants, and 'himſelf the twenty-firſt perſon.

38. 'A ſon, born of a wife by the *Daiva* nuptials, 'redeems ſeven and ſeven in higher and lower de-'grees; of a wife by the *A'rſha* three and three; 'of a wife by the *Prájápatya* ſix and ſix.

39. 'By four marriages, the *Bráhma* and ſo 'forth, in direct order, are born ſons illumi-'ned by the *Véda,* learned men, beloved by the 'learned,

40. 'Adorned with beauty, and with the qua-'lity of goodneſs, wealthy, famed, amply gra-'tified with lawful enjoyments, performing all 'duties, and living an hundred years:

41. 'But in the other *four* baſe marriages, which 'remain, are produced ſons acting cruelly, ſpeak-'ing falſely, abhorring the *Véda,* and the duties 'preſcribed in it.

42. 'From the blameleſs nuptial rites of men 'ſprings a blameleſs progeny; from the reprehen-'ſible, a reprehenſible offspring: let mankind,

'therefore,

'therefore, ſtudiouſly avoid the culpable forms 'of marriage.

43. 'The ceremony of joining hands is appointed for thoſe, who marry women of their 'own claſs; but, with women of a different claſs, 'the following nuptial ceremonies are to be obſerved:

44. 'By a *Cſhatriyà* on her marriage with a '*Bráhmen*, an arrow muſt be held in her hand; 'by a *Vaiſyà* woman, with a bridegroom *of the ſacerdotal or military claſs*, a whip; *and* by a *Súdrà* 'bride, *marrying a prieſt, a ſoldier, or a merchant*, 'muſt be held the ſkirt of a mantle.

45. 'Let the huſband approach his wife in 'due ſeaſon, *that is, at the time fit for pregnancy*; 'let him be conſtantly ſatisfied with her alone; 'but, except on the forbidden days of the moon, 'he may approach her, being affectionately diſpoſed, *even out of due ſeaſon*, with a deſire of conjugal intercourſe.

46. 'Sixteen days and nights in each month, 'with four diſtinct days neglected by the virtuous, are called the natural ſeaſon of women:

47. 'Of thoſe ſixteen, the four firſt, the eleventh, and the thirteenth, are reprehended: the 'ten remaining nights are approved.

48. 'Some ſay, that on the even nights are 'conceived ſons; on the odd nights daughters; 'therefore let the man, who wiſhes for a ſon, 'approach his wife in due ſeaſon on the even 'nights;

49. 'But a boy is in truth produced by the 'greater quantity of the male ſtrength; and a 'girl by a greater quantity of the female; by 'equality, an hermaphrodite, or a boy and a girl;

'by

'by weakneſs or deficiency, is occaſioned a 'failure of conception.

50. 'He, who avoids conjugal embraces on 'the ſix reprehended nights and on eight others, 'is equal in chaſtity to a *Brahmachárì*, in which-'ever of the *two next* orders he may live.

51. 'Let no father, who knows the law, re-'ceive a gratuity, however ſmall, for giving his 'daughter in marriage; ſince the man, who, 'through avarice, takes a gratuity *for that purpoſe*, 'is a ſeller of his offspring.

52. 'Whatever male relations, through delu-'ſion of mind, take poſſeſſion of a woman's 'property, be it only her carriages or her clothes, 'ſuch offenders will ſink to a region of torment.

53. 'Some ſay that the bull and cow *given* in 'the nuptial ceremony of the *Rĭſhis*, are a bribe 'to the father; but this is untrue: a bribe *in-'deed*, whether large or ſmall, is an actual ſale of '*the daughter*.

54. 'When money or goods are given to 'damſels, whoſe kinſmen receive them not for 'their own uſe, it is no ſale: it is merely a token 'of courteſy and affection to the brides.

55. 'Married women muſt be honoured and 'adorned by their fathers and brethren, by their 'huſbands, and by the brethren of their huſbands, 'if they ſeek abundant proſperity:

56. 'Where females are honoured, there the 'deities are pleaſed; but where they are diſho-'noured, there all religious acts become fruitleſs.

57. 'Where female relations are made miſera-'ble, the family of him who makes them ſo, 'very ſoon wholly periſhes; but, where they are 'not unhappy, the family always increaſes.

58. 'On

58. 'On whatever houses the women of a
'family, not being duly honoured, pronounce an
'imprecation, those houses, with all that belong
'to them, utterly perish, as if destroyed by a
'sacrifice for the death of an enemy.

59. 'Let those women, therefore, be con-
'tinually supplied with ornaments, apparel and
'food, at festivals and at jubilees, by men de-
'sirous of wealth.

60. 'In whatever family the husband is con-
'tented with his wife, and the wife with her
'husband, in that house will fortune be assuredly
'permanent.

61. 'Certainly, if the wife be not elegantly
'attired, she will not exhilarate her husband; and
'if her lord want hilarity, offspring will not be
'produced.

62. 'A wife being gaily adorned, her whole
'house is embellished; but, if she be destitute of
'ornament, all will be deprived of decoration.

63. 'By culpable marriages, by omission of
'prescribed ceremonies, by neglect of reading the
'*Véda*, and by irreverence toward a *Bráhmen*,
'great families are sunk to a low state.

64. 'So they are by practising manual arts, by
'*lending at interest and other* pecuniary transactions,
'by begetting children on *Súdras* only, by traffick
'in kine, horses, and carriages, by agriculture
'and by attendance on a king.

65. 'By sacrificing for such as have no right
'to sacrifice, and by denying a future compensa-
'tion for good works, great families, being de-
'prived of sacred knowledge, are quickly de-
'stroyed;

66. 'But families, enriched by a knowledge of

'the

'the *Véda*, though possessing little temporal 'wealth, are numbered among the great, and ac'quire exalted fame.

67. 'LET the house-keeper perform domestic 'religious rites, with the nuptial fire, according 'to law, and the ceremonies of the five great 'sacraments, and the several acts which must day 'by day be performed.

68 'A house keeper has five places of slaughter, '*or where small living creatures may be slain*; his 'kitchen hearth, his grindstone, his broom, his 'pestle and mortar, his water pot; by using 'which, he becomes in bondage to sin:

69. 'For the sake of expiating *offences committed* '*ignorantly* in those places *mentioned* in order, the 'five great sacraments were appointed by eminent 'sages to be performed each day by such as keep 'house.

70. 'Teaching and studying the scripture is 'the sacrament of the *Véda*; offering cakes and 'water, the sacrament of the Manes; an oblation 'to fire, the sacrament of the Deities; giving 'rice or other food to living creatures, the sacra'ment of spirits; receiving guests with honour, 'the sacrament of men;

71. 'Whoever omits not those five great ce'remonies, if he have ability *to perform them*, is 'untainted by the sins of the *five* slaughtering 'places, even though he constantly reside at 'home;

72. 'But whoever cherishes not five orders of 'beings, *namely*, the deities; those, who demand 'hospitality; those, whom he ought by law to 'maintain; his departed forefathers; and him'self; that man lives not even though he 'breathe.

73. 'Some

73. 'Some call the five ſacraments *ahuta* and 'huta, *prahuta*, *bráhmya-huta* and *práſita*:

74. '*Ahuta*, or unoffered, is divine ſtudy; *huta*, 'or offered, is the oblation to fire; *prahuta*, or 'well offered, is the food given to ſpirits; *bráhmya-huta*, is reſpect ſhewn to twice born gueſts; 'and *práſita*, or well eaten, is the offering of rice 'or water to the manes of anceſtors.

75. 'Let every man in this ſecond order employ himſelf daily in reading the ſcripture, and 'in performing the ſacrament of the Gods; for, 'being employed in the ſacrament of deities, he 'ſupports this whole animal and vegetable world;

76. 'Since his oblation of clarified butter, duly 'caſt into the flame, aſcends in ſmoke to the ſun; 'from the ſun it falls in rain; from rain comes 'vegetable food; and from ſuch food animals 'derive their ſubſiſtence.

77. 'As all creatures ſubſiſt by receiving ſupport from air, thus all orders of men exiſt by 'receiving ſupport from houſe-keepers;

78. 'And ſince men of the three other orders 'are each day nouriſhed by them with divine 'learning and with food, a houſe-keeper is for 'this reaſon of the moſt eminent order:

79. 'That order, therefore, muſt be conſtantly 'ſuſtained with great care by the man who ſeeks 'unperiſhable bliſs in heaven, and in this world 'pleaſurable ſenſations; an order which cannot 'be ſuſtained by men with uncontroled organs.

80. 'The divine ſages, the manes, the gods, 'the ſpirits, and gueſts, pray for benefits to 'maſters of families; let theſe honours, therefore, be done to them by the houſe-keeper who 'knows his duty:

81. 'Let

81. 'Let him honour the Sages by ſtudying 'the *Véda*: the Gods, by oblations to fire ordained by law; the Manes, by pious obſequies; 'men by ſupplying them with food; and ſpirits, 'by gifts to all animated creatures.

82. 'Each day let him perform a *ſráddha* 'with boiled rice and the like, or with water, or 'with milk, roots, and fruit; for thus he obtains 'favour from departed progenitors.

83. 'He may entertain one *Bráhmen* in that ſacrement among the five, which is performed for 'the *Pitrĭs*; but, at the oblation to all the Gods, 'let him not invite even a ſingle prieſt.

84. 'In his domeſtic fire for dreſſing the food 'of all the Gods, after the preſcribed ceremony, 'let a *Bráhmen* make an oblation each day to theſe '*following* divinities;

85. 'Firſt to AGNI, god of fire, and to the 'Lunar God, ſeverally; then, to both of them 'at once; next to the aſſembled gods; and afterwards, to DHANWANTARI, god of medicine;

86. 'To CUHU', goddeſs of the day, when the 'new moon is diſcernible; to ANUMATI, goddeſs 'of the day, after the oppoſition; to PRAJA'PATI, 'or the Lord of Creatures; to DYA'VA' and PRITHIVI', goddeſſes of ſky and earth; and laſtly, 'to the fire of the good ſacrifice.

87. 'Having thus, with fixed attention, offered 'clarified butter in all quarters, proceeding *from* '*the eaſt* in a ſouthern direction to INDRA, YAMA, 'VARUNA, and the god SOMA, let him offer his 'gift to animated creatures:

88. '*Saying*, "I ſalute the *Maruts*," or *Winds*, 'let him throw dreſſed rice near the door; *ſaying*, "I ſalute the water gods," in water; and on his

'peſtle

'pestle and mortar, *saying*, "I salute the gods of 'large trees."

89. 'Let him do the like *in the north east, or* 'near his pillow, to SRI', the goddess of abun-'dance; *in the south west, or* at the foot of his bed, 'to the propitious goddess BHADRACA'LI'; in 'the centre of his mansion, to BRAHMA' and his 'household God;

90. 'To all the Gods assembled, let him throw 'up his oblation in the open air; by day, to the 'spirits who walk in light; and by night, to those 'who walk in darkness:

91. In the building on his house top, *or behind* '*his back*, let him cast his oblation for the welfare 'of all creatures; and what remains let him give 'to the *Pitrĭs* with his face toward the south:

92. 'The share of dogs, of outcasts, of dog-'feeders, of sinful men, punished with elephan-'tiasis or consumption, of crows, and of reptiles, 'let him drop on the ground by little and little.

93. 'A *Bráhmen*, who thus each day shall ho-'nour all beings, will go to the highest region in 'a straight path, in an irradiated form.

94. 'When he has performed his duty of mak-'ing oblations, let him cause his guest to take 'food before himself; and let him give a portion 'of rice, as the law ordains, to the mendicant 'who studies the *Véda*:

'95. 'Whatever fruit shall be obtained by that 'student, as the reward of his virtue, when he shall 'have given a cow to his preceptor, according to 'law, the like reward to virtue shall be obtained 'by the twice born house-keeper, when he has 'given a mouthful of rice to the religious men-'dicant.

96. 'To

96. 'To a *Bráhmen* who knows the true principle of the *Véda*, let him present a portion of 'rice, or a pot of water, garnished with fruit and 'flowers, due ceremonies having preceded:

97. 'Shares of oblations to the Gods, or to the 'Manes, utterly perish, when presented, through 'delusion of mind, by men regardless of duty, to 'such ignorant *Bráhmens* as are mere ashes;

98. 'But an offering in the fire of a sacerdotal 'mouth, which richly blazes with true know-'ledge and piety, will release the giver from dis-'tress, and even from deadly sin.

99. 'To the guest who comes of his own 'accord, let him offer a seat and water, with such 'food as he is able to prepare, after the due rites 'of courtesy.

100. 'A *Bráhmen* coming as a guest, and not 'received with just honour, takes to himself all the 'reward of the house-keeper's former virtue, 'even though he had been so temporate as to live 'on the gleanings of harvests, and so pious as to 'make oblations in five distinct fires.

101. 'Grass and earth to sit on, water to wash 'the feet, and, fourthly affectionate speech are at 'no time deficient in the mansions of the good, '*although they may be indigent*.

102. 'A *Bráhmen*, staying but one night as a 'guest, is called an *atit'hi*; since continuing so 'short a time, he is not even a sojourner for a 'whole *tit'hi*, or *day of the moon*.

103. 'The house-keeper must not consider as 'an *atit'hi* a mere visitor of the same town, or a '*Bráhmen*, who attends him on business, even 'though he come to the house where his wife 'dwells, and where his fires are kindled.

104. 'Should

104. 'Should any house-keepers be so senseless, 'as to seek, on pretence of being guests, the food 'of others, they would fall after death, by reason 'of that baseness, to the condition of cattle be- 'longing to the giver of such food.

105. 'No guest must be dismissed in the even- 'ing by a house-keeper; he is sent by the retir- 'ing sun; and, whether he come in fit season or 'unseasonably, he must not sojourn in the house 'without entertainment.

106. 'Let not himself eat any delicate food, 'without asking his guest to partake of it: the 'satisfaction of a guest will assuredly bring the 'house-keeper wealth, reputation, long life, and a 'place in heaven.

107. 'To the highest guests in the best form, 'to the lowest in the worst, to the equal, equally, 'let him offer seats, resting places, couches; giv- 'ing them proportionable attendance, when they 'depart; and honour as long as they stay.

108. 'Should another guest arrive, when the 'oblation to all the Gods is concluded, for him 'also let the house-keeper prepare food, accord- 'ing to his ability; but let him not repeat his 'offerings to animated beings.

109. 'Let no *Bráhmen* guest proclaim his fa- 'mily and ancestry for the sake of an entertain- 'ment; since he, who thus proclaims them, is 'called by the wise a *vántáśi*, or foul-feeding 'demon.

110. 'A military man is not denominated a 'guest in the house of a *Bráhmen*; nor a man of 'the commercial or servile class; nor his fa- 'miliar friend; nor his paternal kinsman; nor 'his preceptor:

111. ‘ But if a warriour come to his houſe in ‘ the form of a gueſt, let food be prepared for ‘ him, according to his deſire, after the before- ‘ mentioned *Brâhmens* have eaten.

112. ‘ Even to a merchant or a labourer, ap- ‘ proaching his houſe in the manner of gueſts, ‘ let him give food, ſhowing marks of benevo- ‘ lence at the ſame time with his domeſticks:

113. ‘ To others, as familiar friends, and the ‘ reſt before-named, who come with affection ‘ to his place of abode, let him ſerve a repaſt at ‘ the ſame time with his wife *and himſelf*, having ‘ amply provided it according to his beſt means.

114. ‘ To a bride, and to a damſel, to the ſick, ‘ and to pregnant women, let him give food, even ‘ before his gueſts, without heſitation.

115. ‘ The idiot, who firſt eats his own meſs, without having preſented food to the perſons ‘ juſt enumerated, knows not, while he crams, that ‘ he will himſelf be food after death for bandogs ‘ and vultures.

116. ‘ After the repaſt of the *Brâhmen* gueſt, ‘ of his kinſmen, and his domeſticks, the married ‘ couple may eat what remains untouched.

117. ‘ The houſe-keeper, having honoured ‘ ſpirits, holy ſages, men, progenitors, and houſe- ‘ hold gods, may feed on what remains after thoſe ‘ oblations.

118. ‘ He, who eats what has been dreſſed for ‘ himſelf only, eats nothing but ſin: a repaſt on ‘ what remains after the ſacrament is called the ‘ banquet of the good.

119. ‘ After a year from the reception of a ‘ viſitor, let the houſe-keeper again honour a ‘ king, a ſacrificer, a ſtudent returned from his preceptor,

'preceptor, a son-in-law, a father-in-law, and 'a maternal uncle, with a *madhuperca,* or present 'of honey, curds, and fruit.

120. 'A king or a *Bráhmen* arriving at the 'celebration of the sacrament, are to be honoured 'with a *madhuperca*; but not, if the sacrament 'be over: this is a settled rule.

121. 'In the evening let the wife make an 'offering of the dressed food, but without pro-'nouncing any text of the *Véda*: one oblation to 'the assembled gods, thence named *Vaiswadéva,* 'is ordained both for evening and morning.

122. 'FROM month to month, on the dark day 'of the moon, let a twice born man, having 'finished the daily sacrament of the *Pitrĭs,* and 'his fire being still blazing, perform the solemn '*sráddha,* called *pindánwáhárya*:

123. 'Sages have distinguished the monthly '*sráddha* by the title of *anwáhárya,* or *after eaten,* 'that is, eaten after the *pinda* or ball of rice; and 'it must be performed with extreme care, and 'with flesh meat in the best condition.

124. 'What *Bráhmens* must be entertained at 'that ceremony, and who must be accepted, how 'many are to be fed, and with what sorts of food, 'on all those articles, without omission, I will fully 'discourse.

125. 'At the *sráddha* of the gods he may en-'tertain two *Bráhmens*; at that of his father, 'paternal grandfather, and paternal great-grand-'father, three; or one only at that of the gods, 'and one at that for his three paternal ancestors: 'though he abound in wealth, let him not be so-'licitous to entertain a large company.

126. 'A large company destroys these five ad-'vantages; reverence to priests, propriety of time

 and

'and place, purity, and the acquisition of virtuous 'Bráhmens: let him not therefore, endeavour to 'feed a superfluous number.

127. 'This act of due honour to departed souls, 'on the dark day of the moon, is famed by the 'appellation of *pitrya*, or ancestral: the legal ce-'remony, in honour of departed spirits, rewards 'with continual fruit, a man engaged in such ob-'sequies.

128. 'Oblations to the gods and to ancestors 'should be given to a most reverend *Bráhmen*, 'perfectly conversant with the *Véda*; since what is 'given to him produces the greatest reward.

129. 'By entertaining one learned man at the 'oblation to the gods and at that to ancestors, he 'gains more exalted fruit than by feeding a mul-'titude, who know not the holy texts.

130. 'Let him inquire into the ancestry, even 'in a remote degree, of a *Bráhmen*, who has ad-'vanced to the end of the *Véda*: such a man, if 'sprung from good men, is a fit partaker of ob-'lations to gods and to ancestors; such a man 'may justly be called an *atit'hi*, or guest.

131. 'Surely, though a million of men, un-'learned in holy texts, were to receive food, yet 'a single man, learned in scripture, and fully sa-'tisfied with his entertainment, would be of more 'value than all of them together.

132. 'Food, consecrated to the gods and the 'manes, must be presented to a theologian of 'eminent learning; for certainly, when hands 'are smeared with blood, they cannot be cleaned 'with blood only, *nor can sin be removed by the 'company of sinners*.

133. 'As many mouthfuls as an unlearned man shall

'shall swallow at an oblation to the gods and to 'ancestors, so many red hot iron balls must the 'giver of the *sráddha* swallow in the next world.

134. 'Some *Bráhmens* are intent on scriptural 'knowledge; others, on austere devotion; some 'are intent both on religious austerity and on the 'study of the *Véda*; others on the performance 'of sacred rites:

135. 'Oblations to the manes of ancestors 'ought to be placed with care before such as are 'intent on sacred learning: but offerings to the 'gods may be presented, with due ceremonies, to '*Bráhmens* of all the four descriptions.

136. 'There may be a *Bráhmen*, whose father 'had not studied the scripture, though the son 'has advanced to the end of the *Véda*; or there 'may be one, whose son has not read the *Véda*, 'though the father had travelled to the end of it:

137. 'Of those two let mankind consider him 'as the superiour, whose father had studied the 'scripture, yet for the sake of performing rites 'with holy texts, the other is worthy of honour.

138. 'Let no man, at the prescribed obsequies, 'give food to an intimate friend; since advantage 'to a friend must be procured by gifts of different 'property: to that *Bráhmen* let the performer of 'a *sráddha* give food, whom he considers neither 'as a friend nor as a foe.

139. 'For him, whose obsequies and offerings 'of clarified butter are provided chiefly through 'friendship, no fruit is reserved in the next life, 'on account either of his obsequies or of his 'offerings.

140. 'The man, who, through delusion of in'tellect, forms temporal connexions by obsequies,

'is excluded from heavenly manſions, as a giver 'of the *ſráddha* for the ſake of friendſhip, and the 'meaneſt of twice born men:

141. 'Such a convivial preſent, by men of the 'three higheſt claſſes, is called the gift of *Piſáchas*, 'and remains fixed here below, like a blind cow 'in one ſtall.

142. 'As a huſbandman, having ſown ſeed in 'a barren ſoil, reaps no grain, thus a performer 'of holy rites, having given clarified butter to 'an unlearned *Bráhmen*, attains no reward in 'heaven;

143. 'But a preſent made, as the law ordains, 'to a learned theologian, renders both the giver 'and the receiver partakers of good fruits in this 'world and in the next.

144. 'If no learned *Bráhmen* be at hand, he 'may at his pleaſure invite a friend to the *ſráddha*; 'but not a foe, be he ever ſo learned; ſince the 'oblation, being eaten by a foe, loſes all fruit in 'the life to come.

145. 'With great care let him give food at 'the *ſráddha* to a prieſt, who has gone through 'the ſcripture, but has chiefly ſtudied the *Rĭgvéda*; 'to one, who has read all the branches, but prin-'cipally thoſe of the *Yajuſh*; or to one who has 'finiſhed the whole, with particular attention to 'the *Sáman*:

146. 'Of that man whoſe oblation has been 'eaten, after due honours, by any one of thoſe 'three *Bráhmens*, the anceſtors are conſtantly 'ſatisfied as high as the ſeventh perſon, *or to the* '*ſixth degree*.

147 'This is the chief rule in offering the '*ſráddha* to the gods and to anceſtors; but the fol-

'lowing

'lowing may be considered as a subsidiary rule, '*where no such learned priests can be found*, and is 'ever observed by good men:

148. 'Let him entertain his maternal grandfather, his maternal uncle, the son of his sister, 'the father of his wife, his spiritual guide, the 'son of his daughter, or her husband, his maternal cousin, his officiating priest, or the performer 'of his sacrifice.

149. 'For an oblation to the gods, let not the 'man, who knows what is law, scrupulously inquire into the parentage of a *Bráhmen*; but for 'a prepared oblation to ancestors let him examine 'it with strict care.

150. 'Those *Bráhmens*, who have committed 'any inferiour theft or any of the higher crimes, 'who are deprived of virility, or who profess a 'disbelief in a future state, MENU has pronounced 'unworthy of honour at a *sráddha* to the gods or 'to ancestors.

151. 'To a student in theology, who has not 'read the *Véda*, to a man *punished for past crimes* '*by being* born without a prepuce, to a gamester, 'and to such as perform many sacrifices for other 'men, let him never give food at the sacred 'obsequies.

152. 'Physicians, image worshippers for gain, 'sellers of meat, and such as live by low traffick, 'must be shunned in oblations both to the deities 'and to progenitors.

153. 'A public servant of the whole town, or 'of the prince, a man with whitlows on his nails, 'or with black yellow teeth, an opposer of his 'preceptor, a deserter of the sacred fire, and an 'usurer,

154. 'A phthisical man, a feeder of cattle, one 'omitting the five great sacraments, a contemner 'of *Bráhmens*, a younger brother married before 'the elder, an elder brother not married before 'the younger, an a man who subsists by the 'wealth of many relations,

155. 'A dancer, one who has violated the 'rule of chastity in the first or fourth order, the 'husband of a *Súdra*, the son of a twice married 'woman, a man who has lost one eye, and a hus'band in whose house an adulterer dwells,

156. 'One who teaches the *Véda* for wages, and 'one who gives wages to such a teacher, the 'pupil of a *Súdra*, and the *Súdra* preceptor, a rude 'speaker, and the son of an adulteress, born either 'before or after the death of the husband,

157. 'A forsaker, without just cause, of his 'mother, father or preceptor, and a man who 'forms a connexion, either by scriptural or 'connubial affinity, with great sinners,

158. 'A house-burner, a giver of poison, an 'eater of food offered by the son of an adulteress, 'a seller of the moon plant, *a species of mountain 'rue,* a navigator of the ocean, a poetical enco'miast, an oilman, and a suborner of perjury,

159. 'A wrangler with his father, an employer 'of gamesters for his own benefit, a drinker of 'intoxicating spirits, a man punished for sin with 'elephantiasis, one of evil repute, a cheat, and a 'seller of liquids,

160. 'A maker of bows and arrows, the hus'band of a younger sister married before the elder '*of the whole blood*, an injurer of his friend, the 'keeper of a gaming-house, and a father instructed 'in the *Véda* by his own son,

161. 'An epileptick perſon, one who has the 'eryſipelas or the leproſy, a common informer, 'a lunatick, a blind man, and a deſpiſer of ſcripture, muſt all be ſhunned.

162. 'A tamer of elephants, bulls, horſes, or 'camels, a man who ſubſiſts by aſtrology, a 'keeper of birds, and one who teaches the uſe 'of arms,

163. 'He, who diverts watercourſes, and he, 'who is gratified by obſtructing them, he, who 'builds houſes for gain, a meſſenger, and a planter of trees *for pay*,

164. 'A breeder of ſporting dogs, a falconer, 'a ſeducer of damſels, a man delighting in miſchief, a *Bráhmen* living as a *Súdra*, a ſacrificer 'to the inferiour gods only,

165. 'He, who obſerves not approved cuſtoms, 'and he, who regards not preſcribed duties, a conſtant importunate aſker of favours, he, who ſupports himſelf by tillage, a clubfooted man, and 'one deſpiſed by the virtuous,

166. 'A ſhepherd, a keeper of buffalos, the 'huſband of a twice married woman, and the remover of dead bodies *for pay*, are to be avoided 'with great care.

167. 'Thoſe loweſt of *Bráhmens*, whoſe manners are contemptible, who are not admiſſible 'into company at a repaſt, an exalted and learned 'prieſt muſt avoid at both *ſráddhas*.

168. 'A *Bráhmen* unlearned in holy writ, is 'extinguiſhed in an inſtant like a fire of dry graſs: 'to him the oblation muſt not be given; for the 'clarified butter muſt not be poured on aſhes.

169. 'What retribution is prepared in the next 'life for the giver of food to men inadmiſſible into company,

'company, at the *sráddha* to the gods and to an-
'cestors, I will now declare without omission.

170. 'On that food, which has been given to '*Bráhmens* who have violated the rules of their 'order, to the younger brother married before the 'elder, and to the rest who are not admissible 'into company, the *Racshases* eagerly feast.

171. 'He, who makes a marriage contract 'with the connubial fire, while his elder brother 'continues unmarried, is called a *perivéttrĭ*; and 'the elder brother a *perivitti*:

172. 'The *perivêttrĭ*, the *perivitti*, the dam-'sel thus wedded, the giver of her in wedlock, 'and, fifthly, the performer of the nuptial sacri-'fice, all sink to a region of torment.

173. 'He, who lasciviously dallies with the 'widow of his deceased brother, though she be le-'gally married to him, is denominated the hus-'band of a *didhishú*.

174. 'Two sons, named a *cunda* and a *gólaca*, 'are born in adultery; the *cunda*, while the husband 'is alive, and the *gôlaca*, when the husband is dead:

175. 'Those animals begotten by adulterers, 'destroy, both in this world and in the next, the 'food presented to them by such as make obla-'tions to the gods or to the manes.

176. 'The foolish giver of a *sráddha* loses, in 'a future life, the fruit of as many admissible 'guests, as a *thief or the like* person, inadmissible 'into company, might be able to see.

177. 'A blind man placed where one with eyes 'might have seen, destroys the reward of ninety; 'he, who has lost one eye, of sixty; a leper, of 'an hundred; one punished with elephantiasis, of 'a thousand.

178. 'Of

178. 'Of the gift at a *sráddha*, to as many 'Bráhmens, as a sacrificer for a *Súdra* might be 'able to touch on the body, the fruit is lost to the 'giver, *if he invite such a wretch*;

179. 'And if a *Bráhmen* who knows the *Véda*, 'receive through covetousness a present from such 'a sacrificer, he speedily sinks to perdition, like a 'figure of unburnt clay in water.

180. 'Food given to a seller of the moon plant, 'becomes ordure in another world; to a physician 'purulent blood; *and the giver will be a reptile 'bred in them*: if offered to an image worshipper, 'it is thrown away; if to an usurer, infamous.

181. 'That which is given to a trader, endures 'neither in this life nor in the next, and that be-'stowed on a *Bráhmen*, who has married a widow, 'resembles clarified butter poured on ashes as an 'oblation to fire.

182. 'That food, which is given to other base 'and inadmissible men, before mentioned, the 'wise have pronounced to be no more than 'animal oil, blood, flesh, skin, and bones.

183. 'Now learn comprehensively, by what '*Bráhmens* a company may be purified, when it has 'been defiled by inadmissable persons; *Bráhmens*, 'the chief of their class, the purifiers of every as-'sembly.

184. 'Those priests must be considered as the 'purifiers of a company who are most learned in 'all the *Védas* and all their *Angas*, together with 'their descendants who have read the whole 'scripture:

185. 'A priest learned in a principal part of 'the *Yajurvéda*; one who keeps the five fires 'constantly burning; one skilled in a principal 'part of the *Rigvéda*; one who explains the six

'*Védángas*;

'*Védángas*; the son of a *Bráhmì*, or woman married by the *Bráhma* ceremony; and one who chants the principal *Sáman*;

186. 'One who propounds the sense of the *Védas*, which he learnt from his preceptor, a student who has given a thousand *cows for pious uses*, and a *Bráhmen* a hundred years old, must all be considered as the purifiers of a party at a *sráddha*.

187. 'On the day before the sacred obsequies, or on the very day when they are prepared, let the performer of them invite, with due honour, such *Bráhmens* as have been mentioned; *usually* one superiour, who has three inferiour to him.

188. 'The *Bráhmen*, who has been invited to a *sráddha* for departed ancestors, must be continually abstemious; he must not even read the *Védas*; and he who performs the ceremony, must act in the same manner.

189. 'Departed ancestors, no doubt, are attendant on such invited *Bráhmens*; hovering around them like pure spirits, and sitting by them, when they are seated.

190. 'The priest who having been duly invited to a *sráddha*, breaks the appointment, commits a grievous offence, and in his next birth becomes a hog.

191. 'He, who caresses a *Súdra* woman, after he has been invited to sacred obsequies, takes on himself all the sin that has been committed by the giver of the repast.

192. 'The *Pitrĭs* or *great progenitors*, are free from wrath, intent on purity, ever exempt from sensual passions, endued with exalted qualities: they are primeval divinities, who have laid arms aside.

193. 'HEAR

193. 'HEAR now completely, from whom they 'sprang; who they are; by whom and by what 'ceremonies they are to be honoured.

194. 'The sons of MARI'CHI and of all the other '*Rĭshis*, who were the offspring of MENU, son of 'BRAHMA', are called the companies of *Pitrĭs*, 'or *forefathers*.

195. 'The *Sómasads*, who sprang from VIRA'J, 'are declared to be the ancestors of the *Sádhybas*; 'and the *Agnishwáttas*, who are famed among 'created beings as the children of MARI'CHI, to 'be the progenitors of the *Dévas*.

196. 'Of the *Daityas*, the *Dánavas*, the *Yac-shas*, the *Gandharvas*, the *Uragas*, or *Serpents*, 'the *Racshashes*, the *Garudas*, and the *Cinnaras*, 'the ancestors are *Barhishads* descended from 'ATRI;

197. 'Of *Bráhmens*, those named *Sómapas*; of '*Cshatriyas*, the *Havishmats*; of *Vaisyas*, those 'called *Abjyapas*; of *Súdras*, the *Sucálins*:

198. 'The *Sómapas* descended from *Me*, BHRĬ-'GU; the *Havishmats*, from ANGIRAS; the *Ajya-pas*, from PULASTYA; the *Sucálins*, from VA-'SISHT'HA.

199. 'Those who are, and those who are not, 'consumable by fire, called *Agnidagdhas*, and '*Anagnidagdhas*, the *Cávyas*, the *Barhishads*, the '*Agnishwáttas*, and the *Saumyas*, let mankind 'consider as the chief progenitors of *Bráhmens*.

200. 'Of those just enumerated, who are ge-'nerally reputed the principal tribes of *Pitrĭs*, 'the sons and grandsons indefinitely, are also in 'this world considered as great progenitors.

201. 'From the *Rĭshis* come the *Pitrĭs*, or 'patriarchs; from the *Pitrĭs*, both *Dévas* and *Dá-navas*;

'*navas*; from the *Dévas*, this whole world of 'animals and vegetables, in due order.

202. 'Mere water, offered with faith to the 'progenitors of men, in veſſels of ſilver, or 'adorned with ſilver, proves the ſource of in-'corruption.

203. 'An oblation by *Bráhmens* to their an-'ceſtors tranſcends an oblation to the deities; 'becauſe that to the deities is conſidered as the 'opening and completion of that to anceſtors:

204. 'As a preſervative of the oblation to the 'patriarchs, let the houſe-keeper begin with an 'offering to the gods; for the *Racſhaſes* rend 'in pieces an oblation which has no ſuch pre-'ſervative.

205. Let an offering to the gods be made at the 'beginning and end of the *ſráddha*: it muſt not 'begin and end with an offering to anceſtors; for 'he who begins and ends it with an oblation to the '*Pitrĭs*, quickly periſhes with his progeny.

206. 'Let the *Bráhmen* ſmear with cow dung 'a purified and ſequeſtered piece of ground; and 'let him, with great care, ſelect a place with a 'declivity toward the ſouth:

207. 'The divine manes are always pleaſed 'with an oblation in empty glades, naturally 'clean, on the banks of rivers, and in ſolitary 'ſpots.

208. 'Having duly made an ablution with 'water, let him place the invited *Bráhmens*, who 'have alſo performed their ablutions, one by 'one, on allotted ſeats purified with *cus'a*-graſs.

209. 'When he has placed them with re-'verence on their ſeats, let him honour them, '(having firſt honoured the Gods) with fragrant 'garlands and ſweet odours.

210. 'Having

210. ' Having brought water for them with ' *cus'a*-grafs and *tila*, let the *Bráhmen*, with the ' *Bráhmens*, pour the oblation, as the law directs, ' on the holy fire.

211. ' First, as it is ordained, having satisfied ' AGNI, SOMA and YAMA, with clairfied butter, ' let him proceed to satisfy the manes of his pro-' genitors.

212. ' If he have no consecrated fire, *as if he be* ' *yet unmarried, or his wife be just deceased*, let him ' drop the oblation into the hand of a *Bráhmen*; ' since, what fire is, even such is a *Bráhmen*; as ' priests who know the *Véda* declare:

213. ' Holy sages call the chief of the twice ' born the gods of obsequies, free from wrath, with ' placid aspects, of a primeval race, employed in ' the advancement of human creatures.

214. ' Having walked in order from east to ' south, and thrown into the fire all the ingredients ' of his oblation, let him sprinkle water on the ' ground with his right hand.

215. ' From the remainder of the clarified ' butter having formed three balls of rice, let him ' offer them, with fixed attention, in the same ' manner as the water, his face being turned to ' the south:

216. ' Then, having offered those balls, after ' due ceremonies and with an attentive mind, *to the* ' *manes of his father, his paternal grandfather, and* ' *great grandfather*, let him wipe the same hand ' with the roots of *cus'a*, which he had before used, ' for the sake of *his paternal ancestors in the fourth,* ' *fifth, and sixth degrees, who are* the partakers of ' the rice and clarified butter *thus* wiped off.

217. ' Having made an ablution, returning to-' ward the north, and thrice suppressing his breath slowly,

'slowly, let him salute the Gods of the six seasons;
'and the *Pitrĭs* also, being well acquainted with
'proper texts of the *Véda*.

218. 'Whatever water remains in his ewer, let 'him carry back deliberately near the cakes of 'rice; and with fixed attention, let him smell 'those cakes, in order as they were offered:

219. 'Then, taking a small portion of the cakes 'in order, let him first, as the law directs, cause 'the *Bráhmens* to eat of them, while they are 'seated.

220. 'If his father be alive, let him offer the '*sráddha* to his ancestors in *three* higher degrees; 'or let him cause his own father to eat, as a '*Bráhmen* at the obsequies:

221. 'Should his father be dead, and his grand- 'father living, let him, in celebrating the name 'of his father, *that is, in performing obsequies to* '*him*, celebrate also his paternal great grand- 'father;

222. 'Either the paternal grandfather may par- 'take of the *sráddha* (so has MENU declared) or 'the grandson, authorized by him, may perform 'the ceremony at his discretion.

223. 'Having poured water, with *cus'a*-grass 'and *tila*, into the hands of the *Bráhmens*, let him 'give them the upper part of the cakes, saying, "*Swadhá* to the manes!"

224. 'Next, having himself brought with both 'hands, a vessel full of rice, let him, still medi- 'tating on the *Pitrĭs*, place it before the *Bráhmens* 'without precipitation.

225. 'Rice taken up, but not supported with 'both hands, the malevolent *Asuras* quickly rend 'in pieces.

226. 'Broths,

226. ' Broths, potherbs, and other eatables ac-' companying the rice, together with milk and ' curds, clarified butter and honey, let him first ' place on the ground, after he has made an ablu-' tion; and let his mind be intent on no other ' object:

227. ' Let him add spiced puddings, and milky ' messes of various sorts, roots of herbs and ripe ' fruits, savoury meats and sweet smelling drinks.

228. ' Then being duly purified, and with per-' fect presence of mind, let him take up all the ' dishes, one by one, and present them in order to ' the *Bráhmens*, proclaiming their qualities.

229. ' Let him at no time drop a tear; let him ' on no account be angry; let him say nothing ' false; let him not touch the eatables with his ' foot; let him not even shake the dishes:

230. ' A tear sends the messes to restless ghosts; ' anger, to foes; falsehood, to dogs; contact with ' his foot, to demons; agitation, to sinners.

231. ' Whatever is agreeable to the *Bráhmens*, ' let him give without envy; and let him discourse ' on the attributes of GOD: such discourse is ex-' pected by the manes.

232. ' At the obsequies to ancestors, he must ' let the *Bráhmens* hear passages from the *Véda*, ' from the codes of law, from moral tales, from ' heroick poems, from the *Purános*, and from ' theological texts.

233. ' Himself being delighted, let him give ' delight to the *Bráhmens*, and invite them to eat ' of the provisions by little and little; attracting ' them often with the dressed rice and other eata-' bles, and mentioning their good properties.

234. ' To the son of his daughter, though a ' student in theology, let him carefully give food

'at the *śráddha*; offering him a blanket from '*Népàl* as his seat, and sprinkling the ground with '*tila*.

235. 'Three things are held pure at such obsequies, the daughter, son, the *Népàl* blanket, 'and the *tila*; and three things are praised in it 'by the wise, cleanliness, freedom from wrath, 'and want of precipitate haste.

236. 'Let all the dressed food be very hot; 'and let the *Bráhmens* eat it in silence; nor let 'them declare the qualities of the food, even 'though asked by the giver.

237. 'As long as the messes continue warm, 'as long as they eat in silence, as long as the qua-'lities of the food are not declared by them, so 'long the manes feast on it.

'238. 'What a *Bráhmen* eats with his head 'covered, what he eats with his face to the south, 'what he eats with sandals on his feet, the demons 'assuredly devour.

239. 'Let not a *Chandála*, a town boar, a cock, 'a dog, a woman in her courses, or an eunuch, 'see the *Bráhmens* eating:

240. 'That which any one of them sees at the 'oblation to fire, at a solemn donation of cows 'and gold, at a repast given to *Bráhmens*, at holy 'rites to the gods, and at the obsequies to ances-'tors, produces not the intended fruit;

241. 'The boar destroys it by his smell; the 'cock, by the air of his wings; the dog, by the 'cast of a look; the man of the lowest class, by 'the touch.

242. 'If a lame man, or a man with one eye, 'or a man with a limb defective or redundant, 'be even a servant of the giver, him also let his 'master remove from the place.

243. 'Should

243. 'Should another *Bráhmen*, or a mendicant, 'come to his house for food, let him, having obtained permission from the invited *Bráhmens*, entertain the stranger to the best of his power.

244. 'Having brought together all the sorts of 'food, as dressed rice and the like, and sprinkling 'them with water, let him place them before the '*Bráhmens*, who have eaten; dropping some *on 'the blades of* cus'a-*grass, which have been spread* 'on the ground.

245. 'What remains in the dishes, and what 'has been dropped on the blades of *cus'a*, must 'be considered as the portion of deceased *Bráh-'mens*, not girt with the sacrificial thread, and of 'such as have deserted unreasonably the women of 'their own tribe.

246. 'The residue, that has fallen on the ground 'at the *sráddha* to the manes, the wise have de-'cided to be the share of all the servants, who are 'not crooked in their ways, nor lazy and ill 'disposed.

247. 'Before the obsequies to ancestors as far 'as the sixth degree, they must be performed to a '*Bráhmen* recently deceased; but the performer of 'them must, *in that case*, give the *sráddha* without 'the ceremony to the gods, and offer only one 'round cake; *and these obsequies for a single ancestor 'should be annually performed on the day of his death*:

248. 'When, *afterwards*, the obsequies to an-'cestors as far as the sixth degree, inclusively of 'him, are performed according to law, then must 'the offering of cakes be made by the descen-'dants in the manner before ordained *for the 'monthly ceremonies*.

249. 'That fool, who, having eaten of the '*sráddha*, gives the residue of it to a man of the

'servile class, falls headlong down to the hell 'named *Cálasútra.*

250. 'Should the eater of a *sráddha* enter, on 'the same day, the bed of a seducing woman, his 'ancestors would sleep for that month on her ex-'crement.

251. 'Having, by the word *swaditam,* asked 'the *Bráhmens* if they have eaten well, let him 'give them, being satisfied, water for an ablution, 'and courteously say to them, "Rest either at 'home or here."

252. 'Then let the *Bráhmens* address him, saying '*swadhá*; for in all ceremonies relating to deceased 'ancestors, the word *swadhá* is the highest benison.

253. 'After that, let him inform those, who 'have eaten of the food that remains; and being 'instructed by the *Bráhmens,* let him dispose of it 'as they may direct.

254. 'At the close of the *sráddha* to his ances-'tors, he must ask if the *Bráhmens* are satisfied, 'by the word *swadita*; after that for his family, 'by the word *susruta*; after that for his own ad-'vancement, by the word *sampanna,* after that 'which has been offered to the gods, by the word '*ruchita.*

255. 'The afternoon, the *cus'a*-grass, the clean-'sing of the ground, the *tilas,* the liberal gifts of 'food, the due preparation for the repast, and the 'company of most exalted *Bráhmens,* are true riches 'in the obsequies to ancestors.

256. 'The blades of *cusa,* the holy texts, the 'forenoon, all the oblations, *which will presently* '*be enumerated,* and the purification before men-'tioned, are to be considered as wealth in the '*sráddha* to the gods:

257. 'Such wild grains as are eaten by hermits, 'milk, the juice of the moonplant, meat untainted,

'and

'and ſalt unprepared by art, are held things fit, in
'their own nature, for the laſt mentioned offering.

258. 'Having diſmiſſed the invited *Bráhmens*, 'keeping his mind attentive, and his ſpeech ſuppreſſed, let him, after an ablution, look toward 'the ſouth, and aſk theſe bleſſings of the *Pitrïs*:

259. "May generous givers abound in our 'houſe! may the ſcriptures be ſtudied, and progeny increaſe in it! may faith never depart from 'us! and may we have much to beſtow on the 'needy!"

260. 'Thus having ended the *ſráddha*, let him 'cauſe a cow, a prieſt, a kid, or the fire, to devour what remains of the cakes; or let him caſt 'them into the waters.

261. 'Some make the offering of the round 'cakes after the repaſt of the *Bráhmens*; ſome 'cauſe the birds to eat what remains, or caſt it 'into water or fire.

262. 'Let a lawful wife, ever dutiful to her 'lord, and conſtantly honouring his anceſtors, eat 'the middlemoſt of the three cakes, *or that offered* '*to his paternal grandfather*, with due ceremonies, 'praying for offspring:

263. 'So may ſhe bring forth a ſon, who will 'be long lived, famed, and ſtrong minded, 'wealthy, having numerous deſcendants, endued 'with the beſt of qualities, and performing all 'duties religious and civil.

264. 'THEN, having waſhed both his hands and 'ſipped water, let him prepare ſome rice for his 'paternal kinſmen; and, having given it them 'with due reverence, let him prepare food alſo 'for his maternal relations.

265. 'Let the reſidue continue in its place, 'until the *Bráhmens* have been diſmiſſed; and

 'then

'then let him perform the *remaining* domestick 'sacraments.

266. 'WHAT sort of oblations, given duly to 'the manes, are capable of satisfying them, for a 'long time or for eternity, I will now declare 'without omission.

267. 'The ancestors of men are satisfied a 'whole month with *tila*, rice, barley, black 'lentils or vetches, water, roots, and fruit, given 'with prescribed ceremonies;

268. 'Two months, with fish; three months, 'with venison; four, with mutton; five, with the 'flesh of *such* birds, *as* the twice born may eat:

269. 'Six months, with the flesh of kids; se-'ven, with that of spotted deer; eight, with that 'of the deer, or antelope, called *éna*; nine, with 'that of the *ruru*:

270. 'Ten months are they satisfied with the 'flesh of wild boars and wild buffalos; eleven, 'with that of rabbits or hares, and of tortoises;

271. 'A whole year with the milk of cows, 'and food made of that milk; from the flesh of 'the long eared white goat, their satisfaction en-'dures twelve years.

272. 'The potherb *cálasáca*, the fish *mahásalca*, 'or the *diodon*, the flesh of a rhinoceros, or of an 'iron-coloured kid, honey, and all such forest 'grains as are eaten by hermits, are formed for 'their satisfaction without end.

273. 'Whatever pure food, mixed with honey, 'a man offers on the thirteenth day of the moon, 'in the season of rain, and under the lunar aste-'rism *Maghà*, has likewise a ceaseless duration.

274. "Oh! may that man, *say the manes*, be 'born in our line, who may give us milky food, 'with honey and pure butter, both on the thir-

'teenth

'teenth of the moon; and when the ſhadow of an
'elephant falls to the eaſt!"

275. 'Whatever a man, endued with ſtrong 'faith, piouſly offers, as the law has directed, 'becomes a perpetual unperiſhable gratification 'to his anceſtors in the other world:

276. 'The tenth and ſo forth, except the 'fourteenth, in the dark half of the month, are 'the lunar days moſt approved for ſacred obſe-'quies: as they *are*, ſo *are* not the others.

277. 'He, who does honour to the manes, on 'even lunar days, and under even lunar ſtations, 'enjoys all his deſires; on odd lunar days, and 'under odd lunar aſteriſms, he procures an illuſ-'trious race.

278. 'As the latter *or dark* half of the month 'ſurpaſſes, for the celebration of obſequies, the 'former, *or bright* half, ſo the latter half of the 'day ſurpaſſes, *for the ſame purpoſe*, the former 'half of it.

279. 'The oblation to anceſtors muſt be duly 'made, even to *the concluſion of it with the diſtri-'bution to* the ſervants, (or even to the cloſe of 'life,) in the form preſcribed, by a *Bráhmen* wear-'ing his thread on his right ſhoulder, proceeding 'from left to right, without remiſſneſs, and with '*cus'a*-graſs in his hand.

280. 'Obſequies muſt not be performed by 'night; ſince the night is called *rácſhasì* or *infeſted 'by demons*; nor while the ſun is riſing or ſetting, 'nor when it has juſt riſen.

281. 'A houſe-keeper, *unable to give a monthly 'repaſt*, may perform obſequies here below, ac-'cording to the ſacred ordinance, only thrice a 'year, in the ſeaſons of *hémanta*, *griſhma*, and

 '*verſhà*;

'*verſhà*; but the five ſacraments he muſt perform
'daily.

282. 'The ſacrificial oblation at obſequies to
'anceſtors, is ordained to be made in no vulgar
'fire; nor ſhou'd the monthly *ſráddha* of that
'*Bráhmen*, who keeps a perpetual fire, be made on
'any day, except on that of the conjunction.

283. 'When a twice born man, having per-
'formed his ablution, offers a ſatisfaction to the
'manes with water only, *being unable to give a*
'*repaſt*, he gains by that offering all the fruit of a
'*ſráddha*.

284. 'The wiſe call our fathers, *Vaſus*; our
'paternal grandfathers, *Rudras*; our paternal great
'grandfathers, *Adityas*; (that is *all are to be re-*
'*vered as deities*,) and to this effect there is a pri-
'meval text in the *Véda*.

285. 'Let a man, who is able, continually feed
'on *vighaſa*, and continually feed on *amrĭta*; by
'*vighaſa* is meant the reſidue of a repaſt at obſe-
'quies; and by *amrĭta*, the reſidue of a ſacrifice
'to the gods.

286. 'This complete ſyſtem of rules, for the
'five ſacraments and the like, has been declared to
'you: now hear the law for thoſe means of ſub-
'ſiſtence, which the chief of the twice born may
'ſeek.

CHAPTER THE FOURTH.

On Economicks; and Private Morals.

1. ' Let a *Bráhmen*, having dwelt with a pre-
' ceptor during the firſt quarter of a man's life,
' paſs the ſecond quarter of human life in his own
' houſe, when he has contracted a legal marriage.

2. ' He muſt live, with no injury, or with the
' leaſt poſſible injury, to animated beings, by
' purſuing thoſe means of gaining ſubſiſtence,
' which are ſtrictly preſcribed by law, except in
' times of diſtreſs:

3. ' For the ſole purpoſe of ſupporting life,
' let him acquire property by thoſe irreproach-
' able occupations, which are peculiar to his claſs,
' and unattended with bodily pain.

4. ' He may live by *rĭta* and *amrĭta*, or, *if ne-*
' *ceſſary*, by *mrĭta* or *pramrĭta*, or even by *ſat-*
' *yanrĭta*; but never let him ſubſiſt by *ſwavrĭtti*:

5. ' By *rĭta*, muſt be underſtood lawful glean-
' ing and gathering; by *amrĭta*, what is given
' unaſked; by *mrĭta*, what is aſked as alms; til-
' lage is called *pramrĭta*;

6. ' Traffick and money lending are *ſatyanrĭta*;
' even by them, *when he is deeply diſtreſſed*, may
' he ſupport life; but ſervice for hire is named
' *ſwavrĭtti*, or *dog living*, and of courſe he muſt by
' all means avoid it.

7. ' He

7. 'He may either ſtore up grain for three 'years; or garner up enough for one year; or 'collect what may laſt three days, or make no 'proviſion for the morrow.

8. 'Of the four *Bráhmens* keeping houſe, *who* '*follow thoſe four different modes*, a preference is 'given to the laſt in order ſucceſſively; as to 'him, who moſt completely by virtue has van- 'quiſhed the world:

9. 'One of them ſubſiſts by all the ſix means 'of livelihood; another by three of them; a 'third by two only; and a fourth lives barely on 'continually teaching the *Véda*.

10. 'He, who ſuſtains himſelf by picking up 'grains and ears, muſt attach himſelf to ſome 'altar of conſecrated fire, but conſtantly perform 'thoſe rites only, which end with the dark and 'bright fortnights and with the ſolſtices.

11. 'Let him never, for the ſake of a ſub- 'ſiſtence, have recourſe to popular converſation; 'let him live by the conduct of a prieſt, neither 'crooked, nor artful, nor blended *with the manners* '*of the mercantile claſs*.

12. 'Let him, if he ſeek happineſs, be firm in 'perfect content, and check all deſire of acquiring 'more *than he poſſeſſes*; for happineſs has its root 'in content, and diſcontent is the root of miſery.

13. 'A *Bráhmen* keeping houſe, *and* ſupport- 'ing himſelf, by any of the *legal* means before- 'mentioned, muſt diſcharge theſe *following* duties, 'which conduce to fame, length of life, and bea- 'titude.

14. 'Let him daily, without ſloth, perform his 'peculiar duty, which the *Véda* preſcribes; for 'he who performs that *duty*, as well as he is able, 'attains the higheſt path to ſupreme bliſs.

15. 'He

15. 'He muſt not gain wealth *by muſick or* '*dancing, or* by any art that pleaſes the ſenſe; nor 'by any prohibited art; nor, whether he be rich 'or poor, *muſt he receive gifts* indiſcriminately.

16. 'Let him not, from a ſelfiſh appetite, be 'ſtrongly addicted to any ſenſual gratification; 'let him, by improving his intellect, ſtudiouſly 'preclude an exceſſive attachment to ſuch plea-'ſures, *even though lawful.*

17. 'All kinds of wealth, that may impede 'his reading the *Véda*, let him wholly abandon, 'perſiſting by all means in the ſtudy of ſcripture; 'for that will be found his moſt beneficial at-'tainment.

18. 'Let him paſs through this life, bringing 'his apparel, his diſcourſe, and his frame of mind, 'to conformity with his age, his occupations, his 'property, his divine knowledge, and his family.

19. 'Each day let him examine thoſe holy 'books, which ſoon give increaſe of wiſdom; and 'thoſe, which teach the means of acquiring wealth; 'thoſe, which are ſalutary to life; and thoſe '*nigamas*, which are explanatory of the *Véda*;

20. 'Since, as far as a man ſtudies completely 'the ſyſtem of ſacred literature, ſo far only can he 'become eminently learned, and ſo far may his 'learning ſhine brightly.

21. 'The ſacramental oblations to ſages, to 'the gods, to ſpirits, to men, and to his anceſtors, 'let him conſtantly perform to the beſt of his 'power.

22. 'Some, who well know the ordinances 'for thoſe oblations, perform not always exter-'nally the five great ſacraments, but continually 'make offerings in their own organs *of ſenſation* '*and intellect*:

23. 'Some

23. 'Some conſtantly ſacrifice their breath in 'their ſpeech, *when they inſtruct others, or praiſe* 'GOD *aloud*, and their ſpeech in their breath, *when* '*they medidate in ſilence*; perceiving in their ſpeech 'and breath, *thus employed*, the unperiſhable fruit 'of a ſacrificial offering:

24. 'Other *Bráhmens* inceſſantly perform thoſe 'ſacrifices with ſcriptural knowledge only; ſeeing 'with the eye of divine learning, that ſcriptural 'knowledge is the root of every ceremonial ob'ſervance.

25. 'Let a *Bráhmen* perpetually make obla'tions to conſecrated fire at the beginning and 'end of day and night, and at the cloſe of each 'fortnight, *or at the conjunction and oppoſition*:

26. 'At the ſeaſon, when old grain is uſually 'conſumed, let him offer new grain for a plenti'ful harveſt; and at the cloſe of the ſeaſon, let 'him perform the rites called *adhvara*; at the 'ſolſtices, let him ſacrifice cattle; at the end of 'the year, let his oblations be made with the 'juice of the moon plant:

27. 'Not having offered grain for the harveſt, 'nor cattle *at the time of the ſolſtice*, let no *Bráh*'*men*, who keeps hallowed fire, and wiſhes for 'long life, taſte rice or fleſh;

28. 'Since the holy fires, not being honoured 'with new grain and with a ſacrifice of cattle, 'are greedy for rice and fleſh, and ſeek to devour 'his vital ſpirits.

29. 'Let him take care, to the utmoſt of his 'power, that no gueſt ſojourn in his houſe un'honoured with a ſeat, with food, with a bed, with 'water, with eſculent roots, and with fruit:

30. 'But let him not honour with his conver'ſation ſuch as do forbidden acts; ſuch as ſubſiſt,

'like

' like cats, *by interested craft*; such as believe
' not the scripture; such as oppugn it by so-
' phisms; or such as live like rapacious water
' birds.

31. ' With oblations to the gods and to an-
' cestors, let him do reverence to *Brâhmens* of the
' second order, who are learned in theology, who
' have returned home from their preceptors, after
' having performed their religious duties and fully
' studied the *Véda*; but men of an opposite de-
' scription let him avoid.

32. ' Gifts must be made by each housekeeper,
' as far as he has ability, to religious mendicants,
' though heterodox; and a just portion must be
' reserved, without inconvenience to his family,
' for all sentient beings, *animal and vegetable.*

33. ' A priest, who is master of a family, and
' pines with hunger, may seek wealth from a
' king *of the military class*, from a sacrificer, or
' his own pupil, but from no person else, *unless*
' *all other helps fail:* thus *will he shew his* respect
' for the law.

34. ' Let no priest, who keeps house, *and is*
' able *to procure food*, ever waste himself with
' hunger; nor, when he has any substance, let
' him wear old or sordid clothes.

35. ' His hair, nails, and beard being clipped;
' *his passions*, subdued; his mantle, white; his
' body, pure; let him diligently occupy himself
' in reading the *Véda*, and be constantly intent on
' such acts, as may be salutary to him.

36. ' Let him carry a staff of *Vénu*, an ewer
' with water in it, a handful of *cus a*-grass, or *a*
' *copy of* the *Vêda*; with a pair of bright golden
' rings in his ears.

37. ' He must not gaze on the sun whether
rising

'rising or setting, or eclipsed, or reflected in 'water, or advanced to the middle of the sky.

38. 'Over a string, to which a calf is tied, let 'him not step; nor let him run while it rains; 'nor let him look on his own image in water: 'this is a settled rule.

39. 'By a mound of earth, by a cow, by an 'idol, by a *Bráhmen*, by a pot of clarified butter, 'or of honey, by a place where four ways meet, 'and by large trees well known in the district, 'let him pass with his right hand toward them.

40. 'Let him not, though mad with desire, 'approach his wife, when her courses appear; 'nor let him then sleep with her in the same bed;

41. 'Since the knowledge, the manhood, the 'strength, the eye-sight, even the vital spirit of 'him, who approaches his wife thus defiled, ut-'terly perish;

42. 'But the knowledge, the manhood, the 'strength, the sight, and the life of him, who 'avoids her in that state of defilement, are greatly 'increased.

43. 'Let him neither eat with his wife, nor 'look at her eating, or sneezing, or yawning, or 'sitting carelessly at her ease;

44. 'Nor let a *Bráhmen*, who desires manly 'strength, behold her setting off her eyes with 'black powder, or scenting herself with essences, 'or baring her bosom, or bringing forth a child.

45. 'Let him not eat his food, wearing only 'a single cloth; nor let him bathe quite naked; 'nor let him eject urine or feces in the highway, 'nor on ashes, nor where kine are grazing.

46. 'Nor on tilled ground, nor in water, nor 'on wood raised for burning, nor, *unless he be in*

great

'*great need*, on a mountain, nor on the ruins of a 'temple, nor at any time on a neſt of white ants,

47. 'Nor in ditches with living creatures in 'them, nor walking, nor ſtanding, nor on the 'bank of a river, nor on the ſummit of a moun- 'tain:

48. 'Nor let him ever eject them, looking at '*things moved by* the wind, or at fire, or at a prieſt, 'or at the ſun, or at water, or at cattle;

49. 'But let him void his excrements, having 'covered the earth with wood, potherbs, *dry* leaves 'and graſs, or the like, carefully ſuppreſſing his 'utterance, wrapping up his breaſt and his head:

50. 'By day let him void them with his face to 'the north; by night, with his face to the ſouth; 'at ſun riſe and at ſun ſet, in the ſame manner as 'by day;

51. 'In the ſhade or in darkneſs, whether by 'day or by night, let a *Bráhmen* eaſe nature with 'his face turned as he pleaſes; and in places where 'he fears injury to life, *from wild beaſts or from* '*reptiles*.

52. 'Of him, who ſhould urine againſt fire, 'againſt the ſun, or the moon, againſt a twice 'born man, a cow, or the wind. all the ſacred 'knowledge would periſh.

53. 'Let him not blow the fire with his mouth; 'let him not ſee his wife naked; let him not 'throw any foul thing into fire; nor let him 'warm his feet in it;

54. 'Nor let him place it *in a chafing diſh* un- 'der *his bed*; nor let him ſtride over it; nor let 'him keep it, *while he ſleeps*, at his feet: let him 'do nothing that may be injurious to life.

55. 'At the time of ſunriſe or ſunſet, let 'him not eat, nor travel, nor lie down to reſt; let

'him not idly draw lines on the ground; nor let 'him take off his own chaplet of flowers.

56. 'Let him not cast into the water either 'urine or ordure, nor saliva, nor cloth, or any 'other thing soiled with impurity, nor blood, nor 'any kinds of poison.

57. 'Let him not sleep alone in an empty 'house; nor let him wake a sleeping man *superiour* '*to himself in wealth and in learning*; nor let him 'speak to a woman at the time of her courses; 'nor let him go to *perform* a sacrifice, unattended '*by an officiating priest*.

58. 'In a temple *of consecrated fire*, in the pas-'ture of kine, in the presence of *Bráhmens*, in 'reading the *Véda*, and in eating his food, let him 'hold out his right arm uncovered.

59. 'Let him not interrupt a cow *while she is* 'drinking, nor give notice to any, *whose milk or* '*water she drinks*; nor let him who knows *right* '*from wrong*, and sees in the sky the bow of INDRA, 'show it to any man.

60. 'Let him not inhabit a town, in which 'civil and religious duties are neglected; nor for 'a long time, one in which diseases are frequent; 'let him not begin a journey alone; let him not 'reside long on a mountain.

61. 'Let him not dwell in a city governed by 'a *Súdra* king, nor in one surrounded with men 'unobservant of their duties, nor in one abounding 'with professed hereticks, nor in one swarming 'with low born outcasts.

62. 'Let him eat no vegetable, from which the 'oil has been extracted; nor indulge his appetite 'to satiety; nor eat either too early or too late; 'nor *take any food* in the evening, if he have eaten 'to fullness in the morning.

63. Let

63. 'Let him make no vain corporeal exertion: let him not ſip water *taken up* with his *cloſed* fingers: let him eat nothing *placed* in his lap: let him never take pleaſure in aſking idle queſtions.

64. 'Let him neither dance, nor ſing, nor play on muſical inſtruments, *except in religious rites*; nor let him ſtrike his arm, or gnaſh his teeth, or make a braying noiſe, though agitated by paſſion.

65. 'Let him not waſh his feet in a pan of mixed yellow metal; nor let him eat from a broken diſh, nor where his mind is diſturbed with anxious apprehenſions.

66. 'Let him not uſe either ſlippers or clothes, or a ſacerdotal ſtring, or an ornament, or a garland, or a water pot, which before have been uſed by another.

67. 'With untrained beaſts of burden let him not travel; nor with ſuch as are oppreſſed by hunger or by diſeaſe; nor with ſuch as have imperfect horns, eyes, or hoofs; nor with ſuch as have ragged tails:

68. 'But let him conſtantly travel with beaſts well trained, whoſe pace is quick, who bear all the marks of a good breed, who have an agreeable colour, and a beautiful form; giving them very little pain with his whip.

69. 'The ſun in the ſign of *Canyà*, the ſmoke of a burning corſe, and a broken ſeat, muſt be ſhunned: he muſt never cut his own hair and nails, nor ever tear his nails with his teeth.

70. 'Let him not break mould or clay *without cauſe*: let him not cut graſs with his nails: let him neither indulge any vain fancy, nor do any act that can bring no future advantage:

 71. 'He

71. 'He, who *thus idly* breaks clay, or cuts 'grafs, or bites his nails, will fpeedily fink to 'ruin; and *fo fhall* a detractor, and an unclean 'perfon.

72. 'Let him ufe no contumelious phrafe; 'let him wear no garland except on his hair: to 'ride on the back of a bull or cow, is in all 'modes culpable.

73. 'Let him not pafs, otherwife than by the 'gate, into a walled town or an enclofed houfe; 'and by night let him keep aloof from the roots 'of trees.

74. 'Never let him play with dice: let him 'not put off his fandals with his hand: let him 'not eat, while he reclines on a bed, nor what is 'placed in his hand, or on a bench;

75. 'Nor, when the fun is fet, let him eat any 'thing mixed with *tila*; nor let him ever, in this 'world, fleep quite naked; nor let him go any 'whither with a remnant of food in his mouth.

76. 'Let him take his food, having fprinkled 'his feet with water; but never let him fleep 'with his feet wet: he, who takes his food with 'his feet fo fprinkled, will attain long life.

77. 'Let him never advance into a place un'diftinguifhable by his eye, or not eafily paffable: 'never let him look at urine or ordure; nor let 'him pafs a river *fwimming* with his arms.

78. 'Let not a man, who defires to enjoy long 'life, ftand upon hair, nor upon afhes, bones, or 'potfherds, nor upon feeds of cotton, nor upon 'hufks of grain.

79. 'Nor let him tarry *even under the fhade of 'the fame tree* with outcafts for great crimes, nor 'with *Chandálas*, nor with *Puccafas*, nor with 'idiots, nor with men proud of wealth, nor with

7 '*wafher-*

'*washermen and other* vile persons, nor with *Antyavasáyins*.

80. 'Let him not give *even temporal* advice to 'a *Súdra*; nor, *except to his own servant*, what remains from his table; nor clarified butter, of 'which part has been offered *to the gods*; nor let 'him *in person* give spiritual counsel to such a 'man, nor *personally* inform him of the legal expiation for his sin:

81. 'Surely he, who declares the law to a 'servile man, and he, who instructs him in the 'mode of expiating sin, *except by the intervention* '*of a priest*, sinks with that very man into the 'hell named *Asamvrĭta*.

82. 'Let him not stroke his head with both 'hands; nor let him even touch it, while food 'remains in his mouth; not without *bathing it*, 'let him bathe his body.

83. 'Let him not *in anger* lay hold of hair, or 'smite any one on the head; nor let him, after 'his head has been rubbed with oil, touch with 'oil any of his limbs.

84. 'From a king, not born in the military 'class, let him accept no gift, nor from such as 'keep a slaughter-house or an oil press, or put out 'a vintner's flag, or subsist by the gain of prostitutes:

85. 'One oil press is as bad as ten slaughter-houses; one vintner's flag, as ten oil presses; 'one prostitute, as ten vintner's flags; one *such* 'king, as ten prostitutes;

86. 'With a slaughterer, *therefore*, who employs ten thousand slaughter-houses, a king, *not* '*a soldier by birth*, is declared to be on a level; '*and*, a gift from him is tremendous.

87. 'He, who receives a present from an ava-

'ricious king and a tranſgreſſor of the ſacred
'ordinances, goes in ſucceſſion to the following
'twenty-one hells:

88. '*Támiſra*, *Andhatámiſra*, *Mahárauravа*, *Rau-*
'*rava*, *Naraca*, *Cálasútra*, and *Mahánaraca*;

89. '*Sanjívana*, *Mahavichi*, *Tapana*, *Samp-*
'*ratápana*, *Sanháta*, *Sacácóla*, *Cudmala*, *Pútim-*
'*rittica*;

90. '*Lóhaſancu*, or *iron ſpiked*, and *Rijíſha*,
'*Pant'hána*, the river *Sálmali*, *Aſipatravana*, or *the*
'*ſword-leaved foreſt*, and *Lóh'ángáraca*, or *the pit*
'*of red hot charcoal*.

91. '*Bráhmens*, who know this *law*, who ſpeak
'the words of the *Véda*, and who ſeek bliſs after
'death, accept no gifts from a king.

92. 'Let the houſe-keeper wake in the time
'ſacred to Bra'hmí, *the goddeſs of ſpeech*, *that is*
'*in the laſt watch of the night*: let him then reflect
'on virtue and virtuous emoluments, on the bo-
'dily labour which they require, and on the
'whole meaning and very eſſence of the *Véda*.

93. 'Having riſen, having done what nature
'makes neceſſary, having then purified himſelf
'and fixed his attention, let him ſtand a long
'time repeating the *gáyatrì* for the firſt *or morning*
'twilight; as he muſt for the laſt *or evening*
'twilight in its proper time.

94. 'By continued repetition of the *gáyatrì*, at
'the twilights, the holy ſages acquire length of
'days, perfect knowledge, reputation during life,
'fame after death, and celeſtial glory.

95. 'Having duly performed the *upácarma*, or
'*domeſtick ceremony with ſacred fire*, at the full moon
'of *Srávana*, or of *Bhádra*, let the *Bráhmen*, fully
'exerting his intellectual powers, read the *Védas*
'during four months and one fortnight:

96. 'Under

96. 'Under the lunar asterism *Pushya*, or on 'the first day of the bright half of *Mágha*, and in 'the first part of the day, let him perform out of 'the town, *the ceremony called* the *utserga* of the '*Védas*.

97. 'Having performed that ceremony out of 'town, as the law directs, let him desist from 'reading for one *intermediate* night winged *with* '*two days*, or for that day and *that following* night 'only;

98. 'But after that *intermission*, let him atten-'tively read the *Védas* in the bright fortnights 'and in the dark fortnights let him constantly 'read all the *Védángas*.

99. 'He must never read the *Véda* without 'accents and letters well pronounced; nor ever in 'the presence of *Súdras*; nor *having begun to read* '*it* in the last watch of the night, must he, though 'fatigued, sleep again.

100. 'By the rule just mentioned let him con-'tinually, with his faculties exerted, read the '*Mantras*, or holy texts, composed in regular 'measures; and, when he is under no restraint, 'let him read both the *Mantras* and the *Bráhmanas*, 'or chapters on the attributes of God.

101. 'Let a reader of the *Véda*, and a teacher 'of it to his pupils, in the form prescribed, al-'ways avoid reading on the following prohibited 'days.

102. 'By night, when the wind meets his ear, 'and by day when the dust is collected, *he must* '*not read* in the season of rain; since both those 'times are declared unfit for reading, by such as 'know when the *Véda* ought to be read.

103. 'In lightning, thunder, *and* rain, or dur-'ing the fall of lage fireballs on all sides, at such

'times MENU has ordained the reading of ſcripture to be deferred till the ſame time next day.

104. 'When the prieſt perceives thoſe accidents occurring at once, while his fires are kindled for *morning and evening* ſacrifices, then let him know, that the *Véda* muſt not be read; and when clouds are ſeen gathered out of ſeaſon.

105. 'On the occaſion of a preternatural ſound from the ſky, of an earthquake, or an obſcuration of the heavenly bodies, even in due ſeaſon, let him know, that his reading muſt be poſtponed till the proper time:

106. 'But if, while his fires are blazing, the ſound of lightning and thunder is heard *without rain*, his reading muſt be diſcontinued, only while the phenomenon laſts; the remaining event, *or rain alſo*, happening, it muſt ceaſe for a night and a day.

107. 'The reading of ſuch, as wiſh to attain the excellent reward of virtue, muſt continually be ſuſpended in towns and in cities, and always where an offenſive ſmell prevails.

108. 'In a diſtrict, through which a corpſe is carried, and in the preſence of an unjuſt perſon, the reading of ſcripture muſt ceaſe; *and* while the ſound of weeping is heard; and in a promiſcuous aſſembly of men.

109. 'In water, near midnight, and while the two natural excretions are made, or with a remnant of food in the mouth, or when the *ſráddha* has recently been eaten, let no man even meditate in his heart *on the holy texts*.

110. 'A learned *Bráhmen*, having received an invitation to the obſequies of a ſingle anceſtor, muſt not read the *Véda* for three days; nor

'when

'when the king has a ſon born; nor when the 'dragon's head cauſes an eclipſe.

111. 'As long as the ſcent and unctuoſity of 'perfumes remain on the body of a learned prieſt, 'who has partaken of an entertainment, ſo long 'he muſt abſtain from pronouncing the texts of 'the *Véda*.

112. 'Let him not read lolling on a couch, 'nor with his feet raiſed on a bench, nor with his 'thighs croſſed, nor having lately ſwallowed 'meat, or the rice and other food *given* on the 'birth or death of a relation;

113. 'Nor in a cloud of duſt, nor while arrows 'whiz, *or a lute ſounds*, nor in either of the twi-'lights, nor at conjunction, nor on the fourteenth 'day, nor at the oppoſition, nor on the eighth 'day of the moon:

114. 'The dark lunar day deſtroys the ſpiritual 'teacher; the fourteenth deſtroys the learner; the 'eighth and the day of the full moon deſtroy *all* '*remembrance of* ſcripture; for which reaſons he 'muſt avoid reading on thoſe lunar days.

115. 'Let no *Bráhmen* read, while duſt falls 'like a ſhower, nor while the quarters of the fir-'mament are inflamed, nor while ſhakals yell, 'nor while dogs bark or yelp, nor while aſſes or 'camels bray, nor while men in company chatter.

116. 'He muſt not read near a cemetery, near 'a town, or in a paſture for kine; nor in a man-'tle worn before a time of dalliance; nor having 'juſt received the preſent uſual at obſequies:

117. 'Be it an animal, or a thing inanimate, or 'whatever be the gift at a *ſráddha*, let him not, 'having lately accepted it, read the *Véda*; for 'ſuch a *Bráhmen* is ſaid to have his mouth in his 'hand.

118. 'When the town is beſet by robbers, or 'an alarm has been raiſed by fire, and in all terrors from ſtrange phenomena, let him know, 'that his lecture muſt be ſuſpended till the due 'time *after the cauſe of terror has ceaſed.*

119. 'The ſuſpenſion of reading ſcripture, after a performance of the *upácarma* and *utſerga,* 'muſt be for three whole nights, *by the man who 'ſeeks virtue more than knowledge*; alſo for one day 'and night, on the eighth lunar days which follow 'thoſe ceremonies, and on the nights at the cloſe 'of the ſeaſons.

120. 'Never let him read on horſeback, nor 'on a tree, nor on an elephant, nor in a boat, nor 'on an aſs, nor on a camel, nor ſtanding on barren ground, nor borne in a carriage;

121. 'Nor during a verbal altercation, nor 'during a mutual aſſault, nor with an army, nor 'in battle, nor after food, *while his hand is moiſt 'from waſhing,* nor with an indigeſtion, nor after 'vomiting, nor with four eructations;

122. 'Nor without notice to a gueſt juſt arrived, 'nor while the wind vehemently blows, nor when 'blood guſhes from his body, nor when it is 'wounded by a weapon.

123. 'While the ſtrain of the *Sáman* meets his 'ear, he ſhall not read the *Rĭch,* or the *Yajuſh*; 'nor any part of the *Véda,* when he has juſt concluded the whole; nor *any other part,* when he 'has juſt finiſhed the book entitled *Aranyáca*:

124. 'The *Rigvéda* is held ſacred to the gods; 'the *Yajurvéda* relates to mankind; the *Sámavéda* 'concerns the manes of anceſtors, and the ſound 'of it, *when chanted,* raiſes therefore a notion of 'ſomething impure.

125. 'Know-

125. 'Knowing this *collection of rules*, let the 'learned read the *Véda* on every *lawful* day, having 'first repeated, in order, the pure essence of the 'three *Védas*, namely, the *pranava*, the *vyáhrĭtis*, 'and the *gáyatrì*.

126. 'If a beast used in agriculture, a frog, a 'cat, a dog, a snake, an ichneumon, or a rat, 'pass between *the lecturer and his pupil*, let him 'know, that the lecture must be intermitted for a 'day and a night.

127. 'Two occasions, when the *Véda* must not 'be read, let a *Bráhmen* constantly observe with 'great care; *namely*, when the place for reading 'it is impure, and when he is himself unpurified.

128. 'On the dark night of the moon, and on 'the eighth, on the night of the full moon, and 'on the fourteenth, let a *Bráhmen*, who keeps 'house, be continually chaste as a student in theo-'logy, even in the season of nuptial embraces.

129. 'Let him not bathe, having just eaten; 'nor while he is afflicted with disease; nor in the 'middle of the night; nor with many clothes; 'nor in a pool of water imperfectly known.

130. 'Let him not intentionally pass over the 'shadow of sacred images, of a natural or spiritual 'father, of a king, of a *Bráhmen*, who keeps house, 'or of any reverend personage; nor of a red-haired '*or copper-coloured* man, nor of one who has just 'performed a sacrifice.

131. 'At noon or at midnight, or having eaten 'flesh at a *sráddha*, or in either of the twilights, 'let him not long tarry where four ways meet.

132. 'He must not stand knowingly near oil 'and other things, with which a man has rubbed 'his body, or water in which he has washed

'himself,

'himſelf, or feces and urine, or blood, or mucus, 'or any thing chewed and ſpitten out, or any 'thing vomited

133. 'Let him ſhew no particular attention to 'his enemy or his enemy's friend, to an unjuſt 'perſon, to a thief, or to the wife of another 'man;

134. 'Since nothing is known in this world ſo 'obſtructive to length of days, as the culpable 'attention of a man to the wife of another.

135. 'Never let him, who deſires an increaſe of 'wealth, deſpiſe a warriour, a ſerpent, or a prieſt 'verſed in ſcripture, how mean ſoever *they may* '*appear*;

136. 'Since thoſe three, when contemned, may 'deſtroy a man; let a wiſe man therefore, always 'beware of treating thoſe three with contempt:

137. 'Nor ſhould he deſpiſe *even* himſelf on 'account of previous miſcarriages; let him pur-'ſue fortune till death, nor ever think her hard 'to be attained.

138. 'Let him ſay what is true, but let him 'ſay what is pleaſing; let him ſpeak no diſagree-'able truth, nor let him ſpeak agreeable falſehood: 'this is a primeval rule.

139. 'Let him ſay "well and good," or let 'him ſay "well" only; but let him not maintain 'fruitleſs enmity and altercation with any man.

140. 'Let him not journey too early in the 'morning or too late in the evening, nor too near 'the mid-day, nor with an unknown companion, 'nor alone, nor with men of the ſervile claſs.

141. Let him not inſult thoſe who want a limb, 'or have a limb redundant, who are unlearned, 'who are advanced in age, who have no beauty,

'who

'who have no wealth, or who are of an ignoble 'race.

142. 'Let no prieſt, unwaſhed after food, touch 'with his hand a cow, a *Bráhmen*, or fire; nor 'being in good health *and* unpurified, let him even 'look at the luminaries in the firmament:

143. 'But, having accidentally touched them 'before his purification, let him ever ſprinkle, 'with water in the palm of his hand, his organs of 'ſenſation, all his limbs, and his navel.

144. 'Not being in pain from diſeaſe, let him 'never without cauſe touch the cavities of his 'body; and carefully let him avoid his concealed 'hair.

145. 'Let him be intent on *thoſe propitious ob-'ſervances which lead to* good fortune, and on the 'diſcharge of his cuſtomary duties, his body 'and mind being pure, and his members kept 'in ſubjection; let him conſtantly without re-'miſſneſs repeat the *gáyatrì*, and preſent his obla-'tion to fire:

146. 'To thoſe who are intent on good fortune 'and on the diſcharge of their duties, who are 'always pure, who repeat the holy text, and 'make oblations to fire, no calamity happens.

147. 'In due ſeaſon, let him ever ſtudy the 'ſcripture without negligence; for the ſages call 'that his principal duty: every other duty is de-'clared to be ſubordinate.

148. 'By reading the *Véda* continually, by 'purity of body and mind, by rigorous devotion, 'and by doing no injury to animated creatures, 'he brings to remembrance his former birth:

149. 'A *Bráhmen*, remembering his former 'birth, again reads the *Véda*, and by reading it 'conſtantly, attains bliſs without end.

150. 'On

150. 'On the days of the conjunction and opposition, let him constantly make those oblations, 'which are hallowed by the *gáyatrì*, and those 'which avert misfortune; but on the eighth and 'ninth lunar days *of the three dark fortnights, after the end of Agrabáyan*, let him always do reverence 'to the manes of ancestors.

151. 'Far from the mansion of holy fire, let him 'remove all ordure; far *let him remove* water, in 'which feet have been washed; far *let him remove* all remnants of food, and all seminal impurity.

152. 'At the beginning of each day let him 'discharge his feces, bathe, rub his teeth, apply 'a collirium to his eyes, adjust his dress, and 'adore the gods.

153. 'On the dark lunar day, and on the 'other monthly *parvans*, let him visit the images 'of deities and *Bráhmens* eminent in virtue, and 'the ruler of the land, for the sake of protection, 'and those whom he is bound to revere.

154. 'Let him humbly greet venerable men, '*who visit him*, and give them his own seat; let 'him sit near them, closing the palms of his 'hands; and when they depart, let him walk 'some way behind them.

155. 'Let him practise, without intermission, 'that system of approved usages, which is the root 'of all duty religious and civil, declared at large 'in the scriptural and sacred law tracts, together 'with the ceremonies peculiar to each act:

156. 'Since by such practice long life is attained; by such practice *is gained* wealth unperishable; such practice baffles every mark of 'ill fortune:

157. 'But

157. 'But by an oppoſite practice, a man ſurely 'ſinks to contempt in this world, has always a 'large portion of miſery, is afflicted with diſeaſe 'and ſhort-lived;

158. 'While the man who is obſervant of ap-'proved uſages, endued with faith in ſcripture, 'and free from a ſpirit of detraction, lives a 'hundred years, even though he bear no bodily 'mark of a proſperous life.

159. 'Whatever act depends on another man, 'that act let him carefully ſhun; but whatever 'depends on himſelf, to that let him ſtudiouſly 'attend:

160. 'ALL THAT DEPENDS ON ANOTHER, 'GIVES PAIN; AND ALL THAT DEPENDS ON 'HIMSELF, GIVES PLEASURE; let him know this 'to be in few words the definition of pleaſure 'and pain.

161. 'When an act, *neither preſcribed nor pro-'hibited*, gratifies the mind of him who performs 'it, let him perform it with diligence, but let 'him avoid its oppoſite.

162. 'Him, by whom he was inveſted with 'the ſacrificial thread, him, who explained the '*Véda*, or even a part of it, his mother, and his 'father, natural or ſpiritual, let him never op-'poſe, nor prieſts, nor cows, nor perſons truly 'devout.

163. 'Denial of a future ſtate, neglect of the 'ſcripture, and contempt of the deities, envy and 'hatred, vanity and pride, wrath and ſeverity, 'let him at all times avoid.

164. 'Let him not, when angry, throw a 'ſtick at another man, nor ſmite him with any 'thing; unleſs he be a ſon or a pupil; thoſe

'two

'two he may chastise for their *improvement* in 'learning.

165. 'A twice born man, who barely assaults 'a *Bráhmen* with intention to hurt him, shall be 'whirled about for a century in the hell named '*Támisra*;

166. '*But*, having smitten him in anger and 'by design, even with a blade of grass, he shall 'be born, in one and twenty transmigrations, 'from the wombs of impure quadrupeds.

167. 'He, who, through ignorance of the law, 'sheds blood from the body of a *Bráhmen*, not 'engaged in battle, shall feel excessive pain in 'his future life:

168. 'As many particles of dust as the blood 'shall roll up from the ground, for so many years 'shall the shedder of that blood be mangled by 'other animals in his next birth.

169. 'Let not him then, who knows *this law*, 'even assault a *Bráhmen* at any time, nor strike 'him even with grass, nor cause blood to gush 'from his body.

170. 'Even here below an unjust man attains 'no felicity; nor he, whose wealth proceeds from 'giving false evidence; nor he, who constantly 'takes delight in mischief.

171. 'Though oppressed by penury, in con-'sequence of his righteous dealings, let him 'never give his mind to unrighteousness; for he 'may observe the speedy overthrow of iniquitous 'and sinful men.

172. 'Iniquity, committed in this world, pro-'duces not fruit immediately, *but*, like the 'earth, *in due season*; and, advancing by little 'and little, it eradicates the man who commit-'ted it.

173. 'Yes;

173. 'Yes; iniquity, once committed, fails 'not of producing fruit to him, who wrought it; 'if not in his own perſon, yet in his ſons; or, if 'not in his ſons, yet in his grandſons:

174. 'He grows rich for awhile through unrighteouſneſs; then he beholds good things; 'then it is, that he vanquiſhes his foes; but he 'periſhes at length from his whole root up'wards.

175. 'LET a man continually take pleaſure in 'truth, in juſtice, in laudable practices, and in 'purity; let him chaſtiſe thoſe whom he may 'chaſtiſe in a legal mode; let him keep in 'ſubjection his ſpeech, his arm, and his ap'petite:

176. 'Wealth and pleaſures, repugnant to law, 'let him ſhun; and even lawful acts, which may 'cauſe future pain, or be offenſive to mankind.

177. 'Let him not have nimble hands, reſtleſs 'feet, or voluble eyes; let him not be crooked in 'his ways; let him not be flippant in his ſpeech, 'nor intelligent in doing miſchief.

178. 'Let him walk in the path of good men; 'the path in which his parents and forefathers 'walked: while he moves in that path he can 'give no offence.

179. 'WITH an attendant on conſecrated fire, 'a performer of holy rites, and a teacher of the '*Véda*, with his maternal uncle, with his gueſt 'or a dependent, with a child, with a man either 'aged or ſick, with a phyſician, with his pa'ternal kindred, with his relations by marriage, 'and with couſins on the ſide of his mother,

180. 'With his mother herſelf, or with his 'father, with his kinſwomen, with his brother, 'with

'with his ſon, his wife, or his daughter, and 'with his whole ſet of ſervants let him have no 'ſtriſe.

181. 'A houſe-keeper, who ſhuns altercation 'with thoſe *juſt mentioned,* is releaſed from all 'ſecret faults; and, by ſuppreſſing all ſuch diſ-'putes, he obtains a victory over the following 'worlds:

182. 'The teacher of the *Véda* ſecures him 'the world of BRAHMA'; his father, the world *of* '*the Sun, or* of the *Prajápetis*; his gueſt, the 'world of INDRA; his attendants on holy fire, 'the world of *Dévas*;

183. 'His female relations, the world of ce-'leſtial nymphs; his maternal couſins, the world 'of the *Viſvadévas*; his relations by affinity, the 'world of waters; his mother and maternal uncle 'give him power on earth;

184. 'Children, old men, poor dependents, 'and ſick perſons, muſt be conſidered as rulers 'of the pure ether; his elder brother, as equal 'to his father; his wife and ſon, as his own 'body;

185. 'His aſſemblage of ſervants, as his own 'ſhadow; his daughter, as the higheſt object 'of tenderneſs: let him therefore, when of-'fended by any of thoſe, bear the offence without 'indignation.

186. 'THOUGH permitted to receive preſents, 'let him avoid a habit of taking them; ſince, by 'taking many gifts, his divine light ſoon fades.

187. 'Let no man of ſenſe, who has not fully 'informed himſelf of the law concerning gifts of '*particular* things, accept a preſent, even though 'he pine with hunger.

188. 'The man who knows not that law, yet

'accepts

'accepts gold or gems, land, a horſe, a cow, 'food, raiment, oils, or clarified butter, becomes 'mere aſhes, like wood conſumed by fire:

189. 'Gold and gems burn up his nouriſhment and life; land and a cow, his body; a 'horſe, his eyes; raiment, his ſkin; clarified 'butter, his manly ſtrength; oils, his progeny.

190. 'A twice born man, void of true devotion, and not having read the *Véda*, yet eager 'to take a gift, ſinks down, together with it, as 'with a boat of ſtone in deep water.

191. 'Let him then, who knows not the law, 'be fearful of preſents from this or that giver; 'ſince an ignorant man, even by a ſmall gift, 'may become helpleſs as a cow in a bog.

192. 'Let no man, apprized of this law, preſent even water to a prieſt, who acts like a cat, 'nor to him, who acts like a bittern, nor to him, 'who is unlearned in the *Véda*;

193. 'Since property, though legally gained, 'if it be given to either of thoſe three, becomes 'prejudicial in the next world, both to the giver 'and receiver:

194. 'As he, who tries to paſs over deep 'water in a boat of ſtone, ſinks to the bottom, 'ſo thoſe two ignorant men, the receiver and the 'giver, ſink to a region of torment.

195. 'A covetous wretch, who continually 'diſplays the flag of virtue, a pretender, a deluder of the people, is declared to be the 'man who acts like a cat; he is an injurious 'hypocrite, a detractor from the merits of all 'men.

196. 'A twice born man, with his eyes dejected, moroſe, intent on his own advantage,

'fly, and falsely demure, is he who acts like a 'bittern.

197. 'Such priests, as live like bitterns, and 'such as demean themselves like cats, fall by 'that sinful conduct into the hell called *Andhatá-misra.*

198. 'LET no man, having committed sin, 'perform a penance under the pretext of austere 'devotion, disguising his crime under fictitious 'religion, and deceiving both women and low 'men:

199. 'Such impostors, though *Bráhmens*, are 'despised in the next life, and in this, by all who 'pronounce holy texts; and every religious act 'fraudulently performed goes to evil beings.

200. 'He, who has no right to distinguishing 'marks, yet gains a subsistence by wearing false 'marks of distinction, takes to himself the sin 'committed by those who are entitled to such 'marks, and shall again be born from the womb 'of a brute animal.

201. 'NEVER let him bathe in the pool of 'another man; for he who bathes in it *without 'licence,* takes to himself a small portion of the 'sins, which the maker of the pool has com'mitted.

202. 'He, who appropriates to his own use 'the carriage, the bed, the seat, the well, the 'garden, or the house of another man, who has 'not delivered them to him, assumes a fourth 'part of the guilt of their owner.

203. 'In rivers, in ponds dug by holy persons, 'and in lakes, let him always bathe; in rivulets 'also, and in torrents.

204. 'A WISE man should constantly discharge 'all

'all the moral duties, though he perform not 'constantly the ceremonies of religion; since he 'falls low, if, while he performs ceremonial acts 'only, he discharge not his moral duties.

205. 'Never let a priest eat part of a sacrifice 'not begun with texts of the *Vĕda*, nor of one 'performed by a common sacrificer, by a woman 'or by an eunuch:

206. 'When those persons offer the clarified 'butter, it brings misfortune to good men, and 'raises aversion in the deities; such *oblations*, 'therefore, he must carefully shun.

207. 'Let him never eat the food of the in-'sane, the wrathful, or the sick; nor that, on 'which lice have fallen; nor that, which has 'designedly been touched by a foot;

208. 'Nor that, which has been looked at by 'the slayer of a priest, *or by any other deadly sinner*, 'or has even been touched by a woman in her 'courses, or pecked by a bird, or approached by 'a dog;

209. 'Nor food which has been smelled by a 'cow; nor particularly that which has been pro-'claimed *for all comers*; nor the food of associated 'knaves, or of harlots; nor that which is con-'temned by the learned in scripture;

210. 'Nor that of a thief or a publick singer, 'of a carpenter, of an usurer, of one who has 'recently come from a sacrifice, or a niggardly 'churl, or of one bound with fetters;

211. 'Of one publickly defamed, of an eunuch, 'of an unchaste woman, or of a hypocrite; nor 'any sweet thing turned acid, nor what has been 'kept a whole night; nor the food of a servile 'man, nor the orts of another;

212. 'Nor the food of a physician, or of a 'hunter, or of a dishonest man, or of an eater 'of orts; nor that of any cruel person; nor of 'a woman in childbed; nor of him, who rises 'prematurely from table to make an ablution; 'nor of her whose ten days of purification have 'not elapsed;

213. 'Nor that, which is given without due 'honour to honourable men; nor any flesh 'which has not been sacrificed; nor the food of 'a woman, who has neither a husband nor a son; 'nor that of a foe, nor that of the whole town, 'nor that of an outcast, nor that on which any 'person has sneezed;

214. 'Nor that of a backbiter, or of a false 'witness; nor of one who sells the reward of his 'sacrifice; nor of a publick dancer, or a tailor; 'nor of him who has returned evil for good;

215. 'Nor that of a blacksmith, or a man of 'the tribe called *Nishàda*, nor of a stage-player, 'nor of a worker in gold or in cane, nor of him 'who sells weapons;

216. 'Nor of those who train hunting dogs, 'or sell fermented liquor; nor of him who 'washes clothes, or who dyes them; nor of 'any malevolent person; nor of one who ig-'norantly suffers an adulterer to dwell under his 'roof;

217. 'Nor of those who knowingly bear 'with the paramours of their own wives, or are 'constantly in subjection to women; nor food 'given for the dead before ten days of purification 'have passed; nor any food whatever, but that 'which satisfies him.

218. 'Food given by a king, impairs his 'manly

'manly vigour; by one of the ſervile claſs, his 'divine light; by goldſmiths, his life; by leather-'cutters, his good name:

219. 'Given by *cooks and the like* mean arti-'zans, it deſtroys his offspring; by a waſher-'man, his muſcular ſtrength; but the food 'of knaviſh aſſociates and harlots excludes him 'from heaven:

220. 'The food of a phyſician is purulent; 'that of a libidinous woman, ſeminal; that of 'an uſurer, feculent; that of a weapon-ſeller, 'filthy:

221. 'That of all others, mentioned in order, 'whoſe food muſt never be taſted, is held equal 'by the wiſe to the ſkin, bones, and hair of the 'dead.

222. 'Having unknowingly ſwallowed the 'food of any ſuch perſons, he muſt faſt during 'three days; but, having eaten it knowingly, he 'muſt perform the ſame harſh penance, as if he 'had taſted any ſeminal impurity, ordure, or 'urine.

223. 'Let no learned prieſt eat the dreſſed 'grain of a ſervile man, who performs no pa-'rental obſequies; but having no other means to 'live, he may take from him raw grain enough 'for a ſingle night.

224. 'The deities, having well conſidered the 'food of a niggard, who has read the ſcripture, 'and that of an uſurer, who beſtows gifts li-'berally, declared the food of both to be equal 'in quality;

225. 'But BRAHMA', advancing towards the 'gods, thus addreſſed them: "Make not that 'equal, which in truth is unequal; ſince the 'food of a liberal man is purified by faith, while

'that of a learned miser is defiled by his want of 'faith in what he has read."

226. 'LET each *wealthy* man continually and 'sedulously perform sacred rites, and consecrate 'pools or gardens with faith; since those two 'acts, accomplished with faith and with riches 'honestly gained, procure an unperishable re-'ward:

227. 'If he meet with fit objects of bene-'volence, let him constantly bestow gifts on 'them, both at sacrifices and consecrations, to 'the best of his power and with a chearful heart;

228. 'Such a gift, how small soever, bestowed 'on request without grudging, passes to a worthy 'object, who will secure the giver from all evil.

229. 'A giver of water obtains content; a 'giver of food, extreme bliss; a giver of *tila*, 'desired offspring; a giver of a lamp, unble-'mished eyesight;

230. 'A giver of land obtains landed pro-'perty; a giver of gems or gold, long life; a 'giver of a house, the most exalted mansion; a 'giver of silver, exquisite beauty;

231. 'A giver of clothes, the same station 'with CHANDRA; a giver of a horse, the same 'station with ASWI; a giver of a bull, eminent 'fortune; a giver of a cow, the mansion of 'SU'RYA;

232. 'A giver of a carriage or a bed, an ex-'cellent consort; a giver of safety, supreme do-'minion; a giver of grain, perpetual delight; 'a giver of scriptural knowledge, union with 'GOD:

233. 'Among all those gifts, of water, food, 'kine, land, clothes, *tila*, gold, clarified butter,

'and

'and the reſt, a gift of ſpiritual knowledge is 'conſequently the moſt important;

234. 'And for whatever purpoſe a man beſtows any gift, for a ſimilar purpoſe he ſhall 'receive, with due honour, a ſimilar reward.

235. 'Both he, who reſpectfully beſtows a 'preſent, and he who reſpectfully accepts it, ſhall 'go to a ſeat of bliſs; but, if they act otherwiſe, 'to a region of horror.

236. 'Let not a man be proud of his rigorous 'devotion; let him not, having ſacrificed, utter 'a falſehood; let him not, though injured, inſult 'a prieſt; having made a donation, let him never 'proclaim it:

237. 'By falſehood, the ſacrifice becomes 'vain; by pride, the merit of devotion is loſt; 'by inſulting prieſts, life is diminiſhed; and by 'proclaiming a largeſs, its fruit is deſtroyed.

238. 'Giving no pain to any creature, let 'him collect virtue by degrees, for the ſake of 'acquiring a companion to the next world, as the 'white ant by degrees builds his neſt;

239. 'For, in his paſſage to the next world, 'neither his father, nor his mother, nor his wife, 'nor his ſon, nor his kinſmen, will remain in 'his company: his virtue alone will adhere 'to him.

240. 'Single is each man born; ſingle he 'dies; ſingle he receives the reward of his good, 'and ſingle the puniſhment of his evil deeds:

241. 'When he leaves his corſe, like a log 'or a lump of clay, on the ground, his kindred 'retire with averted faces; but his virtue ac'companies his ſoul.

242. 'Continually, therefore, by degrees, let

 him

'him collect virtue, for the ſake of ſecuring an 'inſeparable companion; ſince with virtue for 'his guide, he will traverſe a gloom, how hard to 'be traverſed!

243. 'A man, habitually virtuous, whoſe of-'fences have been expiated by devotion, is in-'ſtantly conveyed after death to the higher world, 'with a radiant form and a body of ethereal 'ſubſtance.

244. 'He, who ſeeks to preſerve an exalted 'rank, muſt conſtantly form connexions with the 'higheſt and beſt families, but avoid the worſt 'and the meaneſt;

245. 'Since a prieſt, who connects himſelf 'with the beſt and higheſt of men, avoiding the 'loweſt and worſt, attains eminence; but ſinks, 'by an oppoſite conduct, to the claſs of the ſer-'vile.

246. 'He, who perſeveres in good actions, in 'ſubduing his paſſions, in beſtowing largeſſes, in 'gentleneſs of manners, who bears hardſhips pa-'tiently, who aſſociates not with the malignant, 'who gives pain to no ſentient being, obtains 'final beatitude.

247. 'Wood, water, roots, fruit, and food 'placed before him without his requeſt, he may 'accept from all men; honey alſo, and protec-'tion from danger.

248. 'Gold, or other alms, voluntary brought 'and preſented, but unaſked and unpromiſed, 'Brahma' conſidered as receivable even from a 'ſinner;

249. 'Of him, who ſhall diſdain to accept 'ſuch alms, neither will the manes eat the funeral 'oblations for fifteen years, nor will the fire convey 'the burnt ſacrifice to the gods.

250. 'A

250. 'A bed, houſes, blades of *cuſ'a*, perfumes, 'water, flowers, jewels, butter-milk, ground rice, 'fiſh, new milk, fleſh meat, and green vegetables, 'let him not proudly reject.

251. 'When he wiſhes to relieve his natural 'parents or ſpiritual father, his wife or others, 'whom he is bound to maintain, or when he is 'preparing to honour deities or gueſts, he may 'receive gifts from any perſon, but muſt not 'gratify himſelf with ſuch preſents:

252. 'If his parents, however, be dead, or if 'he live without them in his own houſe, let him, 'when he ſeeks nouriſhment for himſelf, receive 'preſents invariably from good men alone.

253. 'A labourer in tillage, a family friend, a 'herdſman, a ſlave, a barber, a poor ſtranger of-'fering his humble duty, are men of the ſervile 'claſs, who may eat the food of their ſuperiours:

254. 'As the nature of the poor ſtranger is, 'as the work is, which he deſires to perform, and 'as he may ſhow moſt reſpect *to the maſter of the* '*houſe*, even thus let him offer his ſervice;

255. 'For he, who deſcribes himſelf to wor-'thy men, in a manner contrary to truth, is the 'moſt ſinful wretch in this world: he is the worſt 'of thieves, a ſtealer of minds.

256. 'All things have their ſenſe aſcertained 'by ſpeech; in ſpeech they have their baſis; and 'from ſpeech they proceed: conſequently, a falſi-'fier of ſpeech falſifies every thing.

257. 'WHEN he has paid, as the law directs, 'his debts to the ſages, to the manes, and to the 'gods, *by reading the ſcripture, begetting a ſon,* '*and performing regular ſacrifices*, he may reſign 'all to his ſon *of mature age*, and reſide in his

'family,

'family houſe, with no employment, but that of an 'umpire.

258. 'Alone, in ſome ſolitary place, let him 'conſtantly meditate on the divine nature of the 'ſoul, for by ſuch meditation he will attain 'happineſs.

259. 'Thus has been declared the mode, by 'which a *Bráhmen*, who keeps houſe, muſt con'tinually ſubſiſt, together with the rule of de'votion ordained for a pupil returned from his 'preceptor; a laudable rule, which increaſes the 'beſt of *the three* qualities.

260. 'A prieſt, who lives always by theſe 'rules, who knows the ordinances of the *Véda*, 'who is freed from the bondage of ſin, ſhall be 'abſorbed in the divine eſſence.

CHAPTER THE FIFTH.

On Diet, Purification, and Women.

1. THE sages, having heard those laws delivered for the conduct of house-keepers, thus addressed the high-minded BHRĬGU, who proceeded, *in a former birth*, from the genius of fire.

2. 'How, Lord, can death prevail over *Bráhmens*, who know the scriptural ordinances, and 'perform their duties as they have been declared?'

3. Then he, whose disposition was perfect virtue, even BHRĬGU, the son of MENU, thus answered the great *Rĭshis*. 'Hear from what 'sin proceeds the inclination of death, to destroy 'the chief of the twice born:

4. 'Through a neglect of reading the *Véda*, 'through a desertion of approved usages, through 'supine remissness *in performing holy rites*, and 'through various offences in diet, *the genius of* 'death becomes eager to destroy them.

5. 'Garlick, onions, leeks, and mushrooms, '(which no twice born man must eat) and all vegetables raised in dung.

6. 'Red gums or resins, exuding from trees, 'and juices from wounded stems, the fruit *sélu*, 'and the thickened milk of a cow within ten days 'after her calving, a priest must avoid with great 'care.

7. 'Rice

7. 'Rice pudding boiled with *tila*, frumenty, 'rice-milk, and baked bread, which have not 'been first offered to some deity, flesh meat also, 'the food of gods, and clarified butter, which 'have not first been touched, while holy texts 'were recited,

8. 'Fresh milk from a cow, whose ten days are 'not passed, the milk of a camel, or any qua-'druped with a hoof not cloven, that of an ewe, 'and that of a cow in heat, or whose calf is dead 'or absent from her,

9. 'That of any forest beast, except the buffalo, 'the milk of a woman, and any thing naturally 'sweet but acidulated, must all be carefully 'shunned:

10. 'But among such acids, butter-milk may 'be swallowed, and every preparation of butter-'milk, and all acids extracted from pure flowers, 'roots, or fruit *not cut with iron*.

11. 'Let every twice born man avoid carnivo-'rous birds, and such as live in towns, and qua-'drupeds with uncloven hoofs, except those al-'lowed by the *Vêda*, and the bird called *tittibha*;

12. 'The sparrow, the water bird *plava*, the 'phenicopteros, the *chacraváca*, the breed of the 'town cock, the *sárasa*, the *rajjuvála*, the wood-'pecker, and the parot male and female;

13. 'Birds, that strike with their beaks, web-'footed birds, the *cóyashti*, those who wound 'with strong talons, and those who dive to devour 'fish; let him avoid meat kept at a slaughter-'house, and dried meat,

14. 'The heron, the raven, the *c'hanjana*, all 'amphibious fish eaters, tame hogs, and fish of 'every sort, *but those expressly permitted*.

15. 'He,

15. 'He, who eats the flesh of any animal, 'is called the eater of that animal itself; and a 'fish eater is an eater of all flesh; from fish, 'therefore, he must diligently abstain:

16. 'Yet the two fish called *pát'hína* and *róhita*, 'may be eaten *by the guests*, when offered at a re'past in honour of the gods or the manes; and so 'may the *rájíva*, the *sinhatunda*, and the *sasalka* 'of every species.

17. 'Let him not eat the flesh of any solitary 'animals, nor of unknown beasts or birds, though 'by general words declared eatable, nor of any 'creature with five claws;

18. 'The hedgehog and porcupine, the lizard '*gódhá*, the *gandaca*, the tortoise, and the rabbit '*or hare*, wise legislators declare lawful food 'among five toed animals; and all quadrupeds, 'camels excepted, which have but one row of 'teeth.

19. 'The twice born man, who has intention'ally eaten a mushroom, the flesh of a tame hog, 'or a town cock, a leek, or an onion, or garlick, 'is degraded immediately;

20. 'But having undesignedly tasted either of 'those six things, he must perform the penance '*sántapana*, or the *chándráyana*, which anchorets, 'practise; for other things he must fast a whole 'day.

21. 'One of those harsh penances, called *prá'jápatya*, the twice born man must perform an'nually, to purify him from the unknown taint of 'illicit food; but he must do particular penance 'for such food intentionally eaten.

22. 'Beasts and birds of excellent sorts may 'be slain by *Bráhmens* for sacrifice, or for the 'sustenance

'sustenance of those, whom they are bound to 'support; since AGASTYA did this of old.

23. 'No doubt in the primeval sacrifices by 'holy men, and in oblations by those of the 'priestly and military tribes, the flesh of such 'beasts and birds, as may be legally eaten, was 'presented to the deities.

24. 'That which may be eaten or drunk *when 'fresh*, without blame, may be swallowed, if 'touched with oil, though it has been kept a 'whole night; and so may the remains of clari'fied butter:

25. 'And every mess prepared with barley or 'wheat, or with dressed milk, may be eaten by 'the twice born, although not sprinkled with oil.

26. 'Thus has the food, allowed or forbidden 'to a twice born man, been comprehensively men'tioned: I will now propound the *special* rules 'for eating and for avoiding flesh meat.

27. 'He should taste meat, which has been 'hallowed for a sacrifice with appropriated texts, 'and *once only*, when a priest shall desire him, and 'when he is performing a legal act, or in danger 'of losing life.

28. 'For the sustenance of the vital spirit, 'BRAHMA' created all this *animal and vegetable 'system*; and all that is moveable or immoveable, 'that spirit devours.

29. 'Things fixed are eaten by creatures with 'locomotion; toothless animals, by animals with 'teeth; those without hands, by those to whom 'hands were given; and the timid by the bold.

30. 'He, who eats *according to law*, commits 'no sin, even though every day he tastes the flesh 'of such animals, as may lawfully be tasted; 'since both animals, who may be eaten, and those 'who eat them, were equally created by BRAHMA'.

31. 'It

31. ‘ It is delivered as a rule of the gods, that ‘ meat muſt be ſwallowed only for the purpoſe ‘ of ſacrifice; but it is a rule of gigantick de- ‘ mons, that it may be ſwallowed for any other ‘ purpoſe.

32. ‘ No ſin is committed by him, who having ‘ honoured the deities and the manes, eats fleſh ‘ meat, which he has bought, or which he has ‘ himſelf acquired, or which has been given him ‘ by another:

33. ‘ Let no twice born man, who knows the ‘ law, and is not in urgent diſtreſs, eat fleſh with- ‘ out obſerving this rule; for he, unable to ſave ‘ himſelf, will be devoured in the next world by ‘ thoſe animals, whoſe fleſh he has thus illegally ‘ ſwallowed.

34. ‘ The ſin of him, who kills deer for gain, ‘ is not ſo heinous, with reſpect to *the puniſhment* ‘ *in* another life, as that of him, who eats fleſh ‘ meat in vain, *or not previouſly offered as a ſa-* ‘ *crifice*:

35. ‘ But the man, who, engaged *in holy rites* ‘ according to law, refuſes to eat it, ſhall ſink in ‘ another world, for twenty-one births, to the ‘ ſtate of a beaſt.

36. ‘ Never let a prieſt eat the fleſh of cattle ‘ unhallowed with *mantras*, but let him eat it, ‘ obſerving the primeval rule, when it has been ‘ hallowed with thoſe texts of the *Véda*.

37. ‘ Should he have an earneſt deſire to taſte ‘ fleſh meat, he may gratify his fancy by forming ‘ the image of ſome beaſt with clarified butter ‘ thickened, or he may form it with dough, but ‘ never let him indulge a wiſh to kill any beaſt ‘ in vain:

38. ‘ As many hairs as grow on the beaſt, ſo

'many ſimilar deaths ſhall the ſlayer of it, for 'his own ſatisfaction in this world, endure in the 'next from birth to birth.

39. 'By the ſelf-exiſting in perſon were beaſts 'created for ſacrifice; and the ſacrifice *was ordained* for the increaſe of this univerſe: the 'ſlaughterer therefore of beaſts for ſacrifice is in 'truth no ſlaughterer.

40. 'Gramineous plants, cattle, timber-trees, 'amphibious animals, and birds, which have been 'deſtroyed for the purpoſe of ſacrifice, attain in 'the next world exalted births.

41. 'On a ſolemn offering to a gueſt, at a 'ſacrifice and in holy rites to the manes or to the 'gods, but on thoſe occaſions only, may cattle be 'ſlain: this law MENU enacted.

42. 'The twice born man, who knowing the 'meaning and principles of the *Véda*, ſlays cattle 'on the occaſions mentioned, conveys both him-'ſelf and thoſe cattle to the ſummit of beatitude.

43. 'Let no twice born man, whoſe mind is 'improved by learning, hurt animals without the 'ſanction of ſcripture, even though in preſſing 'diſtreſs, whether he live in his own houſe, or in 'that of his preceptor, or in a foreſt.

44. 'That hurt, which the ſcripture ordains, 'and which is done in this world of moveable and 'immoveable creatures, he muſt conſider as no 'hurt at all; ſince law ſhone forth from *the light of* the ſcripture.

45. 'He, who injures animals, that are not 'injurious, from a wiſh to give himſelf pleaſure, 'adds nothing to his own happineſs, living or 'dead;

46. 'While he, who gives no creature willingly 'the pain of confinement or death, but ſeeks the

'the good of all *ſentient beings* enjoys bliſs without 'end.

47. 'He, who injures no animated creature, 'ſhall attain without hardſhip whatever he thinks 'of, whatever he ſtrives for, whatever he fixes 'his mind on.

48. 'Fleſh meat cannot be procured without 'injury to animals, and the ſlaughter of animals 'obſtructs the path to beatitude; from fleſh meat, 'therefore, let man abſtain:

49. 'Attentively conſidering the formation of 'bodies, and the death or confinement of im-'bodied ſpirits, let him abſtain from eating fleſh 'meat of any kind.

50. 'The man who forſakes not the law, and 'eats not fleſh meat, like a blood thirſty demon, 'ſhall attain good will in this world, and ſhall not 'be afflicted with maladies.

51. 'He, who conſents to the death of an 'animal; he, who kills it; he, who diſſects it; 'he, who buys it; he, who ſells it; he, who 'dreſſes it; he, who ſerves it up; and he, who 'makes it his food; theſe are eight principals in 'the ſlaughter.

52. 'Not a mortal exiſts more ſinful than he, 'who without an oblation to the manes or the 'gods, deſires to enlarge his own fleſh with the 'fleſh of another creature.

53. 'The man, who performs annually, for a 'hundred years, an *aſwamédha*, or *ſacrifice of a* '*horſe*, and the man who abſtains from fleſh meat, 'enjoy for their virtue an equal reward.

54. 'By ſubſiſting on pure fruit and on roots, 'and by eating ſuch grains as are eaten by her-'mits, a man reaps not ſo high a reward, as by 'carefully abſtaining from animal food.

55. "Me he (*mán sa*) will devour in the next 'world, whose flesh I eat in this life:" *thus should* '*a flesh eater speak, and* thus the learned pro- 'nounce the true derivation of the word *mánsa*, 'or flesh.

56. 'In lawfully tasting meat, in drinking 'fermented liquor, in caressing women, there is 'no turpitude; for to such enjoyments men are 'naturally prone; but a virtuous abstinence from 'them produces a signal compensation.

57. 'Now will I promulgate the rules of 'purification for the dead, and the modes of puri- 'fying inanimate things, as the law prescribes 'them for the four classes in due order.

58. 'When a child has teethed, and when, 'after teething, his head has been shorn, and 'when he has been girt with his thread, and 'when, being full grown, he dies, all his kindred 'are impure: on the birth of a child the law is 'the same.

59. 'By a dead body, the *sapindas* are rendered 'impure in law for ten days, or until *the fourth* '*day, when* the bones have been gathered up, or 'for three days, or for one day only, *according to* '*the qualities of the deceased:*

60. 'Now the relation of the *sapindas*, or men 'connected by the funeral cake, ceases with the 'seventh person, *or in the sixth degree of ascent or* '*descent*, and that of *samánódacas*, or those con- 'nected by an equal oblation of water, ends only, 'when their births and family names are no longer 'known.

61. 'As this impurity, by reason of a dead 'kinsman, is ordained for *sapindas*, even thus it is 'ordained on a child-birth, for those who seek 'absolute purity.

62. 'Un-

62. 'Uncleanness, on account of the dead, is 'ordained for all; but on the birth of a child, 'for the mother and father: impurity, for ten 'days after the child-birth, affects the mother 'only; but the father, having bathed, becomes 'pure.

63. 'A man, having wasted his manhood, is 'purified by bathing; but after begetting a child 'on a *parapúrvá*, he must meditate for three days 'on his impure state.

64. 'In one day and night, added to nights 'three times three, the *sapindas* are purified after 'touching the corpse; but the *samánódacas* in three 'days.

65. 'A pupil in theology, having performed 'the ceremony of burning his deceased preceptor, 'becomes pure in ten nights: he is equal, in that 'case, to the *sapindas*, who carry out the dead.

66. 'In a number of nights, equal to the 'number of months from conception, a woman 'is purified on a miscarriage; and a woman in 'her courses is rendered pure by bathing, when 'her effusion of blood has quite stopped.

67. 'For deceased male children, whose heads 'have not been shorn, purity is legally obtained 'in one night; but for those, on whom that ce-'remony has been performed, a purification of 'three nights is required.

68. 'A dead child under the age of two years, 'let his kinsmen carry out, having decked him '*with flowers, and bury him* in pure ground, with-'out collecting his bones *at a future time:*

69. 'Let no ceremony with fire be performed 'for him, nor that of sprinkling water; but his 'kindred, having left him like a piece of wood 'in the forest, shall be unclean for three days.

 70. 'For

70. 'For a child under the age of three years, 'the ceremony with water ſhall not be performed 'by his kindred; but if his teeth be completely 'grown, or a name have been given him, they 'may perform it, or not, *at their option.*

71. 'A fellow ſtudent in theology being dead, 'three days of impurity are ordained; and on 'the birth of a *ſamánódaca*, purification is required 'for three nights.

72. 'The relations of *betrothed but* unmarried 'damſels, are in three days made pure; and, in 'as many, are their paternal kinſmen purified '*after their marriage:*

73. 'Let them eat vegetable food without 'factitious, *that is, only with native* ſalt; let them 'bathe for three days at intervals; let them taſte 'no fleſh meat; and let them ſleep apart on the 'ground.

74. 'This rule, which ordains impurity by rea'ſon of the dead, relates to the caſe of one dying 'near his kinſmen; but, in the caſe of one dying 'at a diſtance, the following rule muſt be ob'ſerved by thoſe who ſhare the ſame cake, and 'by thoſe who ſhare only the ſame water:

75. 'The man, who hears that a kinſman is 'dead in a diſtant country, becomes unclean, if 'ten days after the death have not paſſed, for the 'remainder of thoſe ten days only;

76. 'But if the ten days have elapſed, he is 'impure for three nights, and, if a year have 'expired, he is purified merely by touching water.

77. 'If, after the lapſe of ten days, he know 'the death of a kinſman, or the birth of a male 'child, he muſt purify himſelf by bathing together 'with his clothes.

78. 'Should a child, whoſe teeth are not grown,

'grown, or ſhould a *ſamánódaca* die in a diſtant 'region, the kinſman, having bathed with his 'apparel, becomes immediately pure.

79. 'If, during the ten days, another death or 'another birth intervene, a *Bráhmen* remains im-'pure only till thoſe ten days have elapſed.

80 'A ſpiritual teacher being dead, the ſages 'declare his pupil impure for three days; but for 'a day and a night, if the ſon or wife of the 'teacher be deceaſed; ſuch is the ſacred ordi-'nance.

81. 'For a reader of the whole *Véda*, who 'dwells in the ſame houſe, a man is unclean three 'nights; but for a maternal uncle, a pupil, an 'officiating prieſt, and a diſtant kinſman, only 'one night winged *with two days*.

82. 'On the death of a military king, in whoſe 'dominion he lives, *his impurity laſts* while the 'ſun or the ſtars give light; but *it laſts* a whole 'day, on the death of a prieſt who has not read 'the whole *Véda*, or of a ſpiritual guide, who has 'read only part of it, with its *Angas*.

83. 'A man of the ſacerdotal claſs becomes 'pure in ten days; of the warlike, in twelve; 'of the commercial, in five; of the ſervile, in 'a month.

84. 'Let no man prolong the days of impurity; 'let him not intermit the ceremonies to be per-'formed with holy fires; while he performs thoſe 'rites, even though he be a *ſapinda*, he is not 'impure.

85. 'He, who has touched a *Chandála*, a wo-'man in her courſes, an outcaſt for deadly ſin, a 'new born child, a corpſe, or one who has touch-'ed a corpſe, is made pure by bathing.

86. 'If, having ſprinkled his mouth with 'water, and been long intent on his devotion, he 'ſee an unclean perſon, let him repeat, as well as 'he is able, the ſolar texts of the *Vêda*, and thoſe 'which confer purity.

87. 'Should a *Bráhmen* touch a human bone 'moiſt with oil, he is purified by bathing; if it 'be not oily, by ſtroking a cow, or by looking at 'the ſun, having ſprinkled his mouth duly with 'water.

88. 'A ſtudent in theology ſhall not perform 'the ceremony of pouring water at obſequies, un-'til he have completed his courſe of religious acts; 'but if, after the completion of them, he thus 'make an offering of water, he becomes pure in 'three nights.

89. 'For thoſe, who diſcharge not their pre-'ſcribed duties; for thoſe, whoſe fathers were of 'a lower claſs than their mothers; for thoſe, 'who wear a dreſs of religion unauthorized by the '*Vêda*; and for thoſe, who *illegally* kill themſelves, 'the ceremony of giving funeral water is forbid-'den by law;

90. 'And for women imitating ſuch hereticks, 'as wear an unlawful dreſs, and for ſuch women 'as live at their own pleaſure, or have cauſed an 'abortion, or have ſtricken their huſbands, or 'have drunk any ſpirituous liquor.

91. 'A ſtudent violates not the rules of his or-'der, by carrying out, when dead, his own in-'ſtructor in the *Vêdas*, who inveſted him with his 'holy cord, or his teacher of particular chapters, 'or his reverend expounder of their meaning, or 'his father, or his mother.

92. 'Let men carry out a dead *Sûdra* by the 'ſouthern gate of the town; but the twice born,

'in

'in due order, by the western, northern, and 'eastern gates.

93. 'No taint of impurity can light on kings 'or students in theology, *while employed in discharging their several duties*, nor on those who 'have actually begun a sacrifice; for the first are 'then placed on the seat of INDRA, and the others 'are always equally pure with the celestial spirit.

94. 'To a king, on the throne of magnanimity, 'the law ascribes instant purification, because his 'throne was raised for the protection of his people and the supply of their nourishment:

95. 'It is the same with *the kinsmen of* those 'who die in battle, after the king has been slain, 'or have been killed by lightning, or legally by 'the king himself, or in defence of a cow, or of a 'priest; and with all those whom the king 'wishes to be pure.

96. 'The corporeal frame of a king is composed of particles from *Sóma*, AGNI, SU'RYA, 'PAVANA, INDRA, CUVE'RA, VARUNA, and 'YAMA, the eight guardian deities of the world:

97. 'By those guardians of men in substance is 'the king pervaded, and he cannot by law be 'impure; since by those tutelar gods are the 'purity and impurity of mortals both caused and 'removed.

98. 'By a soldier discharging the duties of his 'class, and slain in the field with brandished weapons, the highest sacrifice is, in that instant, 'complete; and so is his purification: this law 'is fixed.

99. 'A priest having performed funeral rites, 'is purified by touching water; a soldier, by 'touching his horse or elephant, or his arms; 'a husbandman, by touching his goad, or the hal-

'ter of his cattle; a servant. by touching his 'staff.

100. 'This mode of purifying *sapindas*, O chief 'of the twice born, has been fully declared to 'you! learn now the purification required on the 'death of kinsmen less intimately connected.

101. 'A *Bráhmen*, having caried out a dead '*Bráhmen*, though not a *sapinda*, with the affection 'of a kinsman, or any of those nearly related to 'him by his mother, becomes pure in three 'days;

102. 'But, if he taste the food offered by their '*sapindas*, he is purified in ten days; and in one 'day, if he neither partake of their food, nor dwell 'in the same house.

103. 'If he voluntarily follow a corpse, whe-'ther of a paternal kinsman or of another, and 'afterwards bathe with his apparel, he is made 'pure by touching fire and tasting clarified 'butter.

104. 'Let no kinsman, whilst any of his own 'class are at hand, cause a deceased *Bráhmen* to be 'carried out by a *Súdra*; since the funeral rite, 'polluted by the touch of a servile man, obstructs 'his passage to heaven.

105. 'Sacred learning, austere devotion, fire, 'holy aliment, earth, the mind, water, smearing 'with cow-dung, air, prescribed acts of religion, 'the sun, and time, are purifiers of imbodied 'spirits;

106. 'But of all pure things, purity in acquir-'ing wealth is pronounced the most excellent: 'since he, who gains wealth with clean hands, is 'truly pure; not he, who is purified merely with 'earth and water.

107. 'By

107. 'By forgiveneſs of injuries, the learned 'are purified; by liberality, thoſe who have neg-'lected their duty; by pious meditation, thoſe 'who have ſecret faults; by devout auſterity, 'thoſe who beſt know the *Véda*.

108. 'By water and earth is purified what 'ought to be made pure; a river, by its current; 'a woman, whoſe thoughts have been impure, by 'her monthly diſcharge, and the chief of twice 'born men, by fixing his mind wholly on GOD.

109. 'Bodies are cleanſed by water; the mind 'is purified by truth; the vital ſpirit, by theology 'and devotion; the underſtanding, by clear 'knowledge.

110. 'Thus have you heard me declare the 'preciſe rules for purifying animal bodies: hear 'now the modes of reſtoring purity to various 'inanimate things.

111. 'Of brilliant metals, of gems, and of every 'thing made with ſtone, the purification, ordained 'by the wiſe, is with aſhes, water, and earth.

112. 'A golden veſſel, not ſmeared, is cleanſed 'with water only; and every thing produced in 'water, *as coral, ſhells or pearls*, and every ſtony 'ſubſtance, and a ſilver veſſel not enchaſed.

113. 'From a junction of water and fire aroſe 'gold and ſilver; and they two, therefore, are beſt 'purified by the elements whence they ſprang.

114. 'Veſſels of copper, iron, braſs, pewter, 'tin and lead, may be fitly cleanſed with aſhes, 'with acids, or with water.

115. 'The purification ordained for all ſorts of 'liquids, is by ſtirring them with *cus'a*-graſs; for 'cloths folded, by ſprinkling them with hallowed 'water; for wooden utenſils, by planeing them.

116. 'For

116. 'For the ſacrificial pots to hold clarified 'butter and juice of the moon plant, by rubbing 'them with the hand, and waſhing them, at 'the time of the ſacrifice:

117. 'Implements to waſh the rice, to contain 'the oblations, to caſt them into the fire, to col'lect, winnow, and prepare the grain, muſt be 'purified with water made hot.

118. 'The purification by ſprinkling is or'dained for grain and cloths in large quantities; 'but to purify them in ſmall parcels, *which a* '*man may eaſily carry*, they muſt be waſhed.

119. 'Leathern utenſils, and ſuch as are made 'with cane, muſt generally be purified in the ſame 'manner with cloths; green vegetables, roots, 'and fruit, in the ſame manner with grain;

120. 'Silk and woollen ſtuff, with ſaline earths; 'blankets from *Népála* with pounded *ariſhtas*, or '*nimba* fruit; veſts and long drawers, with the 'fruit of the *Bilva*; mantles of *cſhumá*, with white 'muſtard ſeeds.

121. 'Utenſils made of ſhells or horn, of bones 'or of ivory, muſt be cleanſed by him who 'knows the law, as mantles of *cſhumá* are puri'fied, with the addition of cows urine or of water.

122. 'Graſs, firewood, and ſtraw, are purified 'by ſprinkling them with water; a houſe, by 'rubbing, bruſhing, and ſmearing with cow-dung; 'an earthen pot, by a ſecond burning:

123. 'But an earthen pot, which has been 'touched with any ſpirituous liquor, with urine, 'with ordure, with ſpittle, with pus, or with 'blood, cannot, even by another burning, be ren'dered pure.

124. 'Land is cleanſed by five modes; by 'ſweeping

'sweeping, by smearing with cow-dung, by sprink-
'ling with cow's urine, by scraping, or by letting
'a cow pass a day and a night on it.

125. 'A thing nibbled by a bird, smelt at by 'a cow, shaken with a foot, sneezed on, or defiled 'by lice, is purified by earth scattered over it.

126. 'As long as the scent or moisture, caused 'by any impurity, remain on the thing soiled, so 'long must earth and water be repeatedly used in 'all purifications of things inanimate.

127. 'The gods declared three pure things 'peculiar to *Bráhmens*; what has been defiled 'without their knowledge, what, in cases of doubt, 'they sprinkle with water; and what they com-'mend with their speech.

128. 'Waters are pure, as far as a cow goes to 'quench her thirst in them, if they flow over 'clean earth, and are sullied by no impurity, but 'have a good scent, colour, and taste.

129. 'The hand of an artist, *employed in his art*, 'is always pure; so is every vendible commodity, 'when exposed to sale; and that food is always 'clean, which a student in theology has begged 'and received: such is the sacred rule.

130. 'The mouth of a woman is constantly 'pure; a bird is pure on the fall of fruit, which 'he has pecked; a sucking animal, on the flowing 'of the milk; a dog, on his catching the deer:

131. 'The flesh of a wild beast slain by dogs, 'MENU pronounces pure; and that of an animal 'slain by other carnivorous creatures, or by men 'of the mixed class, who subsist by hunting.

132. 'All the cavities above the navel are pure, 'and all below it, unclean; so are all excretions 'that fall from the body.

133. 'Gnats, clear drops from the mouth of a 'ſpeaker, a ſhadow, a cow, a horſe, ſun-beams, 'duſt, earth, air and fire, muſt all be conſidered 'as clean, even when they touch an unclean 'thing.

134. 'For the cleanſing of veſſels, which have 'held ordure or urine, earth and water muſt be 'uſed, as long as they are needful; and the ſame 'for cleanſing the twelve corporeal impurities:

135. 'Oily exudations, ſeminal fluids, blood, 'dandruff, urine, feces, ear-wax, nail-parings, 'phlegm, tears, concretions on the eyes, and 'ſweat, are the twelve impurities of the human 'frame.

136. 'By the man who deſires purity, one piece 'of earth, *together with water*, muſt be uſed for the 'conduit of urine, three for that of the feces; ſo, 'ten for one hand, *that is, the left*; then ſeven for 'both: *but if neceſſary, more muſt be uſed.*

137. 'Such is the purification of married men; 'that of ſtudents muſt be double; that of hermits, 'triple; that of men wholly recluſe, quadruple.

138. 'Let each man ſprinkle the cavities of his 'body, and taſte water in due form, when he has 'diſcharged urine or feces; when he is going to 'read the *Véda*; and, invariably, before he takes 'his food:

139. 'Firſt, let him thrice taſte water; then, 'twice let him wipe his mouth, if he *be of a* '*twice born claſs, and* deſire corporeal purity; but 'a woman or ſervile man may once reſpectively 'make that ablution.

140. '*Súdras*, engaged in religious duties, 'muſt perform each month the ceremony of 'ſhaving their heads; their food muſt be the

'orts

'orts of *Bráhmens*; and their mode of purification, the same with that of a *Vaisya*.

141. 'Such drops of water, as fall from the mouth or any part of the body, render it not unclean; nor hairs of the beard that enter the mouth; nor what adheres awhile to the teeth.

142. 'Drops, which trickle on the feet of a man holding water for others, are hold equal to waters flowing over pure earth: by them he is not defiled.

143. 'He, who carries in any manner an inanimate burden, and is touched by any thing impure, is cleansed by making an ablution, without laying his burden down.

144. 'Having vomited, or been purged, let him bathe and taste clarified butter, but, if he have eaten already, let him only perform an ablution: for him, who has been connected with a woman, bathing is ordained by law.

145. 'Having slumbered, having sneezed, having eaten, having spitten, having told untruths, having drunk water, and going to read sacred books, let him, though pure, wash his mouth.

146. 'This perfect system of rules for purifying men of all classes, and for cleansing inanimate things, has been declared to you: hear now the laws concerning women.

147. 'By a girl, or by a young woman, or by a woman advanced in years, nothing must be done, even in her own dwelling place, according to her mere pleasure:

148. 'In childhood must a female be dependent on her father; in youth, on her husband; her lord being dead, on her sons; *if she have no sons, on the near kinsmen of her husband; if he*

'*left*

'*left no kinſmen, on thoſe of her father; if ſhe have*
'*no paternal kinſmen, on the ſovereign:* a woman
'muſt never ſeek independence.

149. 'Never let her wiſh to ſeparate herſelf
'from her father, her huſband, or her ſons; for,
'by a ſeparation from them, ſhe expoſes both
'families to contempt.

150. 'She muſt always live with a cheerful
'temper, with good management in the affairs
'of the houſe, with great care of the houſehold
'furniture, and with a frugal hand in all her
'expences.

151. 'Him, to whom her father has given
'her, or her brother with the paternal aſſent, let
'her obſequiouſly honour, while he lives; and,
'when he dies, let her never neglect him.

152. 'The recitation of holy texts, and the
'ſacrifice ordained by the lord of creatures, are
'uſed in marriages for the ſake of procuring
'good fortune to brides; but the firſt gift, *or*
'*troth plighted* by the huſband, is the primary
'cauſe *and origin* of marital dominion.

153. 'When the huſband has performed the
'nuptial rites with texts from the *Véda*, he gives
'bliſs continually to his wife here below, both in
'ſeaſon and out of ſeaſon; and he will give her
'happineſs in the next world.

154. 'Though inobſervant of approved uſages,
'or enamoured of another woman, or devoid of
'good qualities, yet a huſband muſt conſtantly
'be revered as a god by a virtuous wife.

155. 'No ſacrifice is allowed to women apart
'from their huſbands, no religious rite, no faſt-
'ing: as far only as a wife honours her lord, ſo
'far ſhe is exalted in heaven.

156. 'A

156. 'A faithful wife, who wishes to attain 'in heaven the mansion of her husband, must do 'nothing unkind to him, be he living or dead:

157. 'Let her emaciate her body, by living 'voluntarily on pure flowers, roots, and fruit; 'but let her not, when her lord is deceased, even 'pronounce the name of another man.

158. 'Let her continue till death forgiving all 'injuries, performing harsh duties, avoiding every 'sensual pleasure, and cheerfully practising the 'incomparable rules of virtue, which have been 'followed by such women, as were devoted to 'one only husband.

159. 'Many thousands of *Bráhmens*, having 'avoided sensuality from their early youth, and 'having left no issue in their families, have as-'cended, *nevertheless*, to heaven;

160. 'And, like those abstemious men, a vir-'tuous wife ascends to heaven, though she have 'no child, if, after the decease of her lord, she 'devote herself to pious austerity:

161. 'But a widow, who, from a wish to bear 'children, slights her deceased husband *by marry-'ing again*, brings disgrace on herself here below, 'and shall be excluded from the seat of her lord.

162. 'Issue, begotten on a woman by any 'other *than her husband*, is here declared to be 'no progeny of hers; no more than a child, 'begotten on the wife of another man, *belongs to 'the begetter:* nor is a second husband allowed, 'in any part of this code, to a virtuous woman.

163. 'She, who neglects her former (*púrva*) 'lord, though of a lower class, and takes another '(*para*) of a higher, becomes despicable in this 'world, and is called *parapúrvá*, or *one who had 'a different husband before.*

164. 'A

164. ‘ A married woman, who violates the ‘ duty which ſhe owes to her lord, brings infamy ‘ on herſelf in this life, and, *in the next*, ſhall enter ‘ the womb of a ſhakal, or be afflicted with *ele-* ‘ *phantiaſis, and other* diſeaſes, which puniſh crimes;

165. ‘ While ſhe, who ſlights not her lord, ‘ but keeps her mind, ſpeech, and body, devoted ‘ to him, attains his heavenly manſion, and by ‘ good men is called *ſádhvì*, or *virtuous*.

166. ‘ Yes; by this courſe of life it is, that a ‘ woman, whoſe mind, ſpeech, and body are ‘ kept in ſubjection, acquires high renown in this ‘ world, and, in the next, the ſame abode with ‘ her huſband.

167. ‘ A twice born man, verſed in ſacred ‘ ordinances, muſt burn with hallowed fire and fit ‘ implements of ſacrifice, his wife dying before ‘ him, if ſhe was of his own claſs, and lived by ‘ theſe rules:

168. ‘ Having thus kindled ſacred fires and ‘ performed funeral rites to his wife, who died ‘ before him, he may again marry, and again ‘ light the nuptial fire.

169. ‘ Let him not ceaſe to perform day by ‘ day, according to the preceding rules, the five ‘ great ſacraments; and having taken a lawful ‘ conſort, let him dwell in his houſe during the ‘ ſecond period of his life.

CHAPTER THE SIXTH.

On Devotion ; or on the Third and Fourth Orders.

1. ‘ Having thus remained in the order of a ‘ house-keeper, as the law ordains, let the twice ‘ born man, who had before completed his stu-‘ dentship, dwell in a forest, his faith being firm ‘ and his organs wholly subdued.

2. ‘ When the father of a family, perceives his ‘ muscles become flaccid and his hair gray, and ‘ sees the child of his child, let him then seek ‘ refuge in a forest :

3. ‘ Abandoning all food eaten in towns, and all ‘ his household utensils, let him repair to the ‘ lonely wood, committing the care of his wife to ‘ her sons, or accompanied by her, *if she chuse to* ‘ *attend him.*

4. ‘ Let him take up his consecrated fire, and ‘ all his domestick implements of making oblations ‘ to it, and, departing from the town to the forest, ‘ let him dwell in it with complete power over his ‘ organs *of sense and of action.*

5. ‘ With many sorts of pure food, such as holy ‘ sages used to eat, with green herbs, roots, and

 ‘ fruit,

'fruit, let him perform the five great sacraments 'before mentioned, introducing them with due 'ceremonies.

6. 'Let him wear a black antelopes's hide, or 'a vesture of bark; let him bathe evening and 'morning; let him suffer the hairs of his head, 'his beard, and his nails to grow continually.

7. 'From such food, as himself may eat, let 'him, to the utmost of his power, make offerings 'and give alms; and with presents of water, roots, 'and fruit, let him honour those who visit his 'hermitage.

8. 'Let him be constantly engaged in reading the '*Véda*; patient of all extremities, universally be-'nevolent, with a mind intent on the Supreme 'Being; a perpetual giver, but no receiver of 'gifts; with tender affection for all animated 'bodies.

9. 'Let him, as the law directs, make oblations 'on the hearth with three sacred fires; not omit-'ting, in due time, the ceremonies to be performed 'at the conjunction and opposition of the moon.

10. 'Let him also perform the sacrifice ordained 'in honour of the lunar constellations, make the 'prescribed offering of new grain, and solemnize 'holy rites every four months, and at the winter 'and summer solstices.

11. 'With pure grains, the food of ancient 'sages, growing in the vernal and autumnal sea-'sons, and brought home by himself, let him seve-'rally make, as the law ordains, the oblations of 'cakes and boiled grain;

12. 'And, having presented to the gods, that 'purest oblation which the wild woods produced, 'let him eat what remains, together with some native salt, which himself collected.

13. 'Let

13. 'Let him eat green herbs, flowers, roots, 'and fruit, that grow on earth or in water, 'and the productions of pure trees, and oils 'formed in fruits.

14. 'Honey and flesh meat he must avoid, and 'all sorts of mushrooms, the plant *bhústrĭna*, that 'named *sighruca*, and the fruit of the *sléshmátaca*.

15. 'In the month *Aswina* let him cast away the 'food of sages, which he before had laid up, and 'his vesture, then become old, and his herbs, 'roots, and fruit.

16. 'Let him not eat the produce of plowed 'land, though abandoned by any man *who* '*owns it*, nor fruits and roots produced in a 'town, even though hunger oppress him.

17. 'He may eat what is mellowed by fire, and 'he may eat what is ripened by time; and either 'let him break hard fruits with a stone, or let his 'teeth serve as a pestle.

18. 'Either let him pluck enough for a day, 'or let him gather enough for a month; or let 'him collect enough for six months, or lay up 'enough for a year.

19. 'Having procured food, as he is able, he 'may eat it at eve or in the morning; or he 'may take only every fourth, or every eighth, 'such regular meal;

20. 'Or, by the rules of the lunar penance, he 'may eat a mouthful more each day of the bright, 'and a mouthful less each day of the dark fort-'night; or he may eat only once, at the close of 'each fortnight, a mess of boiled grains:

21. 'Or he may constantly live on flowers and 'roots, and on fruit matured by time, which has 'fallen spontaneously, strictly observing the laws 'ordained for hermits.

22. ‘ Let him ſlide backwards and forwards on ‘ the ground; or let him ſtand a whole day on ‘ tiptoe; or let him continue in motion riſing and ‘ ſitting alternately; but at ſunriſe, at noon, and ‘ at ſunſet, let him go to the waters and bathe.

23. ‘ In the hot ſeaſon, let him ſit expoſed to ‘ five fires, *four blazing around him with the ſun* ‘ *above*; in the rains, let him ſtand uncovered, ‘ *without even a mantle*, where the clouds pour *the* ‘ *heavieſt* ſhowers; and in the cold ſeaſon, let him ‘ wear humid veſture; and let him increaſe by ‘ degrees the auſterity of his devotion:

24. ‘ Performing his ablution at the three *Sava-* ‘ *nas*, let him give ſatisfaction to the manes and ‘ to the gods; and, enduring harſher and ‘ harſher mortifications, let him dry up his bodily ‘ frame.

25. ‘ Then having repoſited his holy fires, as the ‘ law directs, in his mind, let him live without ‘ external fire, without a manſion, wholly ſilent, ‘ feeding on roots and fruit;

26. ‘ Not ſolicitous for the means of gratifica- ‘ tion, chaſte as a ſtudent, ſleeping on the bare ‘ earth, in the haunts of pious hermits, without ‘ one ſelfiſh affection, dwelling at the roots of ‘ trees.

27. ‘ From devout *Bráhmens* let him receive ‘ alms to ſupport life, or from other houſe-keep- ‘ ers of twice born claſſes, who dwell in the ‘ foreſt:

28. ‘ Or the hermit may bring food from a ‘ town, having received it in a baſket of leaves, ‘ in his naked hand, or in a potſherd; and then ‘ let him ſwallow eight mouthfuls.

29. ‘ Theſe and other rules muſt a *Bráhmen*, ‘ who retires to the woods, diligently practiſe;

‘ and,

'and, for the purpose of uniting his soul with the 'Divine Spirit, let him study the various *Upanishads* of scripture, or *chapters on the essence and attributes of God*,

30. 'Which have been studied with reverence 'by anchorites versed in theology, and by house-'keepers, who dwelt afterwards in forests, for the 'sake of increasing their sublime knowledge and 'devotion, and for the purification of their bodies.

31. 'Or, *if he has any incurable disease*, let him 'advance in a straight path, towards the invinci-'ble *nerth eastern* point, feeding on water and air, 'till his mortal frame totally decay, and his soul 'become united with the Supreme.

32. 'A *Bráhmen*, having shuffled off his body 'by any of those modes, which great sages prac-'tised, and becoming void of sorrow and fear, 'rises to exaltation in the divine essence.

33. 'HAVING thus performed religious acts in 'a forest during the third portion of his life, let 'him become a *Sannyási* for the fourth portion of 'it, abandoning all sensual affections, *and wholly 'reposing in the Supreme Spirit:*

34. 'The man who has passed from order to 'order, has made oblations to fire *on his respective 'changes of state*, and has kept his members in 'subjection, but, tired with *so long a course of giving* 'alms and *making* offerings, thus reposes himself 'entirely on GOD, shall be raised, after death, to 'glory.

35. 'When he has paid his three debts *to the 'sages, the manes, and the gods*, let him apply his 'mind to final beatitude; but low shall He fall 'who presumes to seek beatitude without hav-'ing discharged those debts;

 36. 'After

36. ‘ After he has read the *Védas* in the form ‘ prefcribed by law, has legally begotten a fon, ‘ and has performed facrifices to the beft of his ‘ power, he *has paid his three debts, and* may then ‘ apply his heart to eternal blifs;

37. ‘ But if a *Bráhmen* have not read the *Véda*, ‘ if he have not begotten a fon, and if he have not ‘ performed facrifices, yet fhall aim at final bea‘ titude, he fhall fink to a place of degradation.

38. ‘ Having performed the facrifice of PRA‘ JA'PETI, accompanied with a gift of all his ‘ wealth, *and* having repofited in his mind the facri‘ ficial fires, a *Bráhmen* may proceed from his ‘ houfe, *that is, from the fecond order, or he may pro‘ ceed even from the firft*, to the condition of a ‘ *Sannyáfi*.

39. ‘ Higher worlds are illuminated with the ‘ glory of that man, who paffes from his houfe ‘ into the fourth order, giving exemption from ‘ fear to all animated beings, and pronouncing ‘ the *myftick words of* the *Véda*:

40. ‘ To the *Bráhmen*, by whom not even the ‘ fmalleft dread has been occafioned by fentient ‘ creatures, there can be no dread from any quar‘ ter whatever, when he obtains a releafe from ‘ his mortal body.

41. ‘ Departing from his houfe, taking with him ‘ pure implements, *his water-pot and ftaff*, keeping ‘ filence, unallured by defire of the objects near ‘ him, let him enter into the fourth order.

42. ‘ Alone let him conftantly dwell, for the ‘ fake of his own felicity; obferving the happinefs ‘ of a folitary man, who neither forfakes nor is ‘ forfaken, let him live without a companion.

43. ‘ Let him have no culinary fire, no domi‘ cil;

'cil; let him, *when very hungry*, go to the town 'for food; let him patiently bear diſeaſe; let his 'mind be firm; let him ſtudy to know God, and 'fix his attention on God alone.

44. 'An earthen water-pot, the roots of large 'trees, coarſe veſture, total ſolitude, equanimity 'toward all creatures, theſe are the characte-'riſticks of a *Bráhmen* ſet free.

45. 'Let him not wiſh for death; let him not 'wiſh for life; let him expect his appointed time, 'as a hired ſervant expects his wages.

46. 'Let him advance his foot purified by 'looking down, *leſt he touch any thing impure*; let 'him drink water purified by ſtraining with 'a cloth, *leſt he hurt ſome inſect*; let him, *if he 'chuſe to ſpeak*, utter words purified by truth; let 'him by all means keep his heart purified.

47. 'Let him bare a reproachful ſpeech with 'patience; let him ſpeak reproachfully to no 'man; let him not, on account of this *frail and 'feveriſh* body, engage in hoſtility with any one 'living.

48. 'With an angry man, let him not in his turn 'be angry; abuſed, let him ſpeak mildly; nor 'let him utter a word relating to vain illuſory 'things and confined within ſeven gates, *the five 'organs of ſenſe, the heart and the intellect*; *or this 'world, with three above and three below it.*

49. 'Delighted with meditating on the Su-'preme Spirit, ſitting fixed in ſuch meditation, 'without needing any thing earthly, without one 'ſenſual deſire, without any companion but his 'own ſoul, let him live in this world ſeeking the 'bliſs of the next.

50. 'Neither by explaining omens and prodi-

'gies, nor by ſkill in aſtrology and palmiſtry, nor 'by caſuiſtry and expoſitions of holy texts, let 'him at any time gain his daily ſupport.

51. 'Let him not go near a houſe frequented 'by hermits, or prieſts, or birds, or dogs, or other 'beggars.

52. 'His hair, nails, and beard being clipped, 'bearing with him a diſh, a ſtaff, and a water-pot, 'his whole mind being fixed on GOD, let him 'wander about continually, without giving pain 'to *animal or vegetable* beings.

53. 'His diſhes muſt have no fracture, nor 'muſt they be made of bright metals: the puri'fication ordained for them muſt be with water 'alone, like that of the veſſels for a ſacrifice.

54. 'A gourd, a wooden bowl, an earthen diſh, 'or a baſket made of reeds, has MENU, ſon of 'the Self-exiſting, declared fit veſſels to receive 'the food of *Bráhmens* devoted to God.

55. 'Only once a day let him demand food; 'let him not habituate him to eat much at a time; 'for an anchorite, habituated to eat much, be'comes inclined to ſenſual gratifications.

56. 'At the time when the ſmoke of kitchen fires 'has ceaſed, when the peſtle lies motionleſs, when 'the burning charcoal is exinguiſhed, when 'people have eaten, and when diſhes are removed, '*that is, late in the day*, let the *Sannyáſi* always 'beg food.

57. 'For miſſing it, let him not be ſorrowful; 'nor for gaining it, let him be glad; let him care 'only for a ſufficiency to ſupport life, but let him 'not be anxious about his utenſils.

58. 'Let him conſtantly diſdain to receive 'food after humble reverence; ſince, by receiv-

'ing

'ing it in consequence of an humble salutation, a 'Sannyási, though free, becomes a captive.

59. 'By eating little and by sitting in solitary 'places, let him restrain those organs which are 'naturally hurried away by sensual desires.

60. 'By the coercion of his members, by the 'absence of hate and affection, and by giving no 'pain to sentient creatures, he becomes fit for 'immortality.

61. 'Let him reflect on the transmigrations 'of men caused by their sinful deeds, on their 'downfal into a region of darkness, and their 'torments in the mansion of YAMA;

62. 'On their separation from those whom 'they love, and their union with those whom 'they hate, on their strength overpowered by old 'age, and their bodies racked with disease;

63. 'On their agonizing departure from this 'corporeal frame, their formation again in the 'womb, and the glidings of this vital spirit 'through ten thousand millions of uterine pas-'sages;

64. 'On the misery attached to embodied spi-'rits from a violation of their duties, and the un-'perishable bliss attached to them from their 'abundant performance of all duties, religious 'and civil.

65. 'Let him reflect also, with exclusive appli-'cation of mind, on the subtil indivisable essence 'of the Supreme Spirit, and its complete existence 'in all beings, whether extremely high or ex-'tremely low.

66. 'Equal-minded towards all creatures, in 'what order soever *he may have been* placed, let him 'fully discharge his duty though he bear not the

'visible marks of his order: the visible mark, 'or mere name of his order, is by no means an effective discharge of his duty;

67. 'As, although the fruit of the tree *cataca* 'purify water, yet a man cannot purify water by 'merely pronouncing the name of that fruit: *he 'must throw it, when pounded, into the jar.*

68. 'For the sake of preserving minute animals 'by night and by day, let him walk, though with 'pain to his own body, perpetually looking on 'the ground.

69. 'Let a *Sannyási*, by way of expiation for '*the death of* those creatures, which he may have 'destroyed unknowingly by day or by night, 'make six suppressions of his breath, having duly 'bathed:

70. 'Even three suppressions of breath, made 'according to the divine rule, accompanied with 'the triverbal phrase *(bhurbhuvah swah)* and the 'trileteral syllable *(óm)* may be considered as the 'highest devotion of a *Bráhmen*;

71. 'For as the dross and impurities of metal-'lick ores are consumed by fire, thus are the sinful 'acts of the human organ consumed by suppres-'sions of the breath, *while the mystick words, and the 'measures of the* gáyatrì *are revolved in the mind.*

72. 'Let him thus, by such suppressions of 'breath, burn away his offences; by reflecting 'intensely on the steps of ascent to beatitude, *let 'him destroy sin*; by coercing his members, let 'him restrain all sensual attachments; by meditat-'ing on *the intimate union of his own soul and* the 'divine essence, let him extinguish all qualities 'repugnant to the nature of God.

73. 'Let him observe, with extreme applica-'tion

'tion of mind, the progreſs of this internal ſpirit 'through various bodies, high and low; *a progreſs* 'hard to be diſcerned by men with unimproved 'intellects.

74. 'He, who fully underſtands the perpetual 'omnipreſence of God, can be led no more cap- 'tive by criminal acts; but he, who poſſeſſes not 'that ſublime knowledge, ſhall wander again 'through the world.

75. 'By injuring nothing animated, by ſub- 'duing all ſenſual appetites, by devout rites 'ordained in the *Véda*, and by rigorous mortifi- 'cations, men obtain, even in this life, the 'ſtate of beatitude.

76. 'A manſion with bones for its rafters and 'beams; with nerves and tendons, for cords; 'with muſcles and blood, for mortar; with ſkin, 'for its outward covering; filled with no ſweet 'perfume, but loaded with feces and urine;

77. 'A manſion infeſted by age and by ſor- 'row, the ſeat of malady, harraſſed with pains, 'haunted with the quality of darkneſs, and inca- 'pable of ſtanding long; ſuch a manſion of the 'vital ſoul let its occupier always cheerfully 'quit:

78. 'As a tree leaves the bank of a river, '*when it falls in*, or as a bird leaves the branch of 'a tree *at his pleaſure*, thus he, who leaves his 'body *by neceſſity or by legal choice*, is delivered 'from the ravening ſhark, *or crocodile* of the 'world.

79. 'Letting his good acts deſcend (by the 'law of the *Véda*,) to thoſe who love him, 'and his evil deeds, to thoſe who hate him, 'he may attain, through devout meditation, the 'eternal ſpirit.

80. 'When,

80. 'When, having well confidered the nature 'and confequence of fin, he becomes averfe 'from all fenfual delights, he then attains blifs 'in this world; blifs which fhall endure after 'death.

81. 'Thus having gradually abandoned all 'earthly attachments, and indifferent to all pairs 'of oppofite things, *as honour and difhonour, and the 'like,* he remains abforbed in the divine effence.

82. 'All that has now been declared, is ob-'tained by pious meditation; but no man who is 'ignorant of the Supreme Spirit, can gather the 'fruit of mere ceremonial acts.

83. 'Let him conftantly ftudy that part of the '*Véda,* which relates to facrifice; that which 'treats of fubordinate deities; that which reveals 'the nature of the fupreme God; and whatever is 'declared in the *Upanifhads.*

84. 'This holy fcripture is a fure refuge, even 'for thofe who underftand not its meaning, and 'of courfe, for thofe who underftand it; this *Véda* 'is a fure refource for thofe who feek blifs above; 'this *is a fure refource* for thofe who feek blifs 'eternal.

85. 'That *Bráhmen,* who becomes a *Sannyáfi* 'by this difcipline, *announced* in due order, fhakes 'off fin here below, and reaches the moft 'high.

86. 'This *general* law has been revealed to 'you for anchorites with fubdued minds: now 'learn the particular difcipline of thofe who be-'come reclufes according to the *Véda,* that is, *of 'anchorites in the firft of the four degrees.*

87. 'The ftudent, the married man, the her-'mit, and the anchorite, are the offspring, though 'in four orders, of married men keeping houfe;

88. 'And

88. 'And all, or even any of those orders, 'assumed in their turn, according to the sacred 'ordinances, lead the *Bráhmen*, who acts by the 'preceding rules, to the highest mansion:

89. 'But of all those, the house-keeper observ-'ing the regulations of the *Sruti* and *Smriti*, 'may be called the chief; since he supports the 'three *other orders*.

90. 'As all rivers, female and male, run to 'their determined place in the sea, thus men of all '*other* orders, repair to their fixed place in the 'mansion of the house-keeper.

91. 'By *Bráhmens*, placed in these four orders, 'a tenfold system of duties must ever be sedu-'lously practised:

92. 'Content, returning good for evil, resist-'ance to sensual appetites, abstinence from illicit 'gain, purification, coercion of the organs, 'knowledge of scripture, knowledge of the 'Supreme Spirit, veracity, and freedom from 'wrath, form their tenfold system of duties.

93. 'Such *Bráhmens*, as attentively read the 'ten precepts of duty, and after reading, care-'fully practise them, attain the most exalted 'condition.

94. 'A *Bráhmen* having practised with organs 'under command, this tenfold system of duty, 'having heard the *Upanishads* explained, as the 'law directs, and who has discharged his three 'debts, may become an anchorite, *in the house of* '*his son*, according to the *Véda*;

95. 'And, having abandoned all ceremonial 'acts, having expiated all his offences, having ob-'tained a command over his organs, and having 'perfectly understood the scripture, he may live

'at

'at his eaſe, while the houſehold affairs are 'conducted by his ſon.

96. 'When he thus has relinquiſhed all forms, 'is intent on his own occupation, and free from 'every other deſire, when, by devoting himſelf to 'God, he has effaced ſin, he then attains the ſu-'preme path of glory.

97. 'This fourfold regulation for the ſacer-'dotal claſs, has thus been made known to you; 'a juſt regulation, producing endleſs fruit after 'death: next, learn the duty of kings, *or the* '*military claſs.*'

CHAPTER THE SEVENTH.

On Government, and Publick Law; or on the Military Clafs.

---

1. 'I WILL fully declare the duty of kings; 'and ſhow how a ruler of men ſhould conduct 'himſelf, in what manner he was framed, and 'how his ultimate reward *may be attained by him.*

2. 'By a man of the military claſs, who has 'received in due form the inveſtiture which the '*Véda* preſcribes, great care muſt be uſed to 'maintain this whole *aſſemblage of laws.*

3. 'Since, if the world had no king, it would 'quake on all ſides through fear, the ruler of 'this *univerſe*, therefore, created a king, for the 'maintenance of this ſyſtem, both religious and 'civil,

4. 'Forming him of eternal particles drawn 'from the ſubſtance of INDRA, PAVANA, YAMA, 'SU'RYA, of AGNI and VARUNA, of CHANDRA 'and CUVE'RA:

5. 'And ſince a king was compoſed of parti-'cles drawn from thoſe chief guardian deities, he 'conſequently ſurpaſſes all mortals in glory.

6. 'Like the ſun, he burns eyes and hearts; 'nor can any human creature on earth even gaze 'on him.

7. 'He

7. 'He *is* fire and air; he, both ſun and 'moon; he, the god of criminal juſtice; he, 'the genius of wealth; he, the regent of waters; 'he, the lord of the firmament.

8. 'A king, even though a child, muſt not 'be treated lightly, from an idea that he is a 'mere mortal: no; he is a powerful divinity, 'who appears in a human ſhape.

9. 'Fire burns only one perſon, who careleſsly 'goes too near it; but the fire of a king in wrath 'burns a whole family, with all their cattle and 'goods.

10. 'Fully conſidering the buſineſs before 'him, his own force, and the place, and the time, 'he aſſumes in ſucceſſion all ſorts of forms, for 'the ſake of advancing juſtice.

11. 'He, ſure, muſt be the perfect eſſence of 'majeſty, by whoſe favour Abundance riſes on 'her lotos, in whoſe valour dwells conqueſt; in 'whoſe anger, death.

12. 'He, who ſhews hatred of the king, 'through deluſion of mind, will certainly periſh; 'for ſpeedily will the king apply his heart to that 'man's perdition.

13. 'Let the king prepare a juſt compenſa-'tion for the good, and a juſt puniſhment for the 'bad: the rule of ſtrict juſtice let him never 'tranſgreſs.

14. 'For his uſe Brahma' formed, in the be-'ginning of time, the genius of puniſhment, with 'a body of pure light, his own ſon, even ab-'ſtract criminal juſtice, the protector of all created 'things:

15. 'Through fear of that genius, all ſentient 'beings, whether fixed or locomotive, are fitted 'for natural enjoyments and ſwerve not from duty.

16. 'When

16. 'When the king, therefore, has fully considered place and time, and his own ſtrength, 'and the divine ordinance, let him juſtly inflict 'puniſhment on all thoſe who act unjuſtly.

17. 'Puniſhment is an active ruler; he is the 'true manager of publick affairs; he is the diſpenſer of laws; and wiſe men call him the 'ſponſor of all the four orders for the diſcharge 'of their ſeveral duties.

18. 'Puniſhment governs all mankind; puniſhment alone preſerves them; puniſhment wakes, 'while their guards are aſleep; the wiſe conſider 'puniſhment as the perfection of juſtice.

19. 'When rightly and conſiderately inflicted, 'it makes all the people happy; but, inflicted 'without full conſideration, it wholly deſtroys 'them all.

20. 'If the king were not, without indolence, 'to puniſh the guilty, the ſtronger would roaſt 'the weaker, like fiſh, on a ſpit; (*or according to* '*one reading*, the ſtronger would oppreſs the 'weaker, like fiſh in their element;)

21. 'The crow would peck the conſecrated 'offering of rice; the dog would lick the clarified butter; ownerſhip would remain with none; 'the loweſt would overſet the higheſt.

22. 'The whole race of men is kept in order 'by puniſhment; for a guiltleſs man is hard to 'be found; through fear of puniſhment, indeed, 'this univerſe is enabled to enjoy its bleſſings;

23. 'Deities and demons, heavenly ſongſters 'and cruel giants, birds and ſerpents, are made 'capable, by juſt correction, of their ſeveral enjoyments.

24. 'All claſſes would become corrupt; all

'barriers would be deſtroyed, there would be 'total confuſion among men, if puniſhment either 'were not inflicted, or were inflicted unduly:

25. 'But where puniſhment, with a black hue 'and a red eye, advances to deſtroy ſin, there, if 'the judge diſcern well, the people are undiſ-'turbed.

26. 'Holy ſages conſider as a fit diſpenſer of 'criminal juſtice, that king, who invariably ſpeaks 'truth, who duly conſiders all caſes, who under-'ſtands the ſacred books, who knows the diſtinc-'tions of virtue, pleaſure, and riches;

27. 'Such a king, if he juſtly inflict legal 'puniſhments, greatly increaſes thoſe three means 'of happineſs; but puniſhment itſelf ſhall deſtroy 'a king, who is crafty, voluptuous, and wrathful:

28. 'Criminal juſtice, the bright eſſence of 'majeſty, and hard to be ſupported by men with 'unimproved minds, eradicates a king, who 'ſwerves from his duty, together with all his 'race:

29. 'Puniſhment ſhall overtake his caſtles, 'his territories, his peopled land with all fixed 'and moveable things that exiſt on it: even the 'gods and the ſages, *who loſe their oblations*, will 'be afflicted and aſcend to the ſky.

30. 'Juſt puniſhment cannot be inflicted by 'an ignorant and covetous king, who has no wiſe 'and virtuous aſſiſtant, whoſe underſtanding has 'not been improved, and whoſe heart is addicted 'to ſenſuality:

31. 'By a king wholly pure, faithful to his 'promiſe, obſervant of the ſcriptures, with good 'aſſiſtants and ſound underſtanding may puniſh-'ment be juſtly inflicted.

32. 'Let

32. 'Let him in his own domains act with 'justice, chastise foreign foes with rigour, behave 'without duplicity to his affectionate friends, and 'with lenity to *Bráhmens*.

33. 'Of a king thus disposed, even though 'he subsist by gleaning, *or, be his treasure ever so 'small*, the fame is far spread in the world, like 'a drop of oil in water;

34. 'But of a king with a contrary disposition, 'with passions unsubdued, *be his riches ever so 'great*, the fame is contracted in the world, like 'clarified butter in the same element.

35. 'A king was created as the protector of 'all those classes and orders, who from the first 'to the last, discharge their several duties;

36. '*And* all that must be done by him, for 'the protection of his people, with the assistance 'of good ministers, I will declare to you, as the 'law directs, in due order.

37. 'LET the king, having risen at early dawn, 'respectfully attend to *Bráhmens*, learned in the 'three *Védas*, and in the science of ethicks; and 'by their decision let him abide.

38. 'Constantly must he show respect to '*Bráhmens*, who have grown old, *both in years 'and in piety*, who know the scriptures, who *in 'body and mind* are pure; for he, who honours 'the aged, will perpetually be honoured even by 'cruel demons:

39. 'From them, though he may have ac-'quired modest behaviour *by his own good sense 'and by study*, let him continually learn habits 'of modesty and composure; since a king, whose 'demeanour is humble and composed, never 'perishes.

40. 'While, through want of such humble 'virtue, many kings have perished with all their 'possessions, and, through virtue united with 'modesty, even hermits have obtained kingdoms.

41. 'Through want of that virtuous humility 'VE'NA was utterly ruined, and so was the great 'king NAHUSHA, and SUDA'SA, and YAVANA, '(*or by a different reading,* and SUDA'MAN, the son 'of PIYAVANA) and SUMUC'HA, and NIMI;

42. 'But by virtues with humble behaviour, 'PRĬT'HU and MENU acquired sovereignty; 'CUVE'RA, wealth inexhaustible; and VISWA'-'MITRA, son of GA'DHI, the rank of a priest, '*though born in the military class.*

43. 'From those who know the three *Védas,* 'let him learn the triple doctrine comprised in 'them, together with the primeval science of 'criminal justice and sound policy, the systems 'of logick and metaphysicks, and sublime theo-'logical truth: from the people he must learn 'the theory of *agriculture, commerce, and other* 'practical arts.

44. 'Day and night must he strenuously ex-'ert himself to gain complete victory over his 'own organs; since that king alone, whose organs 'are completely subdued, can keep his people 'firm to their duty.

45. 'With extreme care let him shun eighteen 'vices, ten proceeding from love of pleasure, 'eight springing from wrath, and all ending in 'misery;

46. 'Since a king, addicted to vices arising 'from love of pleasure, must lose both his wealth 'and his virtue, and, addicted to vices arising 'from anger, he may lose even his life *from the* '*publick resentment.*

47. 'Hunt-

47. ‘ Hunting, gaming, ſleeping by day, cen-
‘ ſuring rivals, exceſs with women, intoxication,
‘ ſinging, inſtrumental muſick, dancing, and uſe-
‘ leſs travel, are the ten-fold ſet of vices produced
‘ by love of pleaſure:

48. ‘ Tale bearing, violence, inſidious wound-
‘ ing, envy, detraction, unjuſt ſeizure of property,
‘ reviling, and open aſſault, are, in like manner,
‘ the eight-fold ſet of vices to which anger gives
‘ birth.

49. ‘ A ſelfiſh inclination, which all wiſe men
‘ know to be the root of thoſe two ſets, let him
‘ ſuppreſs with diligence: both ſets of vices are
‘ conſtantly produced by it.

50. ‘ Drinking, dice, women, and hunting,
‘ let him conſider as the four moſt pernicious
‘ in the ſet, which love of pleaſure occaſions:

51. ‘ Battery, defamation, and injury to pro-
‘ perty, let him always conſider as the three moſt
‘ heinous in the ſet, which ariſes from wrath;

52. ‘ *And* in this ſeven-fold aſſemblage of vices,
‘ too frequently prevailing in all kingdoms, let
‘ an enlightened prince conſider the firſt, and ſo
‘ forth in order, as the moſt abominable in
‘ each ſet.

53. ‘ On a compariſon between death and
‘ vice, the learned pronounce vice the more
‘ dreadful; ſince, after death, a vicious man ſinks
‘ to regions lower and lower, while a man, free
‘ from vice, reaches heaven.

54. ‘ THE king muſt appoint ſeven or eight
‘ miniſters, who muſt be ſworn *by touching a*
‘ *ſacred image and the like*; men, whoſe anceſtors
‘ were ſervants of kings; who are verſed in the
‘ holy books; who are perſonally brave; who

'are ſkilled in the uſe of weapons; and whoſe lineage is noble.

55. 'Even an act eaſy in itſelf is hard ſometimes to be performed by a ſingle man, eſpecially if he has no aſſiſtant near: how much harder *muſt it be to perform alone the buſineſs of* a kingdom with great revenues!

56. 'Let him perpetually conſult with thoſe miniſters on peace and war, on his forces, on his revenues, on the protection of his people, and on the means of beſtowing aptly the wealth which he has acquired:

57. 'Having aſcertained the ſeveral opinions of his counſellors, *firſt* apart and *then* collectively, let him do what is moſt beneficial for him in publick affairs.

58. 'To one learned *Bráhmen*, diſtinguiſhed among them all, let the king impart his momentous counſel, relating to ſix *principal* articles.

59. 'To him, with full confidence, let him intruſt all tranſactions; and with him, having taken his final reſolution, let him begin all his meaſures.

60. 'He muſt likewiſe appoint other officers; men of integrity, well informed, ſteady, habituated to gain wealth, by honourable means, and tried by experience.

61. 'As many officers as the due performance of his buſineſs requires, not ſlothful men, *but active*, able, and well inſtructed, ſo many, and no more, let him appoint.

62. 'Among thoſe let him employ the brave, the ſkilful, the well born, and the honeſt, in his mines *of gold or gems*, and in other ſimilar works *for amaſſing wealth*; but the puſillanimous, in the receſſes of his palace.

63. 'Let

63. 'Let him likewise appoint an ambassador, 'versed in all the *Sástras*, who understands hints, 'external signs and actions, *whose hand and heart 'are* pure, whose abilities are great, and whose 'birth was illustrious:

64. 'That royal ambassador is applauded most, 'who is generally beloved, pure within and without, dextrous in business, and endued with an 'excellent memory; who knows countries and 'times, is handsome, intrepid and eloquent.

65. 'The forces of the realm must be immediately regulated by the commander in chief; 'the actual infliction of punishment, by the officers of criminal justice; the treasury and the 'country, by the king himself; peace and war, 'by the ambassador;

66. 'For it is the ambassador alone who unites, 'who alone disjoints the united; that is, he transacts the business, by which kingdoms are at 'variance or in amity.

67. 'In the transaction of affairs let the ambassador comprehend the visible signs and hints, and 'discover the acts, of the foreign king, by the 'signs, hints, and acts of his confidential servants, 'and the measures, which that king wishes to 'take by *the character and conduct of* his ministers.

68. 'Thus, having learned completely *from 'his ambassador* all the designs of the foreign 'prince, let the king so apply his vigilant care, 'that he bring no evil on himself.

69. 'Let him fix his abode in a district containing open champaigns; abounding with grain; 'inhabited chiefly by the virtuous; not infected 'with maladies; beautiful to the sight; surrounded by submissive *mountaineers, foresters, or other*

neighbours; a country in which the subjects may live at ease.

70. ‘There let him reside in a capital, having, by way of a fortress, a desert *rather more than twenty miles round it*, or a fortress of earth, a fortress of water, or of trees, a fortress of armed men, or a fortress of mountains.

71. ‘With all possible care let him secure a fortress of mountains; for, among those just mentioned, a fortress of mountains has many transcendent properties.

72. ‘In the three first of them live wild beasts, vermin, and aquatick animals; in the three last, apes, men, and gods, in order as they are named:

73. ‘As enemies hurt them not in the shelter of their several abodes, thus foes hurt not a king who has taken refuge in his *durga*, or *place of difficult access*.

74. ‘One bowman, placed on a wall, is a match in war for a hundred enemies; and a hundred, for ten thousand; therefore is a fort recommended.

75. ‘Let that fort be supplied with weapons, with money, with grain, with beasts, with *Bráhmens*, with artificers, with engines, with grass, and with water.

76. ‘In the centre of it let him raise his own palace, well finished in all its parts, completely defended, habitable in every season, brilliant *with white stucco*, surrounded with water and trees:

77. ‘Having prepared it for his mansion, let him chuse a consort of the same class with himself, endued with all the bodily marks of excellence, born of an exalted race, captivating his heart, adorned with beauty and the best qualities.

78. ‘He must appoint also a domestick priest,

‘ and retain a performer of ſacrifices, who may
‘ ſolemnize the religious rites of his family, and
‘ thoſe performed with three ſacred fires.

79. ‘ Let the king make ſacrifices, accom-
‘ panied with gifts of many different kinds; and
‘ for the full diſcharge of his duty, let him give
‘ the *Bráhmens* both legal enjoyments and mo-
‘ derate wealth.

80. ‘ His annual revenue he may receive from
‘ his whole dominion through his collectors; but
‘ let him in this world obſerve the divine ordi-
‘ nances; let him act as a father to his people.

81. ‘ Here and there he muſt appoint many
‘ ſorts of intelligent ſupervisors, who may inſpect
‘ all the acts of the officers engaged in his buſi-
‘ neſs.

82. ‘ To *Bráhmens* returned from the manſions
‘ of their preceptors, let him ſhow due reſpect;
‘ for that is called a precious unperiſhable gem,
‘ depoſited by kings with the ſacerdotal claſs:

83. ‘ It is a gem, which neither thieves or foes
‘ take away; which never periſhes: kings muſt,
‘ therefore, depoſit with *Bráhmens* that indeſtruc-
‘ tible jewel *of reſpectful preſents*.

84. ‘ An oblation in the mouth, *or hand*, of a
‘ *Bráhmen*, is far better than offerings to holy fire:
‘ it never drops: it never dries: it is never
‘ conſumed.

85. ‘ A gift to one not a *Bráhmen* produces
‘ fruit of a middle ſtandard; to one who calls
‘ himſelf a *Bráhmen*, double; to a well read
‘ *Bráhmen*, a hundred thouſand fold; to one who
‘ has read all the *Védas*, infinite.

86. ‘ Of a gift made with faith in the *Sáſtra*,
‘ to a perſon highly deſerving it, the giver ſhall
‘ indubitably

'indubitably gain the fruit after death, be the 'present ſmall or great.

87. 'A KING, while he protects his people, 'being defied by an enemy of equal, greater, or 'leſs force, muſt by no means turn his face from 'battle, but muſt remember the duty of his mi-'litary claſs:

88. 'Never to recede from combat, to protect 'the people, and to honour the prieſts, is the 'higheſt duty of kings and enſures their felicity.

89. 'Thoſe rulers of the earth, who, deſirous 'of defeating each other, exert their utmoſt 'ſtrength in battle, without ever averting their 'faces, aſcend after death directly to heaven.

90. 'LET no man, engaged in combat, ſmite 'his foe with *ſharp* weapons concealed *in wood*, 'nor with arrows miſchievouſly barbed, nor with 'poiſoned arrows, nor with darts blazing with fire;

91. 'Nor let him *in a car or on horſeback* ſtrike 'his enemy alighted on the ground; nor an ef-'feminate man; nor one who ſues for life with 'cloſed palms; nor one whoſe hair is looſe *and* '*obſtructs his ſight*; nor one, who ſits down *fa-*'*tigued*; nor one, who ſays, "I am thy captive;"

92. 'Nor one, who ſleeps; nor one, who has 'loſt his coat of mail; nor one, who is naked; 'nor one, who is diſarmed; nor one, who is a 'ſpectator, but not a combatant; nor one, who 'is fighting with another man:

93. 'Calling to mind the duty of honourable 'men, let him never ſlay one, who has broken 'his weapon; nor one, who is afflicted *with pri-*'*vate ſorrow*; nor one, who has been grievouſly 'wounded; nor one, who is terrified; nor one, 'who turns his back.

94. 'The

94. ‘ The ſoldier, indeed, who fearing and ‘ turning his back, happens to be ſlain by his ‘ foes in an engagement, ſhall take upon himſelf ‘ all the ſin of his commander, whatever it be ;

95. ‘ And the commander ſhall take to himſelf ‘ *the fruit of* all the good conduct, which the ſol- ‘ dier, who turns his back and is killed, had pre- ‘ viouſly ſtored up for a future life.

96. ‘ CARS, horſes, elephants, umbrellas, habi- ‘ liments, *except the jewels which may adorn them*, ‘ grain, cattle, women, all ſorts of liquids and ‘ metals, except gold and ſilver, are the lawful ‘ prizes of the man who takes them in war ;

97. ‘ But of thoſe prizes, the captors muſt ‘ lay the moſt valuable before the king ; ſuch is ‘ the rule in the *Véda*, concerning them ; and the ‘ king ſhould diſtribute among the whole army ‘ what has not been ſeparately taken.

98. ‘ Thus has been declared the blameleſs ‘ primeval law for military men ; from this law a ‘ king muſt never depart, when he attacks his foes ‘ in battle.

99. ‘ What he has not gained *from his foe*, let ‘ him ſtrive to gain ; what he has acquired, let ‘ him preſerve with care ; what he preſerves, let ‘ him augment ; and what he has augmented, let ‘ him beſtow on the deſerving.

100. ‘ This is the four-fold rule, which he muſt ‘ conſider as the ſure means of attaining the great ‘ object of man, *happineſs* ; and let him practiſe ‘ it fully without intermiſſion, without indolence :

101. ‘ what he has not gained, let him ſtrive ‘ to gain by military ſtrength ; what he has ac- ‘ quired, let him preſerve by careful inſpection ; ‘ what he has preſerved, let him augment by

‘ legal

'legal modes of increaſe; and what he has augmented, let him diſpenſe with juſt liberality.

102. 'Let his troops be conſtantly exerciſed; his proweſs conſtantly diſplayed; what he ought to ſecure, conſtantly ſecured; and the weakneſs of his foe, conſtantly inveſtigated.

103. 'By a king, whoſe forces are always ready for action, the whole world may be kept in awe; let him then, by a force always ready, make all creatures living his own.

104. 'Let him act on all occaſions without guile, and never with inſincerity; but, keeping himſelf ever on his guard, let him diſcover the fraud intended by his foe.

105. 'Let not his enemy diſcern his vulnerable part, but the volunerable part of his enemy let him well diſcern: like a tortoiſe, let him draw in his members under *the ſhell of* concealment, and diligently let him repair any breach that may be made in it.

106. 'Like a heron, let him muſe on gaining advantages; like a lion, let him put forth his ſtrength; like a wolf, let him creep towards his prey; like a hare, let him double to ſecure his retreat.

107. 'When he thus has prepared himſelf for conqueſt, let him reduce all oppoſers to ſubmiſſion by negotiation and three other expedients, *namely, preſents, diviſion, and force of arms:*

108. 'If they cannot be reſtrained by the three firſt methods, then let him firmly, but gradually, bring them to ſubjection by military force.

109. 'Among thoſe four modes of obtaining ſucceſs, the wiſe prefer negotiation and war for the exaltation of kingdoms.

110. 'As

110. ' As a husbandman plucks up weeds and ' preserves his corn, thus let a king destroy his ' opponents and secure his people.

111. ' That king, who, through weakness of ' intellect, rashly oppresses his people, will, to- ' gether with his family, be deprived both of ' kingdom and life :

112. ' As by the loss of bodily sustenance, the ' lives of animated beings are destroyed, thus, ' by the distress of kingdoms, are destroyed even ' the lives of kings.

113. ' For the sake of protecting his domini- ' ons, let the king perpetually observe the follow- ' ing rules ; for, by protecting his dominions, he ' will increase his own happiness.

114. ' Let him place, as the protectors of his ' realm, a company of guards, commanded by an ' approved officer, over two, three, five, or a ' hundred districts, *according to their extent.*

115. ' Let him appoint a lord of one town with ' its district, a lord of ten towns, a lord of twenty, ' a lord of a hundred, and a lord of a thousand.

116. ' Let the lord of one town certify of his ' own accord to the lord of ten towns any *robberies,* ' *tumults, or other* evils, which arise in his dis- ' trict, *and which he cannot suppress* ; and the lord ' of ten, to the lord of twenty :

117. ' Then let the lord of twenty towns no- ' tify them to the lord of a hundred ; and let the ' lord of a hundred transmit the information him- ' self to the lord of a thousand townships.

118. ' Such food, drink, wood, and other ar- ' ticles, as by law should be given each day to the ' king by the inhabitants of the township, let the ' lord of one town receive *as his perquisite :*

119. ' Let

119. 'Let the lord of ten towns enjoy the 'produce of two plough-lands, *or as much ground* '*as can be tilled with two ploughs, each drawn by* '*six bulls*; the lord of twenty, that of five plough-'lands; the lord of a hundred, that of a village 'or small town; the lord of a thousand, that of a 'large town.

120. 'The affairs of those *townships*, either 'jointly or separately transacted, let another mi-'nister of the king inspect; who should be well 'affected, and by no means remiss.

121. 'In every large town or city, let him ap-'point one superintendent of all affairs, elevated in 'rank, formidable in power, distinguished as a 'planet among stars:

122. 'Let that governor from time to time 'survey all the rest in person, and by means of his 'emissaries, let him perfectly know their conduct 'in their several districts.

123. 'Since the servants of the king, whom he 'has appointed guardians of districts, are generally 'knaves, who seize what belongs to other men, 'from such knaves let him defend his people:

124. 'Of such evil minded servants, as wring 'wealth from subjects attending them on business, 'let the king confiscate all the possessions, and 'banish them from his realm.

125. 'For women, employed in the service of 'the king, and for his whole set of menial ser-'vants, let him daily provide a maintenance, 'in proportion to their station and to their 'work:

126. 'One *pana* of copper must be given *each* '*day* as wages to the lowest servant, with two 'cloths *for apparel* every half year, and a *dróna* of

'grain

'grain every month; to the highest *must be given* 'wages *in the ratio of* six *to one*.

127. 'HAVING ascertained the rates of pur-'chase and sale, *the length of* the way, the expen-'ces of food and of condiments, the charges of 'securing the goods carried, and the neat profits 'of trade, let the king oblige traders to pay taxes '*on their saleable commodities:*

128. 'After full consideration, let a king so 'levy those taxes continually in his dominions, 'that both he and the merchant may receive a 'just compensation for their several acts.

129. 'As the leech, the suckling calf, and 'the bee, take their natural food by little and 'little, thus must a king draw from his domi-'nions an annual revenue.

130. 'Of cattle, of gems, of gold and silver, '*added each year to the capital stock*, a fiftieth part 'may be taken by the king; of grain an eighth 'part, a sixth, or a twelfth, *according to the dif-'ference of the soil, and the labour necessary to cul-'tivate it.*

131. 'He may also take a sixth part of the 'clear annual increase of trees, flesh meat, honey, 'clarified butter, perfumes, medical substances, 'liquids, flowers, roots, and fruit,

132. 'Of gathered leaves, potherbs, grass, 'utensils made with leather or cane, earthen pots, 'and all things made of stone.

133. 'A king, even though dying *with want*, 'must not receive any tax from a *Bráhmen* learned 'in the *Védas*, nor suffer such a *Bráhmen*, residing 'in his territories, to be afflicted with hunger:

134. 'Of that king, in whose dominion a learned '*Bráhmen* is afflicted with hunger, the whole

'kingdom

'kingdom will in a short time be afflicted with 'famine.

135. 'The king, having ascertained his know- 'ledge of scripture and good morals, must allot 'him a suitable maintenance, and protect him on 'all sides, as a father protects his own son:

136. 'By that religious duty, which such a *Bráh- 'men* performs each day, under the full protection 'of the sovereign, the life, wealth, and dominions 'of his protector shall be greatly increased.

137. 'Let the king order a mere trifle to be 'paid, in the name of the annual tax, by the 'meaner inhabitants of his realm, who subsists 'by petty traffick:

138. 'By low handicrafts-men, artificers, and 'servile men, who support themselves by labour, 'the king may cause work to be done for a day 'in each month.

139. 'Let him not cut up his own root *by tak- 'ing no revenue,* nor the root of other men by 'excess of covetousness; for by cutting up his 'own root *and theirs,* he makes both himself and 'them wretched.

140. 'Let him, considering the *diversity of* cases, 'be *occasionally* sharp, and *occasionally* mild, since 'a king, duly sharp and mild, becomes univer- 'sally approved.

141. 'When tired of overlooking the affairs 'of men, let him assign the station *of such an in- 'spector* to a principal minister, who well knows 'his duty, who is eminently learned, whose pas- 'sions are subdued, and whose birth is exalted.

142. 'Thus must he protect his people, dis- 'charging, with great exertion, and without 'languor, all those duties, which the law requires 'him to perform.

143. 'That

143. 'That monarch, whose subjects are carried from his kingdom by ruffians, while they 'call aloud for protection, and he barely looks 'on them with his ministers, is a dead, and not 'a living king.

144. 'The highest duty of a military man is 'the defence of his people, and the king who 'receives the consideration just mentioned, is 'bound to discharge that duty.

145. 'Having risen in the last watch of the 'night, his body being pure, and his mind attentive, having made oblations to fire, and shown 'due respect to the priests, let him enter his hall 'decently splendid:

146. 'Standing there, let him gratify his subjects, before he dismiss them, *with kind looks and 'words*; and, having dismissed them all, let him 'take secret council with his principal ministers:

147. 'Ascending up the back of a mountain, 'or going privately to a terrace, a bower, a forest, 'or a lonely place, without listeners, let him consult with them unobserved.

148. 'That prince, of whose weighty secrets all 'assemblies of men are ignorant, shall attain dominion over the whole earth, though *at first* he 'possess no treasure.

149. 'At the time of consultation, let him remove the stupid, the dumb, the blind and the 'deaf, talking birds, decripit old men, women, 'and infidels, the diseased and the maimed;

150. 'Since those, who are disgraced *in this 'life, by reason of sins formerly committed*, are apt to 'betray secret council; so are talking birds; and 'so above all are women: them he must for that 'reason diligently remove.

151. ‘At noon or at midnight, when his fa‘tigues have ceased, and his cares are dispersed, ‘let him deliberate, with those ministers or alone, ‘on virtue, lawful pleasure, and wealth;

152. ‘On the means of reconciling the acqui‘sition of them, when they oppose each other; ‘on bestowing his daughters in marriage, and on ‘preserving his sons *from evil by the best education*;

153. ‘On sending ambassadors and messengers; ‘on the probable events of his measures; on the ‘behaviour *of his women* in the private apart‘ments; and on the acts even of his own emis‘saries.

154. ‘On the whole eightfold business of ‘kings, *relating to the revenue, to their expences,* ‘*to the good or bad conduct of their ministers, to* ‘*legislation in dubious cases, to civil and criminal* ‘*justice, and to expiations for crimes,* let him reflect ‘with the greatest attention; on his five sorts of ‘spies, *or active and artful youths, degraded ancho‘rets, distressed husbandmen, decayed merchants, and* ‘*fictitious penitents, whom he must pay and see pri‘vately*; on the good will or enmity of his neigh‘bours, and on the state of the circumjacent ‘countries.

155. ‘On the conduct of that foreign prince, ‘who has moderate strength *equal to one ordinary* ‘*foe, but no match for two*; on the designs of ‘him, who is willing and able to be a conqueror; ‘on the condition of him, who is pacifick, *but a* ‘*match even for the former unallied*; and on that ‘of his *natural* enemy let him sedulously me‘ditate:

156. ‘Those *four powers*, who, in one word, ‘are the root or *principal strength* of the countries

'round him, added to eight others, *who are called* '*the* branches, *and are as many degrees of allies* '*and opponents variously distinguished*, are declared 'to be twelve chief objects *of the royal con-* '*sideration*;

157. 'And five other heads, namely, their 'ministers, their territories, their strong holds, 'their treasuries, and their armies, being applied 'to each *of those twelve*, there are in all, *together* '*with them*, seventy-two *foreign* objects *to be care-* '*fully investigated.*

158. 'Let the king consider as hostile to him, 'the power immediately beyond him, and the 'favourer of that power; as amicable, the power 'next beyond his *natural* foe; and as neutral, 'the powers beyond that *circle*:

159. 'All those *powers* let him render subser-'vient to his interests by mild measures and the 'other *three* expedients *before mentioned*, either se-'parate or united, but principally by valour and 'policy *in arms and negotiation.*

160. 'Let him constantly deliberate on the six 'measures of a military prince, *namely*, waging 'war, and making peace or alliance, marching to 'battle, and sitting encamped, distributing his 'forces, and seeking the protection of a more 'powerful monarch:

161. 'Having considered the posture of affairs, 'let him occasionally apply to it the measure of 'sitting inactive, or of marching to action, of 'peace, or of war, of dividing his force, or of 'seeking protection.

162. 'A king must know, that there are two 'sorts of alliance and war; two, of remaining en-'camped, and of marching; two likewise, of

'dividing his army, and of obtaining protection
'from another power.

163. 'The two sorts of alliance, attended with 'present and future advantages, are held to be 'those, when he acts in conjunction with his ally, 'and when he acts apart from him.

164. 'War is declared to be of two sorts; 'when it is waged for an injury to himself, and 'when it is waged for an injury to his ally, with a 'view to harass the enemy both in season and out 'of season.

165. 'Marching is of two sorts, when destructive acts are done at his own pleasure by himself 'apart, or when his ally attends him.

166. 'The two sorts of sitting encamped are, '*first*, when he has been gradually weakened by 'the Divine Power, or by the operation of past 'sins, and, *secondly*, when, to favour his ally, he 'remains in his camp.

167. 'A detachment commanded by the king 'in person, and a detachment commanded by a 'general officer, for the purpose of carrying some 'important point, are declared by those, who will 'know the six measures, to be the two modes of 'dividing his army.

168. 'The two modes of seeking protection, 'that his powerful support may be proclaimed in 'all countries, are, *first*, when he wishes to be 'secure from apprehended injury, and, *next*, when 'his enemies actually assail him.

169. 'When the king knows with certainty, 'that at some future time his force will be greatly 'augmented, and when, at the time present, he 'sustains little injury, let him then have recourse 'to peaceful measures;

170. 'But, when he sees all his subjects considerably firm in strength, and feels himself highly

'exalted

'exalted in power, let him protect his dominions 'by war.

171. 'When he perfectly knows his own 'troops to be cheerful and well supplied, and 'those of his enemy quite the reverse, let him 'eagerly march against his foes;

172. 'But when he finds himself weak in 'beasts of burden and in troops, let him then sit 'quiet in camp, using great attention, and paci-'fying his enemy by degrees.

173. 'When a king sees his foe stronger in all 'respects than himself, let him detach a part of 'his army, *to keep the enemy amused*, and secure 'his own safety *in an inaccessible place*;

174. 'But when he is in all places assailable 'by the hostile troops, let him speedily seek the 'protection of a just and powerful monarch.

175. 'Him, who can keep in subjection both 'his own subjects and his foes, let him constantly 'sooth by all sorts of attentive respect, as he 'would honour his father, natural or spiritual:

176. 'But if, even in that situation, he find 'such protection a cause of evil, let him alone, 'though weak, wage vigorous war without fear.

177. 'By all these expedients let a politick 'prince act with such wisdom, that neither allies, 'neutral powers, nor foes, may gain over him 'any great advantage.

178. 'Perfectly let him consider the state of 'his kingdom, both actually present and probably 'future, with the good and bad parts of all his 'actions:

179. 'That king shall never be overcome by 'his enemies, who foresees the good and evil, to 'ensue from his measures; who, on present oc-'casions, takes his resolution with prudent speed,

'and who weighs the various events of his past 'conduct.

180. 'Let him so arrange all his affairs, that 'no ally, neutral prince, or enemy, may obtain 'any advantage over him: this, in a few words, 'is the sum of political wisdom.

181. 'WHEN the king begins his march against 'the domains of his foe, let him gradually ad-'vance, in the following manner, against the 'hostile metropolis.

182. 'Let him set out on his expedition in the 'fine month *Márgasírsha*, or about the month of '*Phálguna* and *Chaitra*, according to *the number* '*of* his forces, *that he may find autumnal or vernal* '*crops in the country invaded by him:*

183. 'Even in other seasons, when he has a 'clear prospect of victory, and when any disaster 'has befallen his foe, let him advance with the 'greater part of his army.

184. 'Having made a due arrangement of 'affairs in his own dominions, and a disposition 'fit for his enterprize, having provided all things 'necessary for his continuance in the foreign 'realms, and having seen all his spies dispatched 'with propriety,

185. 'Having secured the three sorts of ways, '*over water*, *on plains*, *and through forests*, and 'placed his six-fold army, *elephants*, *cavalry*, *cars*, '*infantry*, *officers*, and *attendants*, in complete 'military form, let him proceed by fit journeys 'toward the metropolis of his enemy:

186. 'Let him be much on his guard against 'every secret friend in the service of the hostile 'prince, and against emissaries, who go and re-'turn; for in such friends he may find very 'dangerous foes.

187. 'On

187. 'On his march let him form his troops 'either like a staff, *or in an even column*; like a 'wain, *or in a wedge with the apex foremost*; like 'a boar, *or in a rhomb with the van and rear 'narrow and the centre broad*; like a *Macara* or '*sea monster, that is, in a double triangle with apices 'joined*; like a needle *or in a long line*; or like 'the bird of VISHNU, *that is, in a rhomboid with 'the wings far extended*:

188. 'From whatever side he apprehends 'danger, to that side let him extend his troops; 'and let him always conceal himself in the midst 'of a squadron, formed like a lotos flower.

189. 'Let him cause his generals and the chief 'commander *under himself*, to act in all quarters; 'and from whatever side he perceives a design of 'attacking him, to that side let him turn his front.

190. 'On all sides let him station troops of 'soldiers, in whom he confides, distinguished by 'known *colours and other* marks; who are ex-'cellent both in sustaining a charge and in charg-'ing, who are fearless and incapable of desertion.

191. 'Let him at his pleasure order a few men 'to engage in a close phalanx, or a large number 'of warriours in loose ranks; and, having formed 'them in *a long line like* a needle, or in *three di-'visions like* a thunderbolt, let him give orders 'for battle.

192. 'On a plain, let him fight with his armed 'cars and horses; on watery places, with manned 'boats and elephants; on ground full of trees 'and shrubs, with bows; on cleared ground, with 'swords and targets, and *other* weapons.

193. 'Men born in *Curucshétra*, near *Indrap-'rest'ha*, in *Matsya*, or *Viráta*, in *Panchála*, or '*Cányacubja*, and in *Súrasėna*, in the district of

 '*Mat'burà*

'*Mat'burà*, let him cauſe to engage in the van; 'and men, *born in other countries*, who are tall 'and light.

194. 'Let him, when he has formed his 'troops in array, encourage them *with ſhort animated ſpeeches*; and then let him try them completely: let him know likewiſe how his men ſeverally exert themſelves, while they charge the foe.

195. 'If he block up his enemy, let him ſit 'encamped, and lay waſte the hoſtile country; 'let him continually ſpoil the graſs, water, and 'wood of the adverſe prince.

196. 'Pools, wells, and trenches, let him deſtroy: let him haraſs the foe by day, and alarm 'him by night.

197. 'Let him ſecretly bring over to his party 'all ſuch *leaders* as he can ſafely bring over; let 'him be informed of all that his enemies are 'doing; and, when a fortunate moment is offered by heaven, let him give battle, puſhing 'on to conqueſt and abandoning fear:

198. 'Yet he ſhould be more ſedulous to reduce his enemy by negotiation, by well applied 'gifts, and by creating diviſions, uſing either all 'or ſome of thoſe methods, than by hazarding at 'any time a deciſive action,

199. 'Since victory or defeat are not ſurely 'foreſeen on either ſide, when two armies engage 'in the field: let the king then, *if other expedients prevail*, avoid a pitched battle:

200. 'But, ſhould there be no means of applying the three *before-mentioned* expedients, let 'him, after due preparation, fight ſo valiantly, 'that his enemy may be totally routed.

201. 'Having conquered a country, let him 'reſpect the deities adored in it, and their vir-

'tuous

'tuous priests; let him also distribute largesses '*to the people,* and cause a full exemption from 'terrour to be loudly proclaimed.

202. 'When he has perfectly ascertained the 'conduct and intentions of all the vanquished, let 'him fix in that country a prince of the royal 'race, and give him precise instructions.

203. 'Let him establish the laws of the conquered nation as declared *in their books*; and let 'him gratify the new prince with gems, *and other* '*precious gifts*.

204. 'The seizure of desirable property, though 'it cause hatred, and the donation of it, though 'it cause love, may be laudable or blameable on 'different occasions:

205. 'All this *conduct of human affairs* is con'sidered as dependent on acts ascribed to the 'deity, and on acts ascribed to men; now the 'operations of the deity cannot be known by any 'intenseness of thought, but those of men may be 'clearly discovered.

206. 'Or the victor, considering an ally, ter'ritory, and wealth as the triple fruit of conquest, 'may form an alliance with the vanquished prince, 'and proceed in union with him, using diligent 'circumspection.

207. 'He should pay due attention to the 'prince who supported his cause, and to any 'other prince of the circumjacent region, who 'checked that supporter, so that both from a well'wisher and from an opponent, he may secure the 'fruit of his expedition.

208. 'By gaining wealth and territory a king 'acquires not so great an increase of strength, as 'by obtaining a firm ally, who, though weak, 'may hereafter be powerful.

209. 'That

209. 'That ally, though feeble, is highly eſ-'timable, who knows the whole extent of his 'duties, who gratefully remembers benefits, 'whoſe people are ſatisfied, *or, who has a gentle* '*nature,* who loves his friend, and perſeveres in 'his good reſolutions.

210. 'Him have the ſages declared an enemy 'hard to be ſubdued, who is eminently learned, 'of a noble race, perſonally brave, dextrous in 'management, liberal, grateful, and firm.

211. 'Good nature, knowledge of mankind, 'valour, benignity of heart, and inceſſant libe-'rality, are the aſſemblage of virtues which adorn 'a neutral prince, *whoſe amity muſt be courted.*

212. 'Even a ſalubrious and fertile country, 'where cattle continually increaſe, let a king 'abandon, without heſitation, for the ſake of pre-'ſerving himſelf:

213. 'Againſt misfortune let him preſerve his 'wealth; at the expence of his wealth let him 'preſerve his wife; but let him at all events pre-'ſerve himſelf even at the hazard of his wife and 'his riches.

214. 'A wiſe prince, who finds every ſort of 'calamity ruſhing violently upon him, ſhould 'have recourſe to all juſt expedients, united or 'ſeparate:

215. 'Let him conſider the buſineſs to be ex-'pedited, the expedients collectively, and himſelf 'who muſt apply them; and taking refuge com-'pletely in thoſe three, let him ſtrenuouſly labour 'for his own proſperity.

216. 'Having conſulted with his miniſters, 'in the manner before preſcribed on all this *maſs* '*of publick affairs*; having uſed exerciſe *becoming* '*a warriour*, and having bathed *after it*, let the

'king

'king enter at noon his private apartments for 'the purpose of taking food.

217. 'There let him eat lawful aliment, pre-'pared by servants attached to his person, who 'know the difference of times and are incapable 'of perfidy, after it has been proved innocent *by* '*certain experiments*, and hallowed by texts of the '*Véda*, repulsive of poison.

218. 'Together with all his food let him swal-'low such medical substances as resist venom; 'and let him constantly wear with attention such 'gems as are known to repel it.

219. 'Let his females, well tried and attentive, 'their dress and ornaments having been exa-'mined, *lest some weapon should be concealed in them*, 'do him humble service with fans, water, and 'perfumes:

220. 'Thus let him take diligent care, when 'he goes out in a carriage or on horseback, when 'he lies down to rest, when he sits, when he 'takes food, when he bathes, anoints his body '*with odorous essences*, and puts on all his habili-'ments.

221. 'After eating, let him divert himself with 'his women in the recesses of his palace; and, 'having idled a reasonable time, let him again 'think of publick affairs:

222. When he has dressed himself completely, 'let him once more review his armed men, with 'all their elephants, horses, and cars, their accou-'trements and weapons.

223. 'At sunset, having performed his religious 'duty, let him privately, but well armed, in his 'interior apartment, hear what has been done by 'his reporters and emissaries:

224. 'Then,

224. 'Then, having dismissed those informers, 'and returning to another secret chamber, let him 'go, attended by women, to the inmost recess of 'his mansion for the sake of his evening meal;

225. 'There, having a second time eaten a lit-'tle, and having been recreated with musical 'strains, let him take rest early, and rise refreshed 'from his labour.

226. 'This perfect system of rules let a king, 'free from illness, observe; but when really af-'flicted with disease, he may intrust all these affairs 'to his officers.'

CHAPTER THE EIGHTH.

On Judicature; and on Law, Private and Criminal.

1. 'A KING, desirous of inspecting judicial proceedings must enter his court of justice, composed and sedate in his demeanour, together with *Bráhmens* and counsellors, who know how to give him advice:

2. 'There, either sitting or standing, holding forth his right arm, without ostentation in his dress and ornaments, let him examine the affairs of litigant parties.

3. 'Each day let him decide causes one after another, under the eighteen *principal* titles of law, by arguments and rules drawn from local usages, and from written codes:

4. 'Of those *titles*, the first is debt, on loans for consumption; *the second*, deposits, and loans for use; *the third*, sale without ownership; *the fourth*, concerns among partners; *the fifth*, subtraction of what has been given;

5. '*The sixth*, non-payment of wages or hire; *the seventh*, non-performance of agreements; *the eighth*, rescission of sale and purchase; *the ninth*, disputes between master and servant;

6. '*The tenth*, contests on boundaries; *the eleventh*

'*eleventh and twelfth*, aſſault and ſlander; *the*
'*thirteenth*, larceny; *the fourteenth*, robbery and
'other violence; *the fifteenth*, adultery;

7. '*The ſixteenth*, altercation between man and
'wife, and their ſeveral duties; *the ſeventeenth*,
'the law of inheritance; *the eighteenth*, gaming with
'dice and with living creatures: theſe eighteen
'titles of law are ſettled as the ground work of
'all judicial procedure in this world.

8. 'Among men, who contend for the moſt
'part on the titles juſt mentioned, *and on a few*
'*miſcellaneous heads not compriſed under them*, let
'the king decide cauſes juſtly, obſerving prime-
'val law;

9. 'But when he cannot inſpect ſuch affairs in
'perſon, let him appoint, for the inſpection of
'them, a *Bráhmen* of eminent learning:

10. 'Let that chief judge, accompanied by
'three aſſeſſors, fully conſider all cauſes brought
'before the king; and, having entered the court
'room, let him ſit or ſtand, *but not move back-*
'*wards and forwards*.

11. 'In whatever country three *Bráhmens*,
'particularly ſkilled in the three ſeveral *Védas*, ſit
'together with the very learned *Bráhmen* ap-
'pointed by the king, the wiſe call that *aſſembly*
'the court of BRAHMA' *with four faces*.

12. 'WHEN juſtice, having been wounded by
'iniquity, approaches the court, and the judges
'extract not the dart, they alſo ſhall be wounded
'by it.

13. 'Either the court muſt not be entered *by*
'*judges, parties, and witneſſes*, or law and truth
'muſt be openly declared: that man is criminal,
'who either ſays nothing, or ſays what is falſe
'or unjuſt.

14. 'Where

14. 'Where juſtice is deſtroyed by iniquity, 'and truth by falſe evidence, the judges, who 'baſely look on, *without giving redreſs*, ſhall alſo 'be deſtroyed.

15. 'Juſtice being deſtroyed, will deſtroy; 'being preſerved, will preſerve: it muſt never 'therefore be violated. "Beware, *O judge*, leſt "juſtice being overturned, overturn *both* us and "thyſelf."

16. 'The divine form of juſtice is repreſented 'as *Vriſha*, or *a bull*, and the gods conſider him, 'who violates juſtice, as a *Vriſhala*, or one who 'ſlays a bull: let the king, therefore, and his 'judges beware of violating juſtice.

17. 'The only firm friend, who follows men 'even after death, is juſtice; all others are ex-'tinct with the body.

18. 'Of injuſtice *in deciſions*, one quarter falls 'on the party in the cauſe; one quarter, on his 'witneſſes; one quarter, on all the judges; and 'one quarter on the king;

19. 'But where he, who deſerves condemna-'tion ſhall be condemned, the king is guiltleſs, 'and the judges free from blame: an evil deed 'ſhall recoil on him who committed it.

20. 'A *Bráhmen* ſupported only by his claſs, 'and one barely reputed a *Bráhmen*, but without 'performing any ſacerdotal acts, may, at the king's 'pleaſure, interpret the law to him: *ſo may the* '*two middle claſſes*; but a *Súdra*, in no caſe what-'ever.

21. 'Of that king, who ſtupidly looks on, 'while a *Súdra* decides cauſes, the kingdom it-'ſelf ſhall be embarraſſed, like a cow in deep 'mire.

22. 'The

22. ‘ The whole territory, which is inhabited ‘ by a number of *Súdras*, overwhelmed with ‘ atheists, and deprived of *Bráhmens*, must speedily ‘ perish, afflicted with death and disease.

23. ‘ Let the king *or his judge*, having seated ‘ himself on the bench, his body properly clothed, ‘ and his mind attentively fixed, begin with doing ‘ reverence to the deities, who guard the world; ‘ and then let him enter on the trial of causes:

24. ‘ Understanding what is expedient or in- ‘ expedient, but considering only what is law or ‘ not law, let him examine all disputes between ‘ parties, in the order of their several classes.

25. ‘ By external signs let him see through the ‘ thoughts of men; by their voice, colour, coun- ‘ tenance, limbs, eyes, and action:

26. ‘ From the limbs, the look, the motion ‘ of the body, the gesticulation, the speech, the ‘ changes of the eye and the face, are discovered ‘ the internal workings of the mind.

27. ‘ The property of a student and of an infant, ‘ whether by descent or otherwise, let the king ‘ hold in his custody, until the owner shall have ‘ ended his studentship, or until his infancy shall ‘ have ceased *in his sixteenth year*.

28. ‘ Equal care must be taken of barren ‘ women, of women without sons, *whose husbands* ‘ *have married other wives*, of women without ‘ kindred, or whose husbands are in distant places, ‘ of widows true to their lords, and of women ‘ afflicted with illness.

29. ‘ Such kinsmen, as *by any pretence*, ap- ‘ propriate the fortunes of women during their ‘ lives, a just king must punish with the severity ‘ due to thieves.

30. ‘ Three

30. 'Three years let the king detain the property of which no owner appears, *after a distinct proclamation:* the owner appearing within the three years, may take it; but, after that term, the king may confiscate it.

31. 'He, who says " This is mine," must be duly examined; and if, *before he inspect it*, he declare its form, number, and other circumstances, the owner must have his property;

32. 'But if he show not at what place and time it was lost, and specify not its colour, shape, and dimensions, he ought to be amerced:

33. 'The king may take a sixth part of the property so detained by him, or a tenth, or a twelfth, remembering the duty of good kings.

34. 'Property lost *by one man*, and found *by another*, let the king secure, by committing it to the care of trust-worthy men; and those, whom he shall convict of stealing it, let him cause to be trampled on by an elephant.

35. 'From the man who shall say with truth, " This property, which has been kept, belongs " to me," the king may take a sixth or twelfth part, *for having secured it*;

36. 'But he who shall say so falsely, may be fined either an eighth part of his own property, or else in some small proportion, to the value of the goods falsely claimed, a just calculation having been made.

37. 'A learned *Bráhmen*, having found a treasure formerly hidden, may take it without any deduction; since he is the lord of all;

38. 'But of a treasure anciently reposited under ground, which *any other subject or* the king has discovered, the king may lay up half in his treasury, having given half to the *Bráhmens*.

O 39. 'Of

39. ' Of old hoards, and precious minerals in ' the earth, the king is entitled to half by reason ' of his general protection, and because he is the ' lord paramount of the soil.

40. ' To men of all classes, the king must ' restore their property, which robbers have ' seized; since a king, who takes it for himself, ' incurs the guilt of a robber.

41. ' A king who knows the revealed law, ' must enquire into the particular laws of classes, ' the laws *or usages* of districts, the customs of ' traders, and the rules of certain families, and ' establish their peculiar laws, *if they be not re-* ' *pugnant to the law of* GOD;

42. ' Since all men, who mind their own ' customary ways of proceeding, and are fixed in ' the discharge of their several duties, become ' united by affection with the people at large, ' even though they dwell far asunder.

43. ' Neither the king himself, nor his officers ' must ever promote litigation; nor ever neglect ' a law suit instituted by others.

44. ' As a hunter traces the lair of a *wounded* ' beast by the drops of blood; thus let a king ' investigate the true point of justice by deliberate ' arguments:

45. ' Let him fully consider the nature of ' truth, the state of the case, and his own person; ' and next, the witnesses, the place, the mode, ' and the time; firmly adhering to all the rules ' of practice:

46. ' What has been practised by good men and ' by virtuous *Brâhmens*, if it be not inconsistent ' with the legal customs of provinces or districts, ' of classes and families, let him establish.

47. ' WHEN

47. 'When a creditor ſues before him for the 'recovery of his right from a debtor, let him 'cauſe the debtor to pay what the creditor ſhall 'prove due.

48. 'By whatever lawful means a creditor 'may have gotten poſſeſſion of his own property, 'let the king ratify ſuch payment by the debtor, 'though obtained even by compulſory means:

49. 'By the mediation of friends, by ſuit in 'court, by artful management, or by diſtreſs, a 'creditor may recover the property lent; and 'fifthly, by legal force.

50. 'That creditor, who recovers his right 'from his debtor, muſt not be rebuked by the 'king for retaking his own property.

51. 'In a ſuit for a debt, which the defendant 'denies, let him award payment to the creditor 'of what, by good evidence, he ſhall prove due, 'and exact a ſmall fine, *according to the circum-'ſtances of the debtor.*

52. 'On the denial of a debt, which the de-'fendant has in court been required to pay, the 'plaintiff muſt call a witneſs who was preſent at 'the place of the loan, or produce other evidence, '*as a note and the like.*

53. 'The plaintiff, who calls a witneſs not 'preſent at the place *where the contract was made,* 'or, having knowingly called him, diſclaims him 'as his witneſs; or who perceives not, that he 'aſſerts confuſed and contradictory facts;

54. 'Or who, having ſtated what he deſigns 'to prove, varies afterwards from his caſe; or 'who, being queſtioned on a fact which he had 'before admitted, refuſes to acknowledge that 'very fact;

55. 'Or who has converſed with the witneſſes 'in a place unfit for ſuch converſation; or who 'declines anſwering a queſtion properly put; or 'who departs from the court;

56. 'Or who, being ordered to ſpeak, ſtands 'mute; or who proves not what he has alledged; 'or who knows not what is capable or incapa-'ble of proof; *ſuch a plaintiff* ſhall fail in that 'ſuit.

57. 'Him who has ſaid "I have witneſſes," 'and being told to produce them, produces them 'not, the judge muſt on this account declare 'nonſuited.

58. 'If the plaintiff delay to put in his plaint, 'he may, *according to the nature of the caſe*, be 'corporally puniſhed or juſtly amerced; and if 'the defendant plead not within three fortnights, 'he is by law condemned.

59. 'In the double of that ſum, which the 'defendant falſely denies, or on which the com-'plainant falſely declares, ſhall thoſe two men, 'wilfully offending againſt juſtice, be fined by 'the king.

60. 'When a man has been brought into 'court by a ſuitor for property, and, being called 'on to anſwer, denies the debt, the cauſe ſhould 'be decided by the *Bráhmen* who repreſents the 'king, having heard three witneſſes at leaſt.

61. 'WHAT ſort of witneſſes muſt be pro-'duced by creditors *and others* on the trial 'of cauſes, I will comprehenſively declare; and 'in what manner thoſe witneſſes muſt give true 'evidence.

62. 'Married houſe-keepers, men with male 'iſſue, inhabitants of the ſame diſtrict, either of

'the

'the military, the commercial, or the ſervile claſs, 'are competent, when called by the party, to give 'their evidence; not any perſons indiſcriminately, 'except in *ſuch* caſes of urgency *as will ſoon be 'mentioned.*

63. 'Juſt and ſenſible men of all the *four* claſſes 'may be witneſſes on trials; men, who know 'their whole duty, and are free from covetouſneſs: 'but men of an oppoſite character the judge muſt 'reject.

64. 'Thoſe muſt not be admitted who have a 'pecuniary intereſt; nor familiar friends; nor 'menial ſervants; nor enemies; nor men for-'merly perjured; nor perſons grievouſly diſ-'eaſed; nor thoſe who have committed henious 'offences.

65. 'The king cannot be made a witneſs; nor '*cooks and the like* mean artificers; nor public 'dancers nor ſingers; nor a prieſt of deep learn-'ing in ſcripture; nor a ſtudent in theology; nor 'an anchoret ſecluded from all worldly con-'nexions;

66. 'Nor one wholy dependent; nor one of 'bad fame; nor one who follows a cruel occu-'pation; nor one who acts openly againſt the 'law; nor a decripit old man; nor a child; nor 'one man only, *unleſs he be diſtinguiſhed for virtue*; 'nor a wretch of the loweſt mixed claſs; nor one 'who has loſt the organs of ſenſe;

67. 'Nor one extremely grieved; nor one in-'toxicated; nor a madman; nor one tormented 'with hunger or thirſt; nor one oppreſſed by 'fatigue; nor one excited by luſt; nor one in-'flamed by wrath; nor one who has been con-'victed of theft.

68. 'Women ſhould regularly be witneſſes for 'women; twice born men, for men alike twice 'born; good ſervants and mechanicks, for ſer-'vants and mechanicks; and thoſe of the loweſt 'race, for thoſe of the loweſt;

69. 'But any perſon whatever, who has poſitive 'knowledge *of tranſactions* in the private apart-'ments of a houſe, or in a foreſt, or at a time 'of death, may give evidence between the 'parties:

70. 'On failure *of witneſſes duly qualified*, evi-'dence may, *in ſuch caſes*, be given by a woman, by 'a child, or by an aged man, by a pupil, by a 'kinſman, by a ſlave, or by a hired ſervant;

71. 'Yet of children, of old men, and of the 'diſeaſed, who are all apt to ſpeak untruly, the 'judge muſt conſider the teſtimony as weak; and '*much more*, that of men with diſordered minds:

72. 'In all caſes of violence, of theft and 'adultery, of defamation and aſſault, he muſt not 'examine too ſtrictly the competence of wit-'neſſes.

73. 'If there be contradictory evidence, let the 'king decide by the plurality of credible wit-'neſſes; if equality in number, by ſuperiority in 'virtue; if parity in virtue, by the teſtimony of 'ſuch twice born men as have beſt performed 'publick duties.

74. 'Evidence of what has been ſeen, or of what 'has been heard, *as ſlander and the like*, given by 'thoſe who ſaw or heard it, is admiſſable; and a 'witneſs who ſpeaks truth in thoſe caſes, neither 'deviates from virtue nor loſes his wealth:

75. 'But a witneſs, who knowingly ſays any 'thing, before an aſſembly of good men, differ-'ent from what he had ſeen or heard, ſhall fall

'headlong

'headlong, after death, into a region of horrour, 'and be debarred from heaven.

76. 'When a man fees or hears any thing, 'without being then called upon to atteſt it, yet if 'he be *afterwards* examined as a witneſs, he muſt 'declare it, exactly as *it was* ſeen, *and* as *it was* 'heard.

77. 'One man, untainted with covetouſneſs *and* '*other vices*, may *in ſome caſes* be the ſole witneſs, 'and will have more weight than many women, 'becauſe female underſtandings are apt to waver; 'or than many other men who have been tar'niſhed with crimes.

78. 'What witneſſes declare naturally *or with*'*out bias*, muſt be received on trials; but what 'they improperly ſay, from ſome unnatural bent, 'is inapplicable to the purpoſes of juſtice.

79. 'The witneſſes being aſſembled in the 'middle of the court-room, in the preſence of 'the plaintiff and the defendant, let the judge 'examine them, after having addreſſed them *all* '*together* in the following manner:

80. "What ye know to have been tranſacted "in the matter before us, between the parties re"ciprocally, declare at large and with truth; for "your evidence in this cauſe is required."

81. 'A witneſs, who gives teſtimony with 'truth, ſhall attain exalted ſeats of beatitude 'above, and the higheſt fame here below: ſuch 'teſtimony is revered by BRAHMA' himſelf;

82. 'The witneſs who ſpeaks falſely, ſhall be 'faſt bound, *under water*, in the *ſnaky* cords of 'VARUNA, and be wholly deprived of power *to* '*eſcape torment*, during a hundred tranſmigrations: 'let mankind, therefore, give no falſe teſtimony.

 83. 'By

83. ' By truth is a witneſs cleared of ſin; by ' truth is juſtice advanced: truth muſt, therefore, ' be ſpoken by witneſſes of every claſs.

84. ' The ſoul itſelf is its own witneſs; the ' ſoul itſelf is its own refuge; offend not thy ' conſcious ſoul, the ſupreme internal witneſs of ' men!

85. ' The ſinful have ſaid in their hearts: " None ſees us." Yes; the gods diſtinctly ſee ' them; and ſo does the ſpirit within their breaſts.

86. ' The guardian deities of the firmament, of ' the earth, of the waters, of the human heart, ' of the moon, of the ſun, and of fire, of pu- ' niſhment after death, of the winds, of night, of ' both twilights, and of juſtice, perfectly know ' the ſtate of all ſpirits clothed with bodies.

87. ' In the forenoon let the the judge, being ' purified, ſeverally call on the twice born, being ' purified alſo, to declare the truth, in the pre- ' ſence of *ſome image, a ſymbol* of the divinity, and ' of *Bráhmens*, while the witneſſes turn their faces ' either to the north or to the eaſt.

88. ' To a *Bráhmen* he muſt begin with ſaying, " Declare;" to a *Cſhatriya*, with ſaying " De- " clare the truth;" to a *Vaiſya*, with comparing ' perjury to the crime of ſtealing kine, grain, or ' gold; to a *Súdra*, with comparing it *in ſome or all* ' *of the following ſentences*, to every crime that men ' can commit.

89. " Whatever places of torture have been " prepared for the ſlayer of a prieſt, for the mur- " derer of a woman or of a child, for the injurer " of a friend, and for an ungrateful man, thoſe " places are ordained for a witneſs who gives falſe " evidence.

90. " The

90. " The fruit of every virtuous act, which " thou haſt done, O good man, ſince thy birth, " ſhall depart from thee to dogs, if thou deviate " in ſpeech from the truth.

91. " O friend to virtue, that Supreme Spirit, " which thou believeſt one and the ſame with " thyſelf, reſides in thy boſom perpetually, and is " an all-knowing inſpector of thy goodneſs or " of thy wickedneſs.

92. " If thou beeſt not at variance, *by ſpeaking* " *falſely*, with YAMA, or the ſubduer of all; with " VAIVASWATA, or the puniſher; with that great " divinity who dwells in thy breaſt; go not *on a* " *pilgrimage* to the river *Gangà*, nor to the plains " of CURU, *for thou haſt no need of expiation.*

93. " Naked and ſhorn, tormented with hun-" ger and thirſt, and deprived of ſight, ſhall the " man who gives falſe evidence, go with a " potſherd to beg food at the door of his enemy.

94. " Headlong, in utter darkneſs, ſhall the " impious wretch tumble into hell, who, being " interrogated in a judicial inquiry, anſwers one " queſtion falſely.

95. " He, who in a court of juſtice gives an " imperfect account of any tranſaction, or aſſerts " a fact of which he was no eye-witneſs, ſhall re-" ceive pain *inſtead of pleaſure*, and reſemble a man, " who eats fiſh *with eagerneſs* and ſwallows the " ſharp bones.

96. " The gods are acquainted with no better " mortal in this world, than the man, of whom " the intelligent ſpirit, which pervades his " body, has no diſtruſt, when he prepares to give " evidence.

97. " Hear, honeſt man, from a juſt enumera-" tion

"tion in order, how many kinsmen, in evidence "of different sorts, a false witness kills *or incurs* "*the guilt of killing*:

98. "He kills five by false testimony concern"ing cattle in general; he kills ten by false tes"timony concerning kine; he kills a hundred "by false evidence concerning horses; and a "thousand by false evidence concerning the hu"man race:

99. "By speaking falsely in a cause concerning "gold, he kills the born and the unborn; by "speaking falsely concerning land, he kills "every thing animated: beware then of speaking "falsely in a cause concerning land!

100. "The sages have held false evidence con"cerning water, and the possession or enjoyment "of women, equal to false evidence concerning "land; and it is equally criminal in causes con"cerning *pearls and other* precious things formed "in water, and concerning all things made of "stone.

101. "Marking well all the murders which are "comprehended in the crime of perjury, declare "thou the whole truth with precision, as *it was* "heard, *and* as *it was* seen by thee."

102. '*Bráhmens* who tend herds of cattle, who 'trade, who practise mechanical arts, who profess 'dancing and singing, who are hired servants or 'usurers, let the judge exhort and examine as if 'they were *Súdras*.

103. 'In some cases, a giver of false evidence 'from a pious motive, even though he know the 'truth, shall not lose a seat in heaven; such evi'dence wise men call the speech of the gods.

104. 'Whenever the death of a man, *who had* '*not*

'*not been a grievous offender*, either of the ſervile, 'the commercial, the military, or the ſacerdotal 'claſs, would be occaſioned by true evidence, '*from the known rigour of the king, even though 'the fault aroſe from inadvertence or errour*, falſe-'hood may be ſpoken: it is even preferable to 'truth.

105. 'Such *witneſſes* muſt offer, as oblations to 'SARASWATI', cakes of rice and milk addreſſed 'to the goddeſs of ſpeech; and thus will they 'fully expiate that venial ſin of benevolent falſe-'hood:

106. 'Or ſuch a *witneſs* may pour clarified 'butter into the holy fire, according to the ſacred 'rule, hallowing it with the texts called *cúſhmándá*, 'or with thoſe which relate to VARUNA, begin-'ing with *ud*; or with the three texts appropriated 'to the water gods.

107. 'A MAN who labours not under illneſs, 'yet comes not to give evidence in caſes of loans 'and the like, within three fortnights *after due 'ſummons*, ſhall take upon himſelf the whole debt, 'and pay a tenth part of it as a fine *to the king*.

108. 'The witneſs, who has given evidence, 'and to whom, within ſeven days after, *a misfor-'tune* happens *from* diſeaſe, fire, or the death of 'a kinſman, ſhall be condemned to pay the debt 'and a fine.

109. 'IN caſes, where no witneſs can be 'had, between two parties oppoſing each other, 'the judge may acquire a knowledge of the truth, 'by the oath of the parties; *or* if he cannot *other-'wiſe* perfectly aſcertain it.

110. 'By the *ſeven* great *Rĭſhis*, and by the 'deities themſelves, have oaths been taken, for

'the

'the purpose of judicial proof; and even 'VASISHT'HA, *being accused by* VISWA'MITRA *of* '*murder*, took an oath before the *king* SUDA'MAN, 'son of PIYAVANA.

111. 'Let no man of sense take an oath in 'vain, *that is, not in a court of justice*, on a trifling 'occasion; for the man, who takes an oath in 'vain, shall be punished in this life and in the 'next:

112. 'To women, however, at a time of dal'liance, or on a proposal of marriage, in the 'case of grass or fruit eaten by a cow, of wood 'taken for a sacrifice, or of a promise made for 'the preservation of a *Bráhmen*, it is no deadly sin 'to take a light oath.

113. 'Let the judge cause a priest to swear by his 'veracity; a soldier by his horse or elephant, 'and his weapons; a merchant by his kine, grain, 'and gold; a mechanick, or servile man, by *im*'*precating on his own head, if he speak falsely*, all 'possible crimes;

114. 'Or, *on great occasions*, let him cause the 'party to hold fire, or to dive under water, or 'severally to touch the heads of his children 'and wife:

115. 'He, whom the blazing fire burns not, 'whom the water soon forces not up, or meets with 'no speedy misfortune, must be held veracious in 'his testimony on oath.

116. 'Of the sage VASTA, whom his younger '*half* brother formerly attacked, *as the son of a* '*servile woman*, the fire, which pervades the 'world, burned not even a hair, by reason of his 'perfect veracity.

117. 'WHENEVER false evidence has been 'given in any suit, the king must reverse the

'judgement;

'judgement; and whatever has been done, muſt 'be conſidered as undone.

118. 'Evidence, given from covetouſneſs, 'from diſtraction of mind, from terrour, from 'friendſhip, from luſt, from wrath, from ignorance, 'and from inattention, muſt be held invalid.

119. 'The diſtinctions of puniſhment for a 'falſe witneſs, from either of thoſe motives, I will 'propound fully and in order.

120. 'If he ſpeak falſely through covetouſneſs, 'he ſhall be fined a thouſand *panas*; if through 'diſtraction of mind, *two hundred and fifty*, or the 'loweſt amercements; if through terrour, two 'mean amercements; if through friendſhip, four 'times the loweſt;

121. 'If through luſt, ten times the loweſt 'amercement; if through wrath, three times the 'next *or middlemoſt*; if through ignorance, two 'hundred complete; if through inattention, a 'hundred only.

122. 'Learned men have ſpecified theſe pu-'niſhments, *which were* ordained by ſage legiſla-'tors for perjured witneſſes, with a view to prevent 'a failure of juſtice and to reſtrain iniquity.

123. 'Let a juſt prince baniſh men of the three '*lower* claſſes, if they give falſe evidence, having 'firſt levied the fine; but a *Bráhmen* let him only 'baniſh.

124. 'Menu, ſon of the Self-exiſtent, has named 'ten places of puniſhment, which are appropriated 'to the three *lower* claſſes; but a *Bráhmen* muſt 'depart from the realm unhurt *in any one of* '*them*:

125. 'The part of generation, the belly, the 'tongue, the two hands, and fifthly, the two feet,

'the

'the eye, the nose, both ears, the property, and, *in* 'a capital case, the whole body.

126. 'Let the king, having considered and ascertained the frequency of a similar offence, the 'place and time, the ability of the criminal *to pay* 'or *suffer*, and the crime itself, cause punishment 'to fall on those alone who deserve it.

127. 'Unjust punishment destroys reputation 'during life, and fame after death; it even obstructs, in the next life, the path to heaven: 'unjust punishment, therefore, let the king by all 'means avoid.

128. 'A king who inflicts punishment on such 'as deserve it not, and inflicts no punishment on 'such as deserve it, brings infamy on himself, 'while he lives, and shall sink, when he dies, to a 'region of torment.

129. 'First, let him punish by gentle admonition; afterwards, by harsh reproof; thirdly, by 'deprivation of property; after that, by corporal pain:

130. 'But, when even by corporal punishment 'he cannot restrain such offenders, let him apply 'to them all the four modes with rigour.

131. 'Those names of copper, silver, and 'gold weights, which are commonly used among 'men, for the purpose of worldly business, I will 'now comprehensively explain.

132. 'The very small mote, which may be discerned in a sun-beam passing through a lattice, 'is the least visible quantity, and men call it a '*trasarénu*:

133. 'Eight of those *trasarénus* are supposed 'equal in weight to one minute poppy-seed; three 'of those seeds are equal to one black mustard-seed; 'and three of those least, to a white mustard-seed:

134. 'Six

134. 'Six white muſtard-ſeeds are equal to a 'middle ſized barley-corn; three ſuch barley-'corns to one *ractìcà*, or ſeed of the *Gunjà*; five '*racticas* of gold are one *máſha*, and ſixteen ſuch '*máſhas* one *ſuverna*:

135. 'Four *ſuvernas* make a *pala*; ten *palas* 'a *dharana*; but two *racticas* of ſilver weighed 'together, are conſidered as one *máſhaca*;

136. 'Sixteen of thoſe *máſhacas* are a ſilver '*dharana*, or *purána*; but a *carſha*, or eighty '*racticas* of copper, is called a *pana* or *cárſhápana*.

137. 'Ten *dharanas* of ſilver are known by the 'name of a *ſatamána*; and the weight of four '*ſuvernas* has alſo the appellation of a *niſhca*.

138. 'Now two hundred and fifty *panas* are 'declared to be the firſt *or loweſt* amercement; 'five hundred of them are conſidered as the 'mean; and a thouſand as the higheſt.

139. 'A DEBT being admitted by the de-'fendant, he muſt pay five in the hundred, *as a* '*fine to the king*; but, if it be denied *and proved*, 'twice as much: this law was enacted by MENU.

140. 'A LENDER of money may take, in ad-'dition to his capital, the intereſt allowed by 'VASISHT'HA, *that is*, an eightieth part of a 'hundred, *or one and a quarter* by the month, *if* '*he have a pledge*;

141. 'Or, *if he have no pledge*, he may take 'two in the hundred *by the month*, remembering 'the duty of good men: for, by *thus* taking 'two in the hundred, he becomes not a ſinner 'for gain.

142. 'He may thus take, *in proportion to the* '*riſk, and* in the direct order of the claſſes, two 'in the hundred *from a prieſt*, three *from a ſoldier*, four

'four *from a merchant*; and five *from a mechanick* 'or *servile man*, but never more, as interest by 'the month.

143. 'If he take a beneficial pledge, *or a pledge* '*to be used for his profit*, he must have no other 'interest on the loan; nor, after a great length 'of time, *or when the profits have amounted to the* '*debt*, can he give or sell such a pledge, *though* '*he may assign it in pledge to another*.

144. 'A pledge *to be kept only* must not be 'used by force, *that is, against consent*: the pawner 'so using it must give up his whole interest, or 'must satisfy the pawner, *if it be spoiled or worn* '*out*, by paying him the original price of it; 'otherwise, he commits a theft of the pawn.

145. 'Neither a pledge *without limit*, nor a 'deposit, are lost to the owner by lapse of time: 'they are both recoverable, though they have 'long remained with the bailee.

146. 'A milch cow, a camel, a riding horse, '*a bull, or other beast* which has been sent to be 'tamed for labour, and other things used with 'friendly assent, are not lost, *by length of time*, to 'the owner.

147. '*In general*, whatever chattel the owner 'sees enjoyed by others for ten years, while, 'though present, he says nothing, that chattel he 'shall not recover:

148. 'If he be neither an idiot, nor an infant 'under the full age of fifteen years, and if the 'chattel be adversely possessed in a place where 'he may see it, his property in it is extinct by 'law, and the adverse possessor shall keep it.

149. 'A pledge, a boundary of land, the 'property of an infant, a deposit either open or

in

'in a cheſt ſealed, female ſlaves, the wealth of 'a king, and of a learned *Bráhmen*, are not loſt 'in conſequence of adverſe enjoyment.

150. 'The fool, who ſecretly uſes a pledge 'without, *though not againſt* the aſſent of the 'owner, ſhall give up half of his intereſt, as a 'compenſation for ſuch uſe.

151. 'INTEREST on money received at once, '*not month by month, or day by day, as it ought,* 'muſt never be more than enough to double the 'debt, *that is, more than the amount of the princi- 'pal paid at the ſame time*: on grain, on fruit, on 'wool or hair, on beaſts of burden, *lent to be paid 'in the ſame kind of equal value,* it muſt not be 'more than enough to make the debt quintuple.

152. 'Stipulated intereſt beyond the legal rate, 'and different from the *preceding* rule, is invalid; 'and the wiſe call it an uſurous way *of lending*: 'the lender is entitled, *at moſt*, to five in the 'hundred.

153. 'Let no lender *for a month, or for two or 'three months at a certain intereſt*, receive *ſuch* 'intereſt beyond the year; nor any intereſt, 'which is unapproved; nor intereſt upon intereſt '*by previous agreement*; nor monthly intereſt ex- 'ceeding in time the amount of the principal; 'nor intereſt exacted from a debtor, *as the price 'of the riſk, when there is no publick danger or diſ- 'treſs*; nor immoderate profits from a pledge to 'be uſed by way of intereſt.

154. 'He, who cannot pay the debt *at the 'fixed time*, and wiſhes to renew the contract, 'may renew it in writing, *with the creditor's aſ- 'ſent*, if he pay all the intereſt then due;

155. 'But if *by ſome unavoidable accident*, he 'cannot pay the whole intereſt, he may inſert, *as*

'*principal* in the renewed contract, so much of the 'interest accrued as he ought to pay.

156. 'A lender at interest on *the risk of* safe 'carriage, who has agreed on the place and time, 'shall not receive such interest, if *by accident* the 'goods are not carried to the place, or within 'the time:

157. 'Whatever interest *or price of the risk* 'shall be settled *between the parties*, by men well 'acquainted with sea voyages or journeys by land, 'with times and with places, such interest shall 'have legal force.

158. 'The man who becomes surety for the 'appearance of a debtor in this world, and pro-'duces him not, shall pay the debt out of his 'own property;

159. 'But money due by a surety, or idly 'promised *to musicians and actresses*, or lost at 'play, or due for spirituous liquors, or what re-'mains unpaid of a fine or toll, the son *of the surety* '*or debtor* shall not *in general* be obliged to pay:

160. 'Such is the rule in cases of a surety for 'appearance *or good behaviour*; but if a surety 'for payment should die, the judge may compel 'even his heirs to discharge the debt.

161. 'On what account then is it, that after 'the death of a surety other than for payment, 'the creditor may *in one case* demand the debt '*of the heir*, all the affairs of the deceased being 'known and proved?

162. 'If the surety had received money from 'the debtor, and had enough to pay the debt, 'the son of him who so received it, shall dis-'charge the debt out of his *inherited* property: 'this is a sacred ordinance.

163. 'A contract made by a person intoxicated

'or

'or insane, or grievously disordered, or wholly 'dependent, by an infant or a decrepit old man, 'or *in the name of another*, by a person without 'authority, is utterly null.

164. 'That plaint can have no effect though 'it may be supported by evidence, which con-'tains a cause of action inconsistent with positive 'law or with settled usage.

165. 'When the judge discovers a fraudulent 'pledge or sale, a fraudulent gift and acceptance, 'or in what ever other case he detects fraud, let 'him annul the whole transaction.

166. 'If the debtor be dead, and if the money 'borrowed was expended for the use of his fa-'mily, it must be paid by that family, divided 'or undivided, out of their own estate.

167. 'Should even a slave make a contract '*in the name of his absent master* for the behoof of 'the family, that master, whether in his own 'country or abroad, shall not rescind it.

168. 'What is given by force *to a man who* '*cannot accept it legally*, what is by force enjoyed, 'by force caused to be written, and all other 'things done by force *or against free consent*, MENU 'has pronounced void.

169. 'Three are troubled by means of others, '*namely*, witnesses, sureties, and inspectors of 'causes; and four collect wealth slowly, with 'benefit to others, a *Bráhmen*, a money-lender, 'a merchant, and a king.

170. 'Let no king, how indigent soever, take 'any thing which ought not to be taken; nor 'let him, how wealthy soever, decline taking 'that which he ought to take, be it ever so small:

171. 'By taking what ought not to be taken,

'and by refusing what ought to be received, the 'king betrays his own weakness, and is lost both 'in this world and in the next;

172. 'But by taking his due, by administering 'justice, and by protecting the weak, the king 'augments his own force, and is exalted in the 'next world and in this.

173. 'Therefore, let the king, like YAMA, 'resigning what may be pleasing or unpleasing 'to himself, live by the strict rules of YAMA, 'his anger being repressed, and his organs kept 'in subjection.

174. 'That evil-minded king, who, through 'infatuation, decides causes with injustice, his 'enemies, *through the disaffection of his people*, 'quickly reduce to a state of dependence;

175. 'But him, who subduing both lust and 'wrath, examines causes with justice, his people 'naturally seek, as rivers the ocean.

176. 'THE debtor who complains before the 'king, that his creditor has recovered the debt 'by his own legal act, *as before-mentioned*, shall be 'compelled by the king to pay a quarter of the 'sum *as a fine*, and the creditor shall be left in 'possession of his own.

177. 'Even by personal labour shall the debtor 'pay what is adjudged, if he be of the same class 'with the creditor, or of a lower; but a debtor 'of a higher class must pay it *according to his income*, by little and little.

178. 'By this system of rules let the king 'decide, with equal justice, all disputes between 'men opposing each other, having ascertained 'the truth by evidence or the oaths of the parties.

179. 'A SENSIBLE man should make a deposit 'with

'with some person of high birth, and of good 'morals, well acquainted with law, habitually 'veracious, having a large family, wealthy and 'venerable.

180. Whatever thing, and in whatever manner 'a person shall deposit in the hands of another, 'the same thing, and in the same manner, ought 'to be received back by the owner; as the de-'livery *was*, so *must be* the receipt.

181. 'He, who restores not to the depositor, on 'his request, what has been deposited, may first 'be tried by the judge *in the following manner*, the 'depositor himself being absent.

182. 'On failure of witnesses, let the judge ac-'tually deposit gold, *or precious things*, with the 'defendant, by the artful contrivance of spies, who 'have passed the age of child-hood, and whose 'persons are engaging:

183. 'Should the defendant restore that depo-'sit in the manner and shape in which it was 'bailed *by the spies*, there is nothing in his hands, 'for which others can justly accuse him;

184. 'But if he restore not the gold, or '*precious things*, as he ought, to those emissaries, 'let him be apprehended and compelled to pay 'the value of both deposits; this is a settled rule.

185. 'A deposit, whether sealed up or not, 'should never be redelivered, while the depositor 'is alive, to his heir apparent or presumptive: 'both sorts of deposits, indeed, are extinct, *or can-'not be demanded by the heir*, if the depositor die, '*in that case*; but not, unless he die, *for should the 'heir apparent keep them, the depositor himself may 'sue the bailee*:

186. 'But, if a depositary by his own free act 'shall deliver a deposit to the heir of a deceased

'bailor, he muſt not be haraſſed *with claims of a* '*ſimilar kind*, either by the king, or by that heir;

187. 'And, *if ſimilar claims be made*, the king 'muſt decide the queſtions after friendly admoni- 'tion, *without having recourſe to artifice*; for the 'honeſt diſpoſition of the man being proved, the 'judge muſt proceed with mildneſs.

188. 'Such is the mode of aſcertaining the right 'in all theſe caſes of a depoſit: in the caſe of a 'depoſit ſealed up, the bailee ſhall incur no cen- 'ſure *on the redelivery*, unleſs he have *altered the* '*ſeal or* taken out ſomething.

189. 'If a depoſit be ſeized by thieves *or deſ-* '*troyed by vermine*, or waſhed away by water, or 'conſumed by fire, the bailee ſhall not be obliged 'to make it good, unleſs he took part of it for 'himſelf.

190. 'The defendant, who denies a depoſit, and 'the plaintiff who aſſerts it, let the king try by all 'ſorts of expedients, and by the modes of ordeal 'preſcribed in the *Véda*.

191. 'He who reſtores not a thing really de- 'poſited, and he, who demands what he never 'bailed, ſhall both, *for a ſecond offence*, be pu- 'niſhed as thieves, *if gold, pearls, or the like be* '*demanded*; or, *in the caſe of a trifling demand*, ſhall 'pay a fine equal to the value of the thing claimed:

192. 'For the firſt offence, the king ſhould 'compel a fraudulent depoſitary, without any diſ- 'tinction betweeen a depoſit under ſeal or open, 'to pay a fine equal to its value.

193. 'That man, who, by falſe pretences, gets 'into his hands the goods of another, ſhall, toge- 'ther with his accomplices, be puniſhed by vari- 'ous degrees of whipping or mutilation, or even 'by death.

194. '*Regularly,*

194. ‘ *Regularly*, a depoſit ſhould be produced, ‘ the ſame in kind and quantity as it was bailed, ‘ by the ſame and to the ſame perſon, by whom ‘ and from whom it was received, and before the ‘ ſame company, *who were witneſſes to the depoſit*: ‘ he who produces it, in a different manner, ought ‘ to be fined;

195. ‘ But a thing, privately depoſited, ſhould ‘ be privately reſtored by and to the perſon, by ‘ and from whom it was received: as the bailment ‘ *was*, ſo *ſhould be* the delivery, *according to a rule* ‘ *in the* Véda.

196. ‘ Thus let the king decide cauſes concern- ‘ ing a depoſit, or a friendly loan for uſe, without ‘ ſhowing rigour to the depoſitary.

197. ‘ HIM, who ſells the property of another ‘ man, without the aſſent of the owner, the judge ‘ ſhall not admit as a competent witneſs, but ſhall ‘ treat as a thief, who pretends that he has com- ‘ mitted no theft:

198. ‘ If, indeed he be a near kinſman of the ‘ owner, he ſhall be fined ſix hundred *panas*; but, ‘ if he be neither his kinſman or a claimant under ‘ him, he commits an offence equal to larceny.

199. ‘ A gift or ſale, thus made by any other ‘ than the true owner, muſt, by a ſettled rule, be ‘ conſidered, in judicial proceedings, as not made.

200. ‘ Where occupation *for a time* ſhall be ‘ proved, but no ſort of title ſhall appear, *the ſale* ‘ *cannot be ſupported*: title, not occupation, is ‘ eſſential to its ſupport; *and* this rule *alſo* is fixed.

201. ‘ He who has received a chattel, by pur- ‘ chaſe in open market, before a number of men, ‘ juſtly acquires the abſolute property, by having ‘ paid the price of it, *if he can produce the vendor*;

202. 'But if the vendor be not producible, and 'the vendee prove the publick sale, the latter must 'be dismissed by the king, without punishment; 'and the former owner, who lost the chattel, may 'take it back, *on paying the vendee half its value.*

203. 'One commodity mixed with another, 'shall never be sold as *unmixed*; nor a bad com-'modity as good; nor less *than agreed on*; nor 'any thing kept at a distance or concealed, *lest* '*some defect in it should be discovered.*

204. 'If after one damsel has been shown, another 'be offered to the bridegroom, *who had purchased* '*leave to marry her from her next kinsman,* he may 'become the husband of both for the same price: 'this law MENU ordained.

205. 'The kinsman, who gives a damsel in 'marriage, having first openly told her blemishes, 'whether she be insane, or disordered with ele-'phantiasis, or defiled by connexion with a man, 'shall suffer no punishment.

206. 'IF an officiating priest, actually engaged 'in a sacrifice, abandon his work, a share only, 'in proportion to his work done, shall be given to 'him by his partners in the business, *out of their* '*common pay*:

207. 'But if he discontinue his work *without* '*fraud,* after the time of giving the sacrificial fees, 'he may take his full share, and cause what re-'mains to be performed by another priest.

208. 'Where, on the performance of solemn 'rites, a specifick fee is ordained for each part of 'them, shall he alone, who performs that part, 'receive the fee, or shall all the priests take the 'perquisites jointly?

209. '*At some holy rites,* let the reader of the '*Yajurvéda* take the car, and the *Brahmá,* or su-

' perintending prieſt, the horſe; or, *on another* ' *occaſion*, let the reader of the *Rĭgvéda* take the ' horſe, and the chanter of the *Sámavéda* receive ' the carriage, in which the purchaſed materials ' of the ſacrifice had been brought.

210. ' *A hundred cows being diſtributable among* ' *ſixteen prieſts*, the four chief *or firſt ſet*, are en- ' titled to *near* half, *or forty-eight*; the next four ' to half of that number; the third ſet, to a third ' part of it; and the fourth ſet, to a quarter:

211. ' According to this rule, *or in proportion* ' *to the work*, muſt allotments of ſhares be given ' to men here below, who, *though* in conjunction, ' perform their ſeveral parts of the buſineſs.

212. ' SHOULD money or goods be given, *or* ' *promiſed as a gift*, by one man to another who ' aſks it for ſome religious act, the gift ſhall be ' void, if that act be not afterwards performed:

213. ' If the money be delivered, and the re- ' ceiver, through pride or avarice, refuſe *in that* ' *caſe* to return it, he ſhall be fined one *ſuverna* by ' the king, as a puniſhment for his theft.

214. ' Such, as here declared, is the rule or- ' dained for withdrawing what has been given: ' I will, next, propound the law for non-payment ' of wages.

215. ' THAT hired ſervant or workman, who, ' not from any diſorder but from inſolence, fails ' to perform his work according to his agreement, ' ſhall be fined eight *racticas*, and his wages or ' hire ſhall not be paid.

216. ' But, if he be really ill, and, when reſtored ' to health, ſhall perform his work according to ' his original bargain, he ſhall receive his pay ' even for a very long time;

217. 'Yet, whether he be ſick or well, if the 'work ſtipulated be not performed *by another for 'him or by himſelf*, his whole wages are forfeited, 'though the work want but a little of being 'complete.

218. 'This is the general rule concerning work 'undertaken for wages or hire: next I will fully 'declare the law concerning ſuch men as break 'their promiſes.

219. 'THE man, among the traders and other 'inhabitants of a town or diſtrict, who breaks a 'promiſe through avarice, though he had taken 'an oath to perform it, let the king baniſh from 'his realm:

220. 'Or, *according to circumſtances*, let the 'judge, having arreſted the promiſe-breaker, con-'demn him to pay ſix *niſhcas*, or four *ſuvernas*, or 'one *ſatamána* of ſilver, or all three *if he deſerve 'ſuch a fine*.

221. 'Among all citizens, and in all claſſes, let 'a juſt king obſerve this rule for impoſing fines on 'men who ſhall break their engagements.

222. 'A MAN who has bought or ſold any 'thing in this world, *that has a fixed price, and is 'not periſhable, as land or metals*, and wiſhes to 'reſcind the contract, may give or take back ſuch 'a thing within ten days;

223. 'But, after ten days, he ſhall neither give 'nor take it back: the giver or the taker, *except 'by conſent*, ſhall be fined by the king ſix hundred '*panas*.

224. 'The king himſelf ſhall take a fine of 'ninety-ſix *panas* from him who gives a blemiſhed 'girl *in marriage, for a reward*, without avowing 'her blemiſh;

225. 'But the man, who, through malignity, 'ſays of a damſel, that ſhe is no virgin, ſhall be 'fined a hundred *panas*, if he cannot prove her 'defilement.

226. 'The holy nuptial texts are applied ſolely 'to virgins, and no where on earth to girls who 'have loſt their virginity; ſince thoſe women are '*in general* excluded from legal ceremonies:

227. 'The nuptial texts are a certain rule 'in regard to wedlock, and the bridal contract is 'known by the learned to be complete *and irrevo-'cable*, on the ſeventh ſtep *of the married pair, hand 'in hand, after thoſe texts have been pronounced.*

228. 'By this law, in all buſineſs whatever here 'below, muſt the judge confine, within the path 'of rectitude, a perſon inclined to reſcind his 'contract of ſale and purchaſe.

229. 'I NOW will decide exactly, according to 'principles of law, the conteſts uſually ariſing from 'the fault of ſuch as own herds of cattle, and of 'ſuch as are hired to keep them.

230. 'By day the blame falls on the herdſman; 'by night on the owner, *if the cattle be fed and 'kept* in his own houſe; but, if the place of their 'food and cuſtody be different, the keeper incurs 'the blame.

231. 'That hired ſervant, whoſe wages arn 'paid with milk, may, with the aſſent of the 'own r, milk the beſt cow out of ten: ſuch are 'the wages of herdſmen, unleſs they be paid in a 'different mode.

232. 'The herdſman himſelf ſhall make good 'the loſs of a beaſt, which through his want of 'due care, has ſtrayed, has been deſtroyed by 'reptiles, or killed by dogs, or has died by falling 'into a pit;

233. 'But

233. 'But he shall not be compelled to make 'it good, when robbers have carried it away, if, 'after fresh proclamation and pursuit, he give 'notice to his master in a proper place and season.

234. 'When cattle die, let him carry to his 'master their ears, their hides, their tails, the 'skin below their navels, their tendons, and the 'liquor exuding from their foreheads: let him 'also point out their limbs.

235. 'A flock of goats or of sheep being at-'tacked by wolves, and the keeper not going *to* '*repel the attack*, he shall be responsible for every 'one of them, which a wolf shall violently kill;

236. 'But, if any one of them, while they 'graze together near a wood, and the shepherd 'keeps them in order, shall be suddenly killed 'by a wolf springing on it, he shall not in that case 'be responsible.

237. 'On all sides of a village or small town 'let a space be left for pasture, in breadth either 'four hundred cubits, or three casts of a large 'stick; and thrice that space round a city or con-'siderable town:

238. 'Within that pasture ground, if cattle do 'any damage to grain in a field uninclosed with 'a hedge, the king shall not punish the herds-'man.

239. 'Let the owner of the field inclose it with 'a hedge *of thorny plants*, over which a camel 'could not look; and let him stop every gap, 'through which a dog or a boar could thrust 'his head.

240. 'Should cattle, attended by a herdsman, 'do mischief near a highway, in an inclosed field 'or near the village, he shall be fined a hundred

'*panas*;

'*panas*; but againſt cattle which have no keeper, 'let the owner of the field ſecure it.

241. 'In other fields, the *owner of* cattle *doing 'miſchief* ſhall be fined one *pana* and a quarter; 'but, in all places, the value of the *damaged* 'grain muſt be paid: ſuch is the fixed rule con-'cerning a huſbandman.

242. 'For damage by a cow before ten days 'have paſſed ſince her calving, by bulls kept for 'impregnation, and by cattle conſecrated to the 'deity, whether attended or unattended, MENU 'has ordained no fine.

243. 'If land be injured, by the fault of the 'farmer himſelf, *as if he fails to ſow it in due time,* 'he ſhall be fined ten times as much as the *king's* 'ſhare *of the crop, that might otherwiſe have been 'raiſed*; but only five times as much, if it was 'the fault of his ſervants without his knowledge.

244. 'Theſe rules let a juſt prince obſerve in 'all caſes of tranſgreſſion by maſters, their cattle, 'and their herdſmen.

245. 'IF a conteſt ariſe between two villages, '*or landholders*, concerning a boundary, let the 'king, *or his judge*, aſcertain the limits in the 'month of *Jyaiſht'ha*, when the land-marks are 'ſeen more diſtinctly.

246. '*When boundaries firſt are eſtabliſhed*, let 'ſtrong trees be planted on them, *Vatas*, *Pippalas*, '*Paláſas*, *Sálmalis*, *Sálas* or *Tálas*; or ſuch trees '*(like the* Udumbara *or* Vajradru) as abound in 'milk;

247. 'Or cluſtering ſhrubs, or *Vénus* of differ-'ent ſorts, or *Samí*-trees, and creepers, or *Saras*, 'and clumps of *Cubjacas*: and mounds of earth 'ſhould be raiſed on them, ſo that the land-mark 'may not eaſily periſh:

248. 'Lakes

248. ‘ Lakes and wells, pools and ſtreams,
‘ ought alſo to be made on the common limits,
‘ and temples dedicated to the gods.

249. ‘ The perſons concerned, reflecting on
‘ the perpetual treſpaſſes committed by men here
‘ below through ignorance of boundaries, ſhould
‘ cauſe other land-marks to be concealed *under*
‘ *ground:*

250. ‘ Large pieces of ſtone, bones, tails of
‘ cows, bran, aſhes, potſherds, dried cow-dung,
‘ bricks and tiles, charcoal, pebbles and ſand,

251. ‘ And ſubſtances of all ſorts, which the
‘ earth corrodes not even in a long time, ſhould
‘ be placed *in jars* not appearing *above ground* on
‘ the common boundary.

252. ‘ By ſuch marks, or by the courſe of a
‘ ſtream, and long continued poſſeſſion, the judge
‘ may aſcertain the limit between the lands of two
‘ parties in litigation:

253. ‘ Should there be a doubt, even on the
‘ inſpection of thoſe marks, recourſe muſt be had,
‘ for the deciſion of ſuch a conteſt, to the declara-
‘ tions of witneſſes.

254. ‘ Thoſe witneſſes muſt be examined con-
‘ cerning the land-marks, in the preſence of all
‘ the townſmen or villagers, or of both the con-
‘ tending parties:

255. ‘ What the witneſſes, thus aſſembled and
‘ interrogated, ſhall poſitively declare concerning
‘ the limits, muſt be recorded in writing, together
‘ with all their names.

256. ‘ Let them, putting earth on their heads,
‘ wearing chaplets of red flowers and clad in red
‘ mantles, be ſworn by *the reward of* all their
‘ ſeveral good actions to give correct evidence
‘ concerning the metes and bounds.

257. ‘ Veracious

257. 'Veracious witneſſes, who give evidence 'as the law requires, are abſolved from their ſins; 'but ſuch as give it unjuſtly, ſhall each be fined 'two hundred *panas*.

258. 'If there be no witneſſes, let four men, 'who dwell on all the four ſides of the two vil-'lages, make a deciſion concerning the boundary, 'being duly prepared, *like the witneſſes*, in the 'preſence of the king.

259. 'If there be no ſuch neighbours on all 'ſides, nor any men, nor any men whoſe an-'ceſtors had lived there ſince the villages were 'built, nor other inhabitants of towns, who can 'give evidence on the limits, the judge muſt ex-'amine the following men, who inhabit the woods;

260. 'Hunters, fowlers, herdſmen, fiſhers, 'diggers for roots, catchers of ſnakes, gleaners, 'and other foreſters:

261. 'According to their declaration, when 'they are duly examined, let the king with pre-'ciſion order land-marks to be fixed on the boun-'dary line between the two villages.

262. 'As to the bounds of arable fields, wells 'or pools, gardens and houſes, the teſtimony of 'next neighbours on every ſide muſt be conſidered 'as the beſt means of deciſion:

263. 'Should the neighbours ſay any thing 'untrue, when two men diſpute about a land-'mark, the king ſhall make each of thoſe wit-'neſſes pay the middlemoſt of the three uſual 'amercements.

264. 'He, who by means of intimidation, ſhall 'poſſeſs himſelf of a houſe, a pool, a field, or 'a garden, ſhall be fined five hundred *panas*; but 'only two hundred, if he treſpaſſed through ig-'norance *of the right*.

265. 'If

265. 'If the boundary cannot be *otherwise* ascertained, let the king, knowing what is just, *that is, without partiality, and* consulting the future benefit of both parties, make a bound-line between their lands: this is a settled law.

266. 'Thus has the rule been propounded for decisions concerning land-marks: I next will declare the law concerning defamatory words.

267. 'A SOLDIER, defaming a priest, shall be fined a hundred *panas*; a merchant, *thus offending*, an hundred and fifty, or two hundred; but, *for such an offence*, a mechanick or servile man shall be whipped.

268. 'A priest shall be fined five hundred, if he slander a soldier; twenty-five if a merchant; and twelve if he slander a man of the servile class.

269. 'For abusing one of the same class, a twice born man, shall be fined only twelve; but for ribaldry not to be uttered, even that *and every fine* shall be doubled.

270. 'A once born man, who insults the twice born with gross invectives, ought to have his tongue slit; for he sprang from the lowest part *of* BRAHMA':

271. 'If he mention their names and classes with contumely, *as if he say*, "*Oh* DE'VADATTA, *thou refuse of* Bráhmens," an iron style, ten fingers long, shall be thrust red hot into his mouth.

272. 'Should he, through pride, give instruction to priests concerning their duty, let the king order some hot oil to be dropped into his mouth and his ear.

273. 'He, who falsely denies through insolence, 'the

'the ſacred knowledge, the country, the claſs, or 'the corporeal inveſtiture *of a man, equal in rank,* 'ſhall be compelled to pay a fine of two hundred '*panas.*

274. 'If a man call another blind with one 'eye, or lame, or defective in any ſimilar way, 'he ſhall pay the ſmall fine of one *pana,* even 'though he ſpeak truth.

275. 'He ſhall be fined a hundred, who de-'fames his mother, his father, his wife, his 'brother, his ſon, or his preceptor; and he who 'gives not his preceptor the way.

276. 'For *mutual* abuſe by a prieſt and a 'ſoldier, this fine muſt be impoſed by a learned 'king; the loweſt amercement on the prieſt, 'and the middlemoſt on the ſoldier.

277. 'Such exactly, *as before-mentioned,* muſt 'be the puniſhment of a merchant and a me-'chanick in reſpect of their ſeveral claſſes, except 'the ſlitting of the tongue: this is a fixed rule of 'puniſhment.

278. 'THUS fully has the law been declared 'for the puniſhment of defamatory ſpeech: I 'will next propound the eſtabliſhed law concern-'ing aſſault and battery.

279. 'With whatever member a low born 'man ſhall aſſault or hurt a ſuperiour, even that 'member of his muſt be ſlit, *or cut more or leſs* '*in proportion to the injury:* this is an ordinance 'of MENU.

280. 'He, who raiſes his hand or a ſtaff againſt 'another, ſhall have his hand cut; and he who 'kicks another in wrath, ſhall have an inciſion 'made in his foot.

281. 'A man of the loweſt claſs, who ſhall 'inſolently place himſelf on the ſame ſeat with

'one of the higheſt, ſhall either be baniſhed with 'a mark on his hinder parts, or the king ſhall 'cauſe a gaſh to be made on his buttock:

282. 'Should he ſpit on him through pride, 'the king ſhall order both of his lips to be gaſhed; 'ſhould he urine on him, his penis; ſhould he 'break wind againſt him, his anus.

283. 'If he ſeize the *Bráhmen* by the locks, 'or by the feet, or by the beard, or by the 'throat, or by the ſcrotum, let the king with-'out heſitation cauſe inciſions to be made in his 'hands.

284. 'If any man ſcratch the ſkin *of his equal* '*in claſs*, or fetch blood *from him*, he ſhall be 'fined a hundred *panas*; if he wound a muſcle, 'ſix *niſhcas*; but, if he break a bone, let him be 'inſtantly baniſhed.

285. 'According to the uſe and value of all 'great trees, muſt a fine be ſet for injuring them: 'this is an eſtabliſhed rule.

286. 'If a blow, attended with much pain, 'be given either to human creatures or cattle, 'the king ſhall inflict on the ſtriker a puniſhment 'as heavy as the preſumed ſuffering.

287. 'In all caſes of hurting a limb, wound-'ing, or fetching blood, the aſſailant ſhall pay 'the expence of a perfect cure; or, *on his failure*, 'both full damages and a fine to the ſame 'amount.

288. 'He, who injures the goods of another, 'whether acquainted or unacquainted with the 'owner of them, ſhall give ſatisfaction to the 'owner, and pay a fine to the king equal to the 'damage.

289. 'If injury be done to leather or to

'leathern

'leathern bags, or utensils made of wood or clay, 'the fine shall be five times their value.

290. 'The wise reckon ten occasions, in re-'gard to a carriage, its driver, and its owner, on 'which the fine is remitted; on other occa-'sions a fine is ordained by law:

291. 'The nose-cord or bridle being cut, *by 'some accident without negligence*, or the yoke being 'snapped, on a sudden overturn, or running against 'any thing *without fault*, the axle being broken, 'or the wheel cracked;

292. 'On the breaking of the thongs, of the 'halter, or of the reins, and when the driver has 'called aloud to make way, *on these occasions* has 'Menu declared that no fine shall be set:

293. 'But, where a carriage has been over-'turned by the unskilfulness of the driver, there, 'in the case of any hurt, the master shall be fined 'two hundred *panas*.

294. 'If the driver be skilful, *but negligent*, the 'driver alone shall be fined; and those in the car-'riage shall be fined each a hundred, if the driver 'be clearly unskilful.

295. 'Should a driver, being met in the way 'by another carriage or by cattle, kill any animal '*by his negligence*, a fine shall, without doubt, 'be imposed *by the following rule*:

296. 'For killing a man, a fine, equal to that 'for theft, shall be instantly set; half that amount, 'for large brute animals, as for a bull or cow, 'an elephant, a camel, or a horse;

297. 'For killing very young cattle, the fine 'shall be two hundred *panas*; and fifty, for ele-'gant quadrupeds or beautiful birds, as *antelopes, 'parrots, and the like*;

298. ' For an aſs, a goat, or a ſheep, the fine ' muſt be five ſilver *máſhas* ; and one *máſha* for ' killing a dog or a boar.

299. ' A WIFE, a ſon, a ſervant, a pupil, and ' a *younger* whole brother, may be corrected, ' when they commit faults, with a rope, or the ' ſmall ſhoot of a cane ;

300. ' But on the back part only of their ' bodies, and not on a noble part by any means : ' he who ſtrikes them otherwiſe than by this rule, ' incurs the guilt, *or ſhall pay the fine* of a thief.

301. ' This law of aſſault and battery has been ' completely declared : I proceed to declare the ' rule for the ſettled puniſhment of theft.

302. ' IN reſtraining thieves and robbers, let ' the king uſe extreme diligence; ſince, by ' reſtraining thieves and robbers, his fame and ' his domain are increaſed.

303. ' Conſtantly, no doubt, is that king to be ' honoured, who beſtows exemption from fear ; ' ſince he performs, *as it were*, a perpetual ſacri- ' fice, giving exemption from fear, as a conſtant ' ſacrificial preſent.

304. ' A ſixth part of *the reward for* virtuous ' deeds, performed by the whole people, belongs ' to the king, who protects them ; but, if he ' protect them not, a ſixth part of their iniquity ' lights on him :

305. ' Of *the reward for* what every ſubject ' reads in the *Véda*, for what he ſacrifices, for ' what he gives in charity, for what he performs ' in worſhip, the king juſtly takes a ſixth part in ' conſequence of protection.

306. ' A king, who acts with juſtice in defend- ' ing all creatures, and ſlays only thoſe who ought

' to

'to be ſlain, performs, *as it were*, each day a 'ſacrifice with a hundred thouſand gifts;

307 'But a king, who gives no ſuch protec-'tion, yet receives taxes in kind or in value, mar-'ket duties and tolls, the ſmall daily preſents for 'his houſehold, and fines for offences, falls directly, '*on his death*, to a region of horrour.

308. 'That king, who gives no protection, 'yet takes a ſixth part of the grain as his revenue, 'wiſe men have conſidered as a prince who draws 'to him the foulneſs of all his people.

309. 'Be it known, that a monarch who pays 'no regard to the ſcriptures, who denies a future 'ſtate, who acts with rapacity, who protects not 'his people, yet ſwallows up their poſſeſſions, 'will ſink low indeed *after death*.

310. 'WITH great care and by three methods 'let him reſtrain the unjuſt; by impriſonment, by 'confinement in fetters, and by various kinds of 'corporal puniſhment;

311. 'Since, by reſtraining the bad, and by 'encouraging the good, kings are perpetually 'made pure, as the twice born are purified by ſa-'crificing.

312. 'A KING who ſeeks benefit to his own 'ſoul, muſt always forgive parties litigant, chil-'dren, old men, and ſick perſons, who inveigh 'againſt him.

313. 'He, who forgives perſons in pain, when 'they abuſe him, ſhall, on that account, be exalted 'in heaven; but he, who excuſes them not, 'through the pride of dominion, ſhall for that 'reaſon ſink into hell.

314. 'The ſtealer *of gold from a prieſt* muſt run 'haſtily to the king, with looſened hair, pro-

'claiming the theft: *and adding*; "Thus have I 'sinned, punish me."

315. 'He must bear on his shoulder a pestle of 'stone, or a club of *c'hadira*-wood, or a javelin 'pointed at both ends, or an iron mace:

316. 'Whether the king strike him with it, or 'dismiss him unhurt, the thief is then absolved 'from the crime; but the king, if he punish him 'not, shall incur the guilt of the thief.

317. 'The killer of a priest, *or destroyer of an 'embryo*, casts his guilt on the *willing* eater of his 'provisions; an adulterous wife, on her *negligent* 'husband; a bad scholar and sacrificer, on their '*ignorant* preceptor; and a thief, on the *forgiving* 'prince.

318. 'But men who have committed offences, 'and have received from kings the punishment 'due to them, go pure to heaven, and become as 'clear as those who have done well.

319. 'He, who steals the rope or the water-pot 'from a well, and he, who breaks down a cistern, 'shall be fined a *másha* of gold; and that, *which 'he has taken or injured* he must restore to its 'former condition.

320. 'Corporal punishment shall be inflicted 'on him who steals more than ten *cumbhas* of 'grain, (a *cumbha* is twenty *drónas*, and a *dróna* 'two hundred *palas*:) for less he must be fined 'eleven times as much, and shall pay to the 'owner the amount of his property.

321. 'So shall corporal punishment be inflicted 'for stealing commodities usually sold by weight, 'or more than a hundred head of cattle, or gold, 'or silver, or costly apparel;

322. 'For stealing more than fifty *palas*, it is 'enacted

'enacted that a hand ſhall be amputated; for leſs, 'the king ſhall ſet a fine eleven times as much as 'the value.

323. 'For ſtealing men of high birth, and wo-'men above all, and the moſt precious gems, '*as diamonds or rubies*, the thief deſerves capital 'puniſhment.

324. 'For ſtealing large beaſts, weapons, or 'medicines, let the king inflict *adequate* puniſh-'ment, conſidering the time and the act.

325. 'For taking kine belonging to prieſts, and 'boring their noſtrils, or for ſtealing their other 'cattle, the offender ſhall inſtantly loſe half of 'one foot.

326. 'For ſtealing thread, raw-cotton, mate-'rials to make ſpirituous liquor, cow-dung, mo-'laſſes, curds, milk, butter-milk, water, or graſs,

327. 'Large canes, baſkets of canes, ſalt of 'every kind, earthen pots, clay or aſhes,

328. 'Fiſh, birds, oil, or clarified butter, 'fleſh-meat, honey, or any thing, *as leather, horn,* '*or ivory*, that came from a beaſt,

329. 'Or other things not precious, or ſpiri-'tuous liquors, rice dreſſed with clarified but-'ter, or other meſſes of boiled rice, the fine 'muſt be twice the value of the commodity 'ſtolen.

330. 'For ſtealing *as much as a man can carry* 'of flowers, green corn, ſhrubs, creepers, ſmall 'trees, or other vegetables, encloſed by a hedge, 'the fine ſhall be five *racticas* of gold or ſilver;

331. 'But for corn, pot-herbs, roots, and fruit, 'unencloſed by a fence, the fine is an hundred '*panas*, if there be no ſort of relation *between the* '*taker and the owner*; or half a hundred if there 'be ſuch relation.

332. 'If the taking be violent, and in the sight 'of the owner, it is robbery; if privately in his 'absence, it is only theft, and *it is considered as* '*theft*, when a man, having received any thing, 'refuses to give it back.

333. 'On him who steals the before-mentioned 'things, when they are prepared for use, let the 'king set the lowest amercement *of the three*; 'and *the same* on him who steals only fire from 'the temple.

334. 'With whatever limb a thief commits 'the offence by any means in this world, *as if* '*he break a wall with his hand or his foot*, even 'that limb shall the king amputate for the pre-'vention of a similar crime.

335. 'Neither a father, nor a preceptor, nor 'a friend, nor a mother, nor a wife, nor a son, 'nor a domestick priest, must be left unpunished 'by the king, if they adhere not with firmness to 'their duty.

336. 'Where another man of lower birth 'would be fined one *pana*, the king shall be fined 'a thousand, *and he shall give the fine to the* '*priests, or cast it into the river*: this is a sacred 'rule.

337. 'But the fine of a *Súdra* for theft shall 'be eight-fold; that of a *Vaisya*, sixteen-fold; 'that of a *Cshatriya*, two and thirty-fold.

338. 'That of a *Bráhmen*, four and sixty-fold; 'or a hundred-fold complete, or even twice four 'and sixty-fold; each of them knowing the na-'ture of his offence.

339. 'The taking of roots and fruit from a 'large tree, *in a field or a forest* unenclosed, or of 'wood for a sacrificial fire, or of grass to be eaten 'by cows, Menu has pronounced no theft.

340. 'A

340. 'A PRIEST who willingly receives any 'thing, either for ſacrificing or for inſtructing, 'from the hand of a man who had taken what 'the owner had not given, ſhall be *puniſhed* even 'as the thief.

341. 'A twice born man who is travelling, 'and whoſe proviſions are ſcanty, ſhall not be 'fined for taking only two ſugar canes, or two 'eſculent roots, from the field of another man.

342. 'He who ties the unbound, or looſes 'the bound *cattle of another*, and he who takes a 'ſlave, a horſe, or a carriage *without permiſſion*, 'ſhall be puniſhed as for theft.

343. 'A king, who by *enforcing* theſe laws 'reſtrains men from committing theft, acquires 'in this world fame, and in the next beatitude.

344. 'LET not the king who ardently de-'ſires a ſeat with INDRA, and wiſhes for glory, 'which nothing can change or diminiſh, endure 'for a moment the man who has committed 'atrocious violence, as by robbery, arſon, or 'homicide.

345. 'He who commits great violence, muſt 'be conſidered as a more grievous offender than 'a defamer, a thief, or a ſtriker with a ſtaff:

346. 'That king who endures a man convict-'ed of ſuch atrocity, quickly goes to perdition, 'and incurs publick hate.

347. 'Neither on account of friendſhip, nor 'for the ſake of great lucre, ſhall the king diſmiſs 'the perpetrators of violent acts, who ſpread 'terrour among all creatures.

348. 'THE twice born may take arms when 'their duty is obſtructed by force; and when in 'ſome evil time a diſaſter has befallen the twice-'born claſſes;

349. 'And

349. 'And in their own defence; and in a 'war for just cause; and in defence of a woman 'or a priest; he who kills justly, commits no 'crime.

350. 'Let a man without hesitation slay ano-'ther, *if he cannot otherwise escape*, who assails him 'with intent to murder, whether young or old, 'or his preceptor, or a *Bráhmen* deeply versed in 'the scripture.

351. 'By killing an assassin, who attempts to 'kill, whether in public or in private, no crime 'is committed by the slayer: fury recoils upon 'fury.

352. 'Men who commit overt-acts of adul-'terous inclinations for the wives of others, let 'the king banish from his realm, having pu-'nished them with such bodily marks as excite 'aversion;

353. 'Since adultery causes, to the general 'ruin, a mixture of classes among men: thence 'arises violation of duties; and thence is the root 'of felicity quite destroyed.

354. 'A man before noted for such an offence, 'who converses in secret with the wife of ano-'ther, shall pay the first of the three usual amerce-'ments;

355. 'But a man, not before noted, who thus 'converses with her for some reasonable cause, 'shall pay no fine; since in him there is no 'transgression.

356. 'He, who talks with the wife of another 'man at a place of pilgrimage, in a forest or a 'grove, or at the confluence of rivers, incurs the 'guilt of an adulterous inclination:

357. 'To send her flowers or perfumes, to 'sport and jest with her, to touch her apparel and 'ornaments,

'ornaments, to ſit with her on the ſame couch, 'are held adulterous acts on his part;

358. 'To touch a married woman on *her* '*breaſts or* any *other* place, which ought not to be 'touched, or, being touched unbecomingly by 'her, to bear it complacently, are adulterous acts 'with mutual aſſent.

359. 'A man of the ſervile claſs, who com- 'mits actual adultery with the wife of a prieſt, 'ought to ſuffer death: the wives, indeed, of all 'the four claſſes muſt ever be moſt eſpecially 'guarded.

360. 'Mendicants, encomiaſts, men prepared 'for a ſacrifice, and *cooks and other* artiſans, are 'not prohibited from ſpeaking to married women.

361. 'Let no man converſe, after he has been 'forbidden, with the wives of others: he, who 'thus converſes, *after a huſband or father has* for- 'bidden *him*, ſhall pay a fine of one *ſuverna*.

362. 'Theſe laws relate not to the wives of 'publick dancers or ſingers, or of ſuch baſe men 'as live by intrigues of their wives; men, who 'either carry women to others, or, lying con- 'cealed at home, permit them to hold a culpable 'intercourſe:

363. 'Yet he, who has a private connexion with 'ſuch women, or with ſervant-girls kept by one 'maſter, or with female anchorets *of an heretical* '*religion*, ſhall be compelled to pay a ſmall fine.

364. 'He, who vitiates a damſel without her 'conſent, ſhall ſuffer corporal puniſhment in- 'ſtantly; but he, who enjoys a willing damſel, 'ſhall not be corporally puniſhed, if his claſs be 'the ſame with hers.

365. 'From a girl, who makes advances to

'a man

'a man of a high claſs, let not the king take the 'ſmalleſt fine; but her, who firſt addreſſes a low 'man, let him conſtrain to live in her houſe 'well guarded.

366. 'A low man, who makes love to a dam-'ſel of high birth, ought to be puniſhed corpo-'rally; but he who addreſſes a maid of equal 'rank, ſhall give the nuptial preſent *and marry* '*her*, if her father pleaſe.

367. 'Of the man, who through inſolence 'forcibly contaminates a damſel, let the king in-'ſtantly order two fingers to be amputated, and 'condemn him to pay a fine of ſix hundred '*panas*:

368. 'A man of equal rank, who defiles a con-'ſenting damſel, ſhall not have his fingers am-'putated, but ſhall pay a fine of two hundred '*panas*, to reſtrain him from a repetition of his 'offence.

369. 'A damſel polluting another damſel, muſt 'be fined two hundred *panas*, pay the double 'value of her nuptial preſent, and receive ten 'laſhes with a whip;

370. 'But a woman, polluting a damſel, ſhall 'have her head inſtantly ſhaved, and two of her 'fingers chopped off; and ſhall ride, mounted on 'an aſs, *through the publick ſtreet*.

371. 'Should a wife, proud of her family 'and the great qualities of her kinſmen, actually 'violate the duty which ſhe owes to her lord, 'let the king condemn her to be devoured by 'dogs in a place much frequented;

372. 'And let him place the adulterer on an 'iron bed well heated, under which the execu-'tioners ſhall throw logs continually, till the 'ſinful wretch be there burned *to death*.

373. 'Of

373. ‘ Of a man once convicted, and a year after guilty *of the ſame crime*, the fine muſt be doubled: *ſo it muſt* if he be connected with the daughter of an outcaſt or with a *Chándálí* woman.

374. ‘ A mechanick or ſervile man, having an adulterous connexion with a woman of a twice born claſs, whether guarded at home or unguarded, *ſhall thus be puniſhed*; if ſhe was unguarded, *he* ſhall loſe the part *offending*, and his whole ſubſtance; if guarded, *and a prieſteſs*, every thing, *even his life*.

375. ‘ *For adultery with a guarded prieſteſs*, a merchant ſhall forfeit all his wealth after impriſonment for a year; a ſoldier ſhall be fined a thouſand *panas*, and be ſhaved with *the* urine *of an aſs*:

376. ‘ But, if a merchant or a ſoldier commit adultery with a woman of the ſacerdotal claſs, whom her huſband guards not at home, the king ſhall only fine the merchant five hundred, and the ſoldier a thouſand:

377. ‘ Both of them, however, if they commit that offence with a prieſteſs *not only* guarded, *but eminent for good qualities*, ſhall be puniſhed like men of the ſervile claſs, or be burned in a fire of dry graſs or reeds.

378. ‘ A *Bráhmen*, who carnally knows a guarded woman without her free will, muſt be fined a thouſand *panas*, but only five hundred if he knew her with her free conſent.

379. ‘ Ignominious tonſure is ordained, inſtead of capital puniſhment, for an adulterer of the prieſtly claſs, where the puniſhment of other claſſes may extend to loſs of life.

380. ‘ Never

380. 'Never ſhall the king ſlay a *Bráhmen* 'though convicted of all poſſible crimes: let him 'baniſh the offender from his realm, but with all 'his property ſecure, and his body unhurt:

381. 'No greater crime is known on earth 'than ſlaying a *Bráhmen*; and the king, therefore, 'muſt not even form in his mind an idea of kill'ing a prieſt.

382. 'If a merchant converſe criminally with 'a guarded woman of the military, or a ſoldier 'with one of the mercantile claſs, they both de'ſerve the ſame puniſhment as in the caſe of a 'prieſteſs unguarded:

383. 'But a *Bráhmen*, who ſhall commit adul'tery with a guarded woman of thoſe two claſſes, 'muſt be fined a thouſand *panas*; and, for the 'like offence with a guarded woman of the ſervile 'claſs, the fine of a ſoldier or a merchant ſhall 'alſo be one thouſand.'

384. 'For adultery with a woman of the mi'litary claſs, if unguarded, the fine of a merchant 'is five hundred; but a ſoldier, *for the converſe of* '*that offence*, muſt be ſhaved with urine, or pay 'the fine *juſt mentioned*.

385. 'A prieſt ſhall pay five hundred *panas* if 'he connect himſelf criminally with an unguarded 'woman of the military, commercial, or ſervile 'claſs; and a thouſand *for ſuch a connexion with* a 'woman of vile *mixed* breed.

386. 'That king, in whoſe realm lives no 'thief, no adulterer, no defamer, no man guilty 'of atrocious violence, and no committer of aſ'ſaults, attains the manſion of Sacra.

387. 'By ſuppreſſing thoſe five in his dominion, 'he gains royalty paramount over men of the

'ſame

'same kingly rank, and spreads his fame through 'the world.

388. 'THE sacrificer who forsakes the officiating priest, and the officiating priest who abandons the sacrificer, each being able to do his 'work, and guilty of no grievous offence, must 'each be fined a hundred *panas*.

389. 'A mother, a father, a wife, and a son, 'shall not be forsaken: he, who forsakes either of 'them, unless guilty of a deadly sin, shall pay 'six hundred *panas* as a fine to the king.

390. 'LET not a prince, who seeks the good 'of his own soul, *hastily and alone* pronounce the 'law, on a dispute concerning any legal observance, among twice born men in their several 'orders;

391. '*But* let him, after giving them due honour according to their merit, and, at first, having soothed them by mildness, apprise them of 'their duty with the assistance of *Bráhmens*.

392. 'THE priest who gives an entertainment 'to twenty men of the three first classes, without 'inviting his next neighbour, and his neighbour 'next but one, if both be worthy of an invitation, 'shall be fined one *másha* of silver.

393. 'A *Bráhmen* of deep learning in the *Véda* 'who invites not another *Bráhmen*, both learned 'and virtuous, to an entertainment *given on some* '*occasion* relating to his wealth, *as the marriage of* '*his child, and the like*, shall be made to pay him 'twice the value of the repast, and be fined a '*másha* of gold.

394. 'NEITHER a blind man, nor an idiot, nor 'a cripple, nor a man full seventy years old, nor 'one who confers great benefits on priests of emi-

'nent learning, ſhall be compelled by any *king* to 'pay taxes.

395. 'Let the king always do honour to a 'learned theologian, to a man either ſick or 'grieved, to a little child, to an aged or indigent 'man, to a man of exalted birth, and to a man of 'diſtinguiſhed virtue.

396. 'LET a waſherman waſh *the* clothes *of his* '*employers* by little and little, *or piece by piece, and* '*not haſtily*, on a ſmooth board of *Sálmali*-wood: 'let him never mix *the* clothes *of one perſon* with '*the* clothes *of another*, nor ſuffer any *but the owner* 'to wear them.

397. 'LET a weaver who has received ten '*palas* of cotton thread, give them back increaſed 'to eleven *by the rice water and the like uſed in* '*weaving*: he who does otherwiſe, ſhall pay a 'fine of twelve *panas*.

398. 'As men verſed in caſes of tolls, and ac-'quainted with all marketable commodities, ſhall 'eſtabliſh the price of ſaleable things, let the king 'take a twentieth part of *the profit on ſales at* that 'price.

399. 'Of the trader, who, through avarice, 'exports commodities, of which the king juſtly 'claims the pre-emption, or on which he has 'laid an embargo, let the ſovereign confiſcate the 'whole property.

400. 'Any ſeller or buyer, who *fraudulently* 'paſſes by the toll office at *night*, *or* any *other* im-'proper time, or who makes a falſe enumeration '*of the articles bought*, ſhall be fined eight times 'as much as their value.

401. 'Let the king eſtabliſh rules for the ſale 'and purchaſe of all marketable things, having 'duly conſidered whence they come, *if imported*;

'and,

'and, *if exported*, whither they muſt be ſent; 'how long they have been kept; what may be 'gained by them; and what has been expended 'on them.

402. 'Once in five nights, or at the cloſe of 'every half month, *according to the nature of the 'commodities*, let the king make a regulation for 'market prices in the preſence of thoſe *experi-'enced men*:

403. 'Let all weights and meaſures be well 'aſcertained by him; and once in ſix months let 'him re-examine them.

404. 'The toll at a ferry is one *pana* for an 'empty cart; half a *pana*, for a man with a load; 'a quarter, for a beaſt uſed in agriculture, or for 'a woman; and an eighth, for an unloaded man.

405. 'Waggons filled with goods packed up, 'ſhall pay toll in proportion to their value; but 'for empty veſſels and bags, and for *poor* men ill-'apparelled, a very ſmall toll ſhall be demanded.

406. 'For a long paſſage, the freight muſt be 'proportioned to places and times; but this 'muſt be underſtood of paſſages up and down 'rivers: at ſea there can be no ſettled freight.

407. 'A woman, who has been two months 'pregnant, a religious beggar, a foreſter in the 'third order, and *Bráhmens*, *who are* ſtudents in 'theology, ſhall not be obliged to pay toll for 'their paſſage.

408. 'Whatever ſhall be broken in a boat, by 'the fault of the boatmen, ſhall be made good by 'thoſe men collectively, each paying his portion.

409. 'This rule, ordained for ſuch as paſs 'rivers in boats, relates to the culpable neglect of 'boatmen on the water: in the caſe of inevitable 'accident, there can be no damages recovered.

410. 'The king should order each man of the 'mercantile class to practise trade, or money- 'lending, or agriculture and attendance on cattle; 'and each man of the servile class to act in the 'service of the twice born.

411. 'Both him of the military, and him of the 'commercial class, if distressed for a livelihood, 'let some wealthy *Bráhmen* support, obliging them 'without harshness to discharge their several duties.

412. 'A *Bráhmen*, who, by his power and 'through avarice, shall cause twice born men, 'girt with the sacrificial thread, to perform ser- 'vile acts, *such as washing his feet*, without their 'consent, shall be fined by the king six hundred '*panas*;

413. 'But a man of the servile class whether 'bought or unbought, he may compel to perform 'servile duty; because such a man was created 'by the Self-existent for the purpose of serving '*Bráhmens*:

414. 'A *Súdra*, though emancipated by his 'master, is not released from a state of servitude; 'for of a state which is natural to him, by whom 'can he be divested?

415. 'There are servants of seven sorts; one 'made captive under a standard *or in battle*, one 'maintained in consideration of service, one born 'of a female slave in the house, one sold, or 'given, or inherited from ancestors, and one en- 'slaved by way of punishment *on his inability to* '*pay a large fine*.

416. 'Three persons, a wife, a son, and a slave, 'are declared by law to have *in general* no wealth 'exclusively their own: the wealth, which they 'may earn, is *regularly* acquired for the man to 'whom they belong.

417. 'A

417. ‘ A *Bráhmen* may ſeize without heſitation, ‘ *if he be diſtreſſed for a ſubſiſtence*, the goods of his ‘ *Súdra* ſlave; for as that ſlave can have no pro- ‘ perty, his maſter may take his goods.

418. ‘ With vigilant care ſhould the king ex- ‘ ert himſelf in compelling merchants and mecha- ‘ nicks to perform their reſpective duties; for ‘ when ſuch men ſwerve from their duty, they ‘ throw this world into confuſion.

419. ‘ Day by day muſt the king, *though en-* ‘ *gaged in forenſick buſineſs*, conſider the great ob- ‘ jects of publick meaſures, and inquire into the ‘ ſtate of his carriages, *elephants, horſes, and cars*, his ‘ conſtant revenues and neceſſary expences, his ‘ mines *of precious metals or gems*, and his treaſury:

420. ‘ Thus, bringing to a concluſion all theſe ‘ weighty affairs, and removing *from his realm and* ‘ *from himſelf* every taint of ſin, a king reaches the ‘ ſupreme path of beatitude.’

CHAPTER THE NINTH.

On the ſame; and on the Commercial and Servile Claſſes.

1. ‘ I NOW will propound the immemorial ‘ duties of man and woman, who muſt both re‘ main firm in the legal path, whether united or ‘ ſeparated.

2. ‘ Day and night muſt women be held by ‘ their protectors in a ſtate of dependence; but ‘ in *lawful and innocent* recreations, though rather ‘ addicted to them, they may be left at their own ‘ diſpoſal.

3. ‘ Their fathers protect them in child-hood; ‘ their huſbands protect them in youth; their ‘ ſons protect them in age: a woman is never fit ‘ for independence.

4. ‘ Reprehenſible is the father, who gives not ‘ his daughter in marriage at the proper time; ‘ and the huſband, who approaches not his wife ‘ in due ſeaſon; reprehenſible alſo is the ſon, ‘ who protects not his mother after the death of ‘ her lord.

5. ‘ Women muſt, above all, be reſtrained from ‘ the ſmalleſt illicit gratification; for, not being

'thus reſtrained, they bring ſorrow on both fa-
'milies:

6. 'Let huſbands conſider this as the ſupreme 'law, ordained for all claſſes; and let them, 'how weak ſoever, diligently keep their wives 'under lawful reſtrictions;

7. 'For he who preſerves his wife *from vice*, 'preſerves his offspring *from ſuſpicion of baſtardy*, 'his ancient uſages *from neglect*, his family *from* '*diſgrace*, himſelf *from anguiſh*, and his duty *from* '*violation*.

8. 'The huſband, after conception by his wife, 'becomes himſelf an embryo, and is born a 'ſecond time here below; for which reaſon the 'wife is called *jáyá*, ſince by her *(jáyaté)* he is 'born again:

9. 'Now the wife brings forth a ſon endued 'with ſimilar qualities to thoſe of the father; 'ſo that with a view to an excellent offspring, 'he muſt vigilantly guard his wife.

10. 'No man, indeed, can wholly reſtrain 'women by violent meaſures; but, by theſe 'expedients, they may be reſtrained:

11. 'Let the huſband keep his wife employed in 'the collection and expenditure of wealth, in puri- 'fication and female duty, in the preparation of 'daily food, and the ſuper-intendence of houſe- 'hold utenſils.

12. 'By confinement at home, even under 'affectionate and obſervant guardians, they are 'not ſecure; but thoſe women are truly ſecure, 'who are guarded by their own good inclina- 'tions.

13. 'Drinking *ſpirituous liquor*, aſſociating with 'evil perſons, abſence from her huſband, ram-

'bling

'bling abroad, unſeaſonable ſleep, and dwelling 'in the houſe of another, are ſix faults which 'bring infamy on a married woman:

14. 'Such *women* examine not beauty, nor pay 'attention to age; whether *their lover be* hand-'ſome or ugly, they think it is enough that he is 'a man, and purſue their pleaſures.

15. 'Through their paſſion for men, their 'mutable temper, their want of ſettled affection, 'and their perverſe nature, (let them be guarded 'in this world ever ſo well) they ſoon become 'alienated from their huſbands.

16. 'Yet ſhould their huſbands be diligently 'careful in guarding them; though they well 'know the diſpoſition with which the lord of 'creation formed them:

17. 'MENU allotted to ſuch women a love 'of their bed, of their ſeat, and of ornament, 'impure appetites, wrath, weak flexibility, deſire 'of miſchief, and bad conduct.

18. 'Women have no buſineſs with the texts 'of the *Véda*; thus is the law fully ſettled: 'having therefore no evidence *of law*, and no '*knowledge of* expiatory texts, ſinful women muſt 'be as foul as falſehood itſelf; and this is a fixed 'rule.

19. 'To this effect, many texts, which may 'ſhow their true diſpoſition, are chanted in the '*Védas*: hear now their expiation for ſin.

20. "That pure blood, which my mother "defileth by adulterous deſire, frequenting the "houſes of other men, and violating her duty "to her lord, that blood may my father purify!" 'Such is the tenour of the holy text, *which her 'ſon, who knows her guilt, muſt pronounce for her*;

21. ' *And* this expiation has been declared for ' every unbecoming thought, which enters her ' mind, concerning infidelity to her husband, ' since that is *the beginning of* adultery.

22. ' Whatever be the qualities of the man ' with whom a woman is united by lawful mar- ' riage, such qualities even she assumes; like a ' river *united* with the sea.

23. ' ACSHAMA'LA', a woman of the lowest ' birth, being thus united to VASISHT'HA, and ' SA'RANGÍ, being united to MANDAPA'LA, were ' entitled to very high honour:

24. ' These and other females of low birth, ' have attained eminence in this world by the ' respective good qualities of their lords,

25. ' Thus has the law, ever pure, been pro- ' pounded for the civil conduct of men and wo- ' men: hear next the laws concerning children, ' by obedience to which may happiness be at- ' tained in this and the future life.

26. ' WHEN good women united with husbands ' in expectation of progeny, eminently fortunate ' and worthy of reverence, irradiate the houses ' of their lords, between them, and goddesses of ' abundance, there is no diversity whatever.

27. ' The production of children, the nurture ' of them when produced, and the daily super- ' intendence of domestick affairs are peculiar to ' the wife:

28. ' From the wife alone proceed offspring, ' good household management, solicitous atten- ' tion, most exquisite caresses, and that heavenly ' beatitude which she obtains for the manes of ' ancestors, and for *the husband* himself.

29. ' She who deserts not her lord, but keeps ' in

'in ſubjection to him her heart, her ſpeech, and 'her body, ſhall attain his manſion in heaven; and, 'by the virtuous in this world, be called *Sádhwì, 'or good and faithful*;

30. 'But a wife, by diſloyalty to her huſ'band, ſhall incur diſgrace in this life, and be 'born *in the next* from the womb of a ſhakal, or 'be tormented with horrible diſeaſes, which pu'niſh vice

31. 'LEARN now that excellent law, univer'ſally ſalutary, which was declared concerning 'iſſue, by great and good ſages, formerly born.

32. 'They conſider the male iſſue of a woman 'as the ſon of the lord; but, on the ſubject of 'that lord, a difference of opinion is mentioned 'in the *Véda*; ſome giving that name to the real 'procreator of the child, and others applying it 'to the married poſſeſſor of the woman.

33. 'The woman is conſidered in law as the 'field, and the man as the grain: now vegetable 'bodies are formed by the united operation of the 'ſeed and the field.

34. 'In ſome caſes the prolifick power of the 'male is chiefly diſtinguiſhed; in others, the re'ceptacle of the female; but, when both are 'equal in dignity, the offspring is moſt highly 'eſteemed:

35. 'In general, as between the male and fe'male powers of procreation, the male is held 'ſuperiour; ſince the offspring of all procreant 'beings is diſtinguiſhed by marks of the male 'power.

36. 'Whatever be the quality of ſeed, ſcattered 'in a field prepared in due ſeaſon, a plant of the 'ſame quality ſprings in that field, with peculiar 'viſible properties.

37. 'Certainly

37. 'Certainly this earth is called the primeval 'womb of many beings; but the feed exhibits 'not in its vegetation any properties of the womb.

38. 'On earth here below, even in the fame 'ploughed field, feeds of many different forms, 'having been fown by hufbandmen in the proper 'feafon, vegetate according to their nature:

39. 'Rice plants, mature in fixty days, and 'thofe which require tranfplantation, *mudga, tila,* '*máſha*, barley, leaks, and fugar-canes, all fpring 'up according to the feeds.

40. 'That one plant fhould be fown, and ano-'ther produced cannot happen: whatever feed 'may be fown, even that produces its proper ftem.

41. 'Never muft it be fown in another man's 'field by him, who has natural good fenfe, who 'has been well inftructed, who knows the *Véda* 'and its *Angas*, who defires long life:

42. 'They who are acquainted with paftimes, 'have preferved, on this fubject, holy ftrains 'chanted by every breeze, *declaring*, that "feed "muft not be fown in the field of another man."

43. 'As the arrow of that hunter is vain, who 'fhoots it into the wound which another had made 'juft before in the antelope, thus inftantly pe-'rifhes the feed which a man throws into the 'foil of another:

44. 'Sages, who know former times, confider 'this earth *(Prĭt'hivì)* as the wife of king PRĬTHU; 'and thus they pronounce cultivated land to be 'the property of him who cut away the wood, *or* '*who cleared and tilled it*; and the antelope, of the 'firft hunter, who mortally wounded it.

45. 'Then only is a man perfect, when he 'confifts of *three perfons united*, his wife, himfelf, 'and his fon; and thus have learned *Bráhmens*

'announced

'announced this *maxim*: "The huſband is even "one perſon with his wife," *for all domeſtick and religious, not for all civil purpoſes.*

46. 'Neither by ſale nor deſertion can a wife be 'releaſed from her huſband: thus we fully ac-'knowledge the law enacted of old by the Lord 'of creatures.

47. 'Once is the partition of an inheritance 'made; once is a damſel given in marriage; and 'once does a man ſay "I give:" theſe three 'are, by good men, done once for all *and ir-revocably.*

48. 'As with cows, mares, female camels, 'ſlave-girls, milch buffalos, ſhe goats, and 'ewes, it is not the owner of the *bull, or other* 'father, who owns the offspring, even thus is it 'with the wives of others.

49. 'They who have no property in the field, 'but having grain in their poſſeſſion, ſow it in ſoil 'owned by another, can receive no advantage 'whatever from the corn, which may be pro-'duced:

50. 'Should a bull beget a hundred calves on 'cows not owned by his maſter, thoſe calves be-'long ſolely to the proprietors of the cows; and 'the ſtrength of the bull was waſted:

51. 'Thus men, who have no marital pro-'perty in women, but ſow in the fields owned 'by others, may raiſe up fruit to the huſbands; 'but the procreator can have no advantage 'from it.

52. 'Unleſs there be a ſpecial agreement be-'tween the owners of the land and of the ſeed, 'the fruit belongs clearly to the land-owner, for 'the receptacle is more important than the ſeed:

'53. 'But

53. ‘ But the owners of the seed and of the soil ‘ may be considered in this world as joint owners ‘ of the crop, which they agree, by special com- ‘ pact in consideration of the seed, to divide ‘ between them.

54. ‘ Whatever man owns a field, if seed, con- ‘ veyed into it by water or wind, should germinate, ‘ the plant belongs to the land-owner: the mere ‘ sower takes not the fruit.

55. ‘ Such is the law concerning the offspring ‘ of cows, and mares, of female camels, goats, ‘ and sheep, of slave girls, hens, and milch buf- ‘ falos, *unless there be a special agreement.*

56. ‘ Thus has the comparative importance of ‘ the soil and the seed been declared to you; I will ‘ next propound the law concerning women, who ‘ have no issue *by their husbands.*

57. ‘ The wife of an elder brother is considered ‘ as mother-in-law to the younger; and the wife ‘ of the younger as daughter-in-law to the elder:

58. ‘ The elder brother, amorously approach- ‘ ing the wife of the younger, and the younger, ‘ caressing the wife of the elder, are both degraded, ‘ even though authorized *by the husband or spiritual* ‘ *guide*, except when such wife has no issue.

59. ‘ On failure of issue by the husband, *if he* ‘ *be of the servile class*, the desired offspring may be ‘ procreated, either by his brother or some other ‘ *sapinda*, on the wife, who has been duly au- ‘ thorized:

60. ‘ Sprinkled with clarified butter, silent in ‘ the night, let the kinsman thus appointed beget ‘ one son, but a second by no means, on the ‘ widow *or childless wife:*

61. ‘ Some sages, learned in the laws concern- ‘ ing

'ing women, thinking it poſſible, that the great 'object of that appointment may not be obtained '*by the birth of a ſingle ſon*, are of opinion, that the 'wife and appointed kinſman may legally pro- 'create a ſecond.

62. 'The firſt object of the appointment being 'attained according to law, both *the brother and* '*the widow* muſt live together like a father and a 'daughter by affinity.

63. 'Either brother, appointed for this pur- 'poſe, who deviates from the ſtrict rule, and acts 'from carnal deſire, ſhall be degraded, as having 'defiled the bed of his daughter-in-law or of his 'father.

64. 'By men of twice born claſſes no widow, '*or childleſs wife*, muſt be authorized to conceive 'by any other than her lord, for they, who au- 'thorize her to conceive by any other, violate the 'primeval law.

65. 'Such a commiſſion *to a brother or other* '*near kinſman* is no where mentioned in the nuptial 'texts of the *Véda*; nor is the marriage of a 'widow even named in the laws concerning 'marriage.

66. 'This practice, fit only for cattle, is repre- 'hended by learned *Bráhmens*; yet it is declared 'to have been the practice even of men, while 'VE'NA had ſovereign power:

67. 'He, poſſeſſing the whole earth, and *thence* '*only called* the chief of ſage monarchs, gave riſe 'to a confuſion of claſſes, when his intellect be- 'came weak through luſt.

68. 'Since his time the virtuous diſapprove of 'that man, who, through deluſion of mind, di- 'rects a widow *to receive the careſſes of another* for 'the ſake of progeny.

69. The

69. 'The damſel, *indeed,* whoſe huſband ſhall 'die after troth verbally plighted, *but before con-'ſummation,* his brother ſhall take in marriage ac-'cording to this rule:

70. 'Having eſpouſed her in due form of law, 'ſhe being clad in a white robe, and pure in her 'moral conduct, let him approach her once in 'each proper ſeaſon, and until iſſue *be had.*

71. 'Let no man of ſenſe, who has once 'given his daughter to a ſuitor, give her again to 'another; for he, who gives away his daughter, 'whom he had before given, incurs the guilt and 'fine of ſpeaking falſely in a cauſe concerning 'mankind.

72. 'Even though a man have married a 'young woman in legal form, yet he may aban-'don her, if he find her blemiſhed, afflicted with 'diſeaſe, or previouſly deflowered, and given to 'him with fraud:

73. 'If any man give a faulty damſel in 'marriage, without diſcloſing her blemiſh, the 'huſband may annul that act of her ill-minded 'giver.

74. 'Should a man have buſineſs abroad, let 'him aſſure a fit maintenance to his wife, and 'then reſide *for a time* in a foreign country; ſince 'a wife, even though virtuous, may be tempted 'to act amiſs, if ſhe be diſtreſſed by want of 'ſubſiſtence:

75. 'While her huſband, having ſettled her 'maintenance, reſides abroad, let her continue 'firm in religious auſterities; but, if he leave her 'no ſupport, let her ſubſiſt by *ſpinning and other* 'blameleſs arts.

76. 'If he live abroad on account of ſome

' sacred duty, let her wait for him eight years; ' if on account of knowledge or fame, six; if on ' account of pleasure, three: *after those terms have* ' *expired she must follow him.*

77. ' For a whole year let a husband bear with ' his wife, who treats him with aversion; but, ' after a year, let him deprive her of her separate ' property, and cease to cohabit with her.

78. ' She, who neglects her lord, though ' addicted to gaming, fond of spirituous liquors, ' or diseased, must be deserted for three months, ' and deprived of her ornaments and household ' furniture:

79. ' But she who is averse from a mad hus-' band, or a deadly sinner, or an eunuch, or one ' without manly strength, or one afflicted with ' such maladies as punish crimes, must neither ' be deserted nor stripped of her property.

80. ' A wife, who drinks any spirituous li-' quors, who acts immorally, who shows hatred ' *to her lord,* who is *incurably* diseased, who is mis-' chievous, who wastes his property, may at all ' times be superseded by another wife.

81. ' A barren wife may be superseded by ano-' ther in the eighth year: she, whose children are ' all dead, in the tenth; she, who brings forth *only* ' daughters, in the eleventh; she, who speaks ' unkindly, without delay;

82. ' But she, who, though afflicted with ill-' ness, is beloved and virtuous, must never be ' disgraced, though she may be superseded by ' another wife with her own consent.

83. ' If a wife, legally superseded, shall depart ' in wrath from the house, she must either in-' stantly be confined, or abandoned in the pre-' sence of the whole family:

84. ' But

84. ‘ But ſhe, who having been forbidden, ‘ addicts herſelf to intoxicating liquor even at ‘ jubilees, or mixes in crowds at theatres, muſt be ‘ fined ſix *ractica's* of gold.

85. ‘ When twice born men take wives, both ‘ of their own claſs and others, the precedence, ‘ honour and habitation of thoſe wives, muſt be ‘ ſettled according to the order of their claſſes :

86. ‘ To all ſuch married men, the wives of ‘ the ſame claſs only (not wives of a different ‘ claſs by any means) muſt perform the duty of ‘ perſonal attendance, and the daily buſineſs re- ‘ lating to acts of religion ;

87. ‘ For he who fooliſhly cauſes thoſe duties ‘ to be performed by any other than his wife of ‘ the ſame claſs, when ſhe is near at hand, has ‘ been immemorially conſidered as a mere *Chán-* ‘ *dala* begotten on a *Bráhmenì.*

88. ‘ To an excellent and handſome youth of ‘ the ſame claſs, let every man give his daughter ‘ in marriage, according to law ; even though ‘ ſhe have not attained her age *of eight years* :

89. ‘ *But* it is better that the damſel, though ‘ marriageable, ſhould ſtay at home till her death, ‘ than that he ſhould ever give her in marriage ‘ to a bridegroom void of excellent qualities.

90. ‘ Three years let a damſel wait, though ‘ ſhe be marriageable ; but, after that term, let ‘ her chuſe for herſelf a bridegroom of equal ‘ rank :

91. ‘ If not being given in marriage, ſhe chuſe ‘ her bridegroom, neither ſhe, nor the youth ‘ choſen, commits any offence ;

92. ‘ But a damſel, thus electing her huſband, ‘ ſhall not carry with her the ornaments which

‘ ſhe

'she received from her father, nor those given 'by her mother, or brethren: if she carry 'them away she commits theft.

93. 'He who takes to wife a damsel of full 'age, shall not give a nuptial present to her fa- 'ther; since the father lost his dominion over 'her, by detaining her at a time when she might 'have been a parent.

94. 'A man aged thirty years, may marry a 'girl of twelve, *if he find one* dear to his heart; 'or a man of twenty-four years a damsel of 'eight: but if *he finish his studentship earlier and* 'the duties *of his next order* would otherwise be 'impeded, let him marry immediately.

95. 'A wife given by the gods *who are named* '*in the bridal texts*, let the husband receive and 'support constantly, if she be virtuous, though he 'married her not from inclination: such conduct 'will please the gods.

96. 'To be mothers were women created; 'and to be fathers, men; religious rites therefore 'are ordained in the *Véda* to be performed *by the* '*husband* together with the wife.

97. 'If a nuptial gratuity has actually been 'given to a damsel, and he, who gave it should 'die *before marriage*, the damsel shall be married 'to his brother if she consent;

98. 'But even a man of the servile class ought 'not to receive a gratuity when he gives his 'daughter in marriage; since a father who 'takes a fee *on that occasion*, tacitly sells his 'daughter.

99. 'Neither ancients nor moderns who were 'good men, have ever given a damsel in mar- 'riage after she had been promised to another 'man;

100. ‘ Nor, even in former creations, have we ‘ heard *the virtuous approve* the tacit sale of a ‘ daughter for a price, under the name of a nuptial ‘ gratuity.

101. “ Let mutual fidelity continue till death:” ‘ this, in few words, may be considered as the su- ‘ preme law between husband and wife.

102. ‘ Let a man and woman, united by mar- ‘ riage, constantly beware, lest at any time dis- ‘ united, they violate their mutual fidelity.

103. ‘ Thus has been declared to you the law, ‘ abounding in the purest affection, for the con- ‘ duct of man and wife; together with the prac- ‘ tice of raising up offspring *to a husband of the* ‘ *servile class* on failure *of issue by him begotten:* ‘ learn now the law of inheritance.

104. ‘ After the death of the father and the ‘ mother, the brothers being assembled, may di- ‘ vide among themselves the paternal *and ma-* ‘ *ternal* estate; but they have no power over it, ‘ while their parents live, *unless the father chuse* ‘ *to distribute it.*

105. ‘ The eldest brother may take entire ‘ possession of the patrimony; and the others ‘ may live under him as *they lived* under their ‘ father, *unless they chuse to be separated.*

106. ‘ By the eldest, at the moment of his ‘ birth, the father having begotten a son, dis- ‘ charges his debt to his own progenitors; the ‘ eldest son, therefore, ought *before partition* to ‘ manage the whole patrimony:

107. ‘ That son alone, by whose birth he dis- ‘ charges his debt, and through whom he attains ‘ immortality, was begotten from a sense of duty: ‘ all the rest are considered by the wife as begotten ‘ from love of pleasure.

108. 'Let the father alone support his sons; 'and the first-born, his younger brothers, and let 'them behave to the eldest according to law, as 'children *should behave* to their father.

109. 'The first-born, *if virtuous*, exalts the 'family, or, *if vitious*, destroys it: the first-born 'is in this world the most respectable; and the 'good never treat him with disdain.

110. 'If an elder brother act as an elder 'brother ought, he is *to be revered* as a mother, 'as a father; and, even if he have not the be-'haviour of a good elder brother, he should be 'respected as a *maternal uncle, or other* kinsman.

111. 'Either let them thus live together, or, 'if they desire *separately to perform* religious rites, 'let them live apart; since religious duties are 'multiplied in separate houses, their separation is, 'therefore, legal *and even laudable.*

112. 'The portion deducted for the eldest is 'a twentieth part *of the heritage*, with the best of 'all the chattels; for the middlemost, half of that, '*or a fortieth*; for the youngest, a quarter of it, *or* '*an eightieth.*

113. 'The eldest and youngest respectively 'take their just mentioned portions; and if there 'be more than one between them, each of the 'intermediate sons has the mean portion, *or the* '*fortieth.*

114. 'Of all the goods collected let the first-'born, *if he be transcendently learned and virtuous*, 'take the best article, whatever is most excellent 'in its kind, and the best of ten *cows or the like*:

115. 'But among brothers equally skilled in 'performing their several duties, there is no de-'duction of the best in ten, *or the most excellent*

 chattel;

'*chattel*; though some trifle, as a mark of greater 'veneration, should be given to the first-born.

116. 'If a deduction be thus made, let equal 'shares of the residue be ascertained *and received*; 'but, if there be no deduction, the shares must 'be distributed in this manner:

117. 'Let the eldest have a double share, and 'the next born, a share and a half, *if they clearly* '*surpass the rest in virtue and learning*; the younger 'sons must have each a share: *if all be equal in* '*good qualities, they must all take share and share* '*alike.*

118. 'To the *unmarried* daughters *by the same* '*mother*, let their brothers give portions out of 'their own allotments respectively, *according to* '*the classes of their several mothers*: let each give 'a fourth part of his own distinct share; and 'they who refuse to give it shall be degraded.

119. 'Let them never divide *the value of* a 'single goat or sheep, or a single beast with 'uncloven hoofs: a single goat or sheep *remain-* '*ing after an equal distribution*, belongs to the first- 'born.

120. 'Should a younger brother, *in the manner* '*before mentioned*, have begotten a son on the wife 'of his *deceased* elder brother, the division must 'then be made equally *between that son who re-* '*presents the deceased, and his natural father*: thus 'is the law settled.

121. 'The representative is not *so far* wholly 'substituted by law in the place of the *deceased* 'principal, *as to have the portion of an elder son*; 'and the principal became a father in consequence 'of the procreation *by his younger brother*; the son, 'therefore, is entitled by law to an equal share, '*but not to a double portion.*

122. 'A

122. 'A younger ſon being born of a firſt married wife, after an elder ſon had been born of a wife laſt married, *but of a lower claſs*, it may be a doubt in that caſe, how the diviſion ſhall be made:

123. 'Let the ſon born of the elder wife, take one moſt excellent bull deducted from the inheritance; the next excellent bulls are for thoſe who *were born firſt, but* are inferior on account of their mothers *who were married laſt*.

124. 'A ſon, indeed, who was firſt born, and brought forth by the wife firſt married, may take, *if learned and virtuous*, one bull and fifteen cows; and the other ſons may then take, each in right of his ſeveral mother: ſuch is the fixed rule.

125. 'As between ſons, born of wives equal in their claſs, *and* without *any other* diſtinction, there can be no ſeniority in right of the mother; but the ſeniority ordained by law is according to the birth.

126. 'The right of invoking INDRA by the texts, called *ſwabráhmanyá*, depends on actual priority of birth; and of twins alſo, *if any ſuch be conceived* among *different* wives, the eldeſt is he, who was firſt actually born.

127. 'HE, who has no ſon, may appoint his daughter in this manner to raiſe up a ſon for him, *ſaying*, "the male child, who ſhall be born from her in wedlock, ſhall be mine for the purpoſe of performing my obſequies."

128. 'In this manner DACSHA himſelf, lord of created beings, anciently appointed all his *fifty* daughters to raiſe up ſons to him, for the ſake of multiplying his race:

129. 'He gave ten to DHERMA, thirteen to 'CASYAPA, twenty-seven to SÓMA king *of Bráhmens and medical plants,* after doing honour to 'them with an affectionate heart.

130. 'THE son of a man is even as himself; 'and as the son, such is the daughter *thus appointed:* how then, *if he have no son,* can any inherit his property, but a daughter who is closely 'united with his own soul?

131. 'Property, given to the mother on her 'marriage, is inherited by her *unmaried* daughter; 'and the son of a daughter, *appointed in the manner just mentioned,* shall inherit the whole estate of 'her father, who leaves no son *by himself begotten:*

132. 'The son, however, of *such* a daughter, 'who succeeds to all the wealth of her father 'dying without a son, must offer two funeral 'cakes, one to his own father, and one to the 'father of his mother.

133. 'Between a son's son and the son of *such* 'a daughter, there is no difference in law; since 'their father and their mother both sprang from 'the body of the same man:

134. 'But a daughter having been oppointed 'to produce a son forher father, and a son, *begotten by himself,* being afterwards born, the division of 'the heritage must in that case be equal; since 'there is no right of primogeniture for a woman.

135. 'Should a daughter, thus appointed to 'raise up a son for her father, die by any accident 'without a son, the husband of that daughter 'may, without hesitation, possess himself of her 'property.

136. 'By that male child, whom a daughter 'thus appointed, either by an implied intention

'or

'or a plain declaration, ſhall produce from an 'huſband of an equal claſs, the maternal grandfather becomes in law the father of a ſon: let 'that ſon give the funeral cake and poſſeſs the 'inheritance.

137. 'By a ſon, a man obtains victory over all 'people; by a ſon's ſon, he enjoys immortality; 'and, afterward, by the ſon of that granſdon, he 'reaches the ſolar abode.

138. 'Since the ſon *(tráyaté)* delivers his father 'from the hell named *put*, he was, therefore 'called *puttra* by BRAHMA' himſelf:

139. 'Now between the ſons of his ſon and of 'his daughter *thus appointed*, there ſubſiſts in this 'world no difference, for even the ſon of *ſuch* a 'daughter delivers him in the next, like the ſon 'of his ſon.

140. 'Let the ſon of ſuch a daughter offer the 'firſt funeral cake to his mother; the ſecond to her 'father; the third to her paternal grandfather.

141. 'OF the man, to whom a ſon has been 'given, *according to a ſubſequent law*, adorned 'with every virtue, that ſon ſhall take *a fifth or* '*ſixth part of* the heritage, though brought from 'a different family.

142. 'A given ſon muſt never claim the family 'and eſtate of his natural father: the funeral cake 'follows the family and eſtate; but of him who 'has given away his ſon, the funeral oblation is 'extinct.

143. 'THE ſon of a wife, not authorized to 'have iſſue by another, and the ſon begotten, by 'the brother of the huſband, on a wife who has 'a ſon then living, are both unworthy of the heritage; one being the child of an adulterer, and 'the other produced through mere luſt.

144. 'Even the ſon of a wife duly authorized, 'not begotten according to the law *already* '*propounded*, is unworthy of the paternal eſtate; 'for he was procreated by an outcaſt:

145. 'But the ſon *legally* begotten on a wife, au- 'thorized for the purpoſe *before mentioned*, may 'inherit *in all reſpects, if he be virtuous and learned*, 'as a ſon begotten by the huſband; ſince, *in that* '*caſe*, the ſeed and the produce belong of right to 'the owner of the field.

146 'He, who keeps the *fixed and moveable* 'eſtate of his *deceaſed* brother, maintains the 'widow, and raiſes up a ſon to that brother, muſt 'give that ſon, *at the age of fifteen*, the whole of 'his brother's *divided* property.

147. 'Should a wife, even though legally au- 'thorized, produce a ſon by the brother, or any 'other *ſapinda*, of her huſband, that ſon, if begot- 'ten with *amorous embraces, and tokens of* impure 'deſire, the ſages proclaim baſe-born and incapa- 'ble of inheriting.

1.8. 'This law, *which has preceded*, muſt be 'underſtood of a diſtribution among ſons begotten 'on women of the ſame claſs: hear now the 'law concerning *ſons by* ſeveral women of differ- 'ent claſſes.

149. 'If there be four wives of a *Bráhmen* in 'the direct order of the claſſes, and ſons are pro- 'duced by them all, this is the rule of partition '*among them*:

150. 'The chief ſervant in huſbandry, the bull 'kept for impregnating cows, the riding horſe or 'carriage, the *ring and other* ornaments, and the 'principal meſſuage, ſhall be deducted from the 'inheritance and given to the *Bráhmen*-ſon,

'together

'together with a larger ſhare by way of pre-'eminence.

151. 'Let the *Bráhmen* take three ſhares of the 'reſidue; the ſon of a *Cſhatriyá* wife, two ſhares; 'the ſon of the *Vaiſyá* wife, a ſhare and a half; 'and the ſon of the *Súdra* wife may take one ſhare.

152. 'Or, *if no deduction be made*, let ſome per-'ſon learned in the law divide the whole collected 'eſtate into ten parts, and make a legal diſtribu-'tion by this *following* rule:

153. 'Let the ſon of the *Bráhmanì* take four 'parts; the ſon of the *Cſhatriyá* three; let the 'ſon of the *Vaiſyá* have two parts; let the ſon of 'the *Súdra* take a ſingle part, *if he be virtuous.*

154. 'But whether the *Bráhmen* have ſons, or 'have no ſons, *by wives of the three firſt claſſes*, no 'more than a tenth part muſt be given to the ſon 'of a *Súdra*.

155. 'The ſon of a *Bráhmen*, a *Cſhatriya*, or a '*Vaiſya* by a woman of the ſervile claſs, ſhall 'inherit no part of the eſtate, *unleſs he be virtuous;* '*nor jointly with other ſons, unleſs his mother was* '*lawfully married*: whatever his father may give 'him, let that be his own.

156. 'All the ſons of twice born men, pro-'duced by wives of the ſame claſs, muſt divide 'the heritage equally, after the younger brothers 'have given the firſt-born his deducted allot-'ment.

157. 'For a *Súdra* is ordained a wife of his 'own claſs, *and* no other: all produced by her 'ſhall have equal ſhares, though ſhe have a hun-'dred ſons.

158. 'Of the twelve ſons of men, whom 'Menu, ſprung from the Self-exiſtent, has named,

'ſix

'six are kinsman and heirs; six not heirs, *except to* '*their own fathers*, but kinsmen.

159. 'The son begotten by a man himself *in* '*lawful wedlock*, the son of his wife begotten *in* '*the manner before described*, a son given *to him*, 'a son made *or adopted*, a son of concealed birth, '*or whose real father cannot be known*, and a son 'rejected *by his natural parents*, are the six kins'men and heirs:

160. 'The son of a young woman *unmarried*, 'and the son of a pregnant bride, a son bought, 'a son by a twice married woman, a son self'given, and a son by a *Súdra*, are the six kinsmen, 'but not heirs *to collaterals*.

161. 'Such advantage, as a man would gain, 'who should attempt to pass deep water in a 'boat made of woven reeds, the father obtains, 'who passes the gloom of death, leaving only 'contemptible sons, *who are the eleven, or at least* '*the six last mentioned*.

162. 'If the two heirs of one man be the son 'of his own body and a son of his wife by a kins'man, *the former of whom was begotten after his* '*recovery from an illness thought incurable*, each of 'the sons, exclusively of the other, shall succeed 'to the whole estate of his natural father.

163. 'The son of his own body is the sole heir 'to his estate, but, that all evil may be removed, 'let him allow a maintenance to the rest;

164. 'And, when the son of the body has taken 'an account of the paternal inheritance, let 'him give a sixth part of it to the son of the 'wife begotten by a kinsman, *before his father's* '*recovery*; or a fifth part, *if that son be eminently* '*virtuous*.

165. 'The son of the body, and the son of the

'wife,

'wife, may ſucced *immediately* to the paternal 'eſtate *in the manner juſt mentioned*; but the ten 'other ſons can only ſucceed in order to the fa- 'mily duties, and to their ſhare of the inheritance, '*thoſe laſt named being excluded by any one of the* '*preceding*.

166. 'HIM, whom a man has begotten on his 'own wedded wife, let him know to be the firſt 'in rank, as the ſon of his body.

167. 'He who was begotten, according to law, 'on the wife of a man deceaſed, or impotent, or 'diſordered, after due authority given to her, is 'called the lawful ſon of the wife.

168. 'He, whom his father, or mother *with* '*her huſbands aſſent*, gives to another as his ſon, 'provided that the donee have no iſſue, if the boy 'be of the ſame claſs and affectionately diſpoſed, 'is conſidered as a ſon given, *the gift being con-* '*firmed* by *pouring* water.

169. 'He is conſidered as a ſon made *or adopted*, 'whom a man takes as his own ſon, the boy being 'equal in claſs, endued with filial virtues, ac- 'quainted with *the* merit *of performing obſequies* '*to his adopter*, and with *the* ſin *of omitting them*.

170. 'In whoſe manſion ſoever a male child 'ſhall be brought forth *by a married woman, whoſe* '*huſband has long been abſent*, if the real father 'cannot be diſcovered, *but if it be probable that* '*he was of an equal claſs*, that child belongs to the 'lord of the *unfaithful* wife, and is called a ſon of 'concealed birth in his manſion.

171. 'A boy, whom a man receives as his own 'ſon, after he has been deſerted *without juſt cauſe* 'by his parents, or by either of them, *if one be* '*dead*, is called a ſon rejected.

172. 'A

172. ‘ A ſon, whom the daughter of any man ‘ privately brings forth in the houſe of her father, ‘ if ſhe *afterwards* marry her lover, is deſcribed as ‘ a ſon begotten on an unmarried girl.

173. ‘ If a pregnant young woman marry, ‘ whether her pregnancy be known or unknown, ‘ the male child in her womb belongs to the bride-‘ groom, and is called a ſon received with his ‘ bride.

174. ‘ He is called a ſon bought, whom a man, ‘ for the ſake of having a ſon *to perform his obſe-‘ quies*, purchaſes from his father and mother, ‘ whether the boy be equal or unequal *to himſelf ‘ in good qualities, for in claſs all adopted ſons muſt ‘ be equal.*

175. ‘ He, whom a woman, either forſaken by ‘ her lord or a widow, conceived by a ſecond ‘ huſband, whom ſhe took by her own deſire, ‘ *though againſt law*, is called the ſon of a woman ‘ twice married:

176. ‘ If, *on her ſecond marriage*, ſhe be ſtill a ‘ virgin, or if ſhe left her huſband under the age ‘ of puberty and return to him at his full age, ſhe ‘ muſt again perform the nuptial ceremony *either* ‘ with her ſecond, *or her young and deſerted*, ‘ huſband.

177. ‘ He, who has loſt his parents, or been ‘ abandoned *by them* without juſt cauſe, and offers ‘ himſelf to a man *as his ſon* is called a ſon ſelf-‘ given.

178. ‘ A ſon, begotten through luſt on a *Súdra* ‘ by a man of the prieſtly claſs, is even as a corpſe, ‘ though alive, and is thence called in law a living ‘ corpſe:

179. ‘ But a ſon begotten by a man of the ſer-‘ vile claſs on his female ſlave, or on the female

'slave of his male slave, may take a share of the 'heritage, if permitted *by the other sons:* thus is 'the law established.

180. 'These eleven sons (the son of the wife 'and the rest, as enumerated) are allowed by wise 'legislators to be substitutes *in order* for sons of 'the body, for the sake of preventing a failure of 'obsequies;

181. 'Though such, as are called sons for that 'purpose, but were produced from the manhood 'of others, belong in truth to the father, from 'whose manhood they severally sprang, and to no 'other, *except by a just fiction of law.*

182. 'If among several brothers of the whole 'blood, one have a son born, Menu pronounces 'them all fathers of a male child by means of 'that son; *so that if such nephew would be the 'heir, the uncles have no power to adopt sons:*

183. '*Thus,* if, among all the wives of the same 'husband, one bring forth a male child, Menu 'has declared them all, by means of that son, 'to be mothers of male issue.

184. 'On failure of the best, *and* of the *next* 'best, *among those twelve sons,* let the inferiour 'in order take the heritage; but if there be 'many of equal rank, let all be sharers of the 'estate.

185. 'Not brothers, nor parents, but sons, *if 'living, or their male issue,* are heirs to the de-'ceased, but of him, who leaves no son, *nor a 'wife, nor a daughter,* the father shall take the 'inheritance; and *if he leave neither father nor 'mother,* the brothers.

186. 'To three *ancestors* must water be given 'at their obsequies; for three *(the father, his 'father, and the paternal grandfather)* is the funeral 'cake

'cake ordained: the fourth *in descent* is the giver '*of oblations to them and their heir, if they die without nearer descendants*; but the fifth has no concern *with the gift of the funeral cake.*

187. 'To the nearest *sapinda, male or female,* 'after him in the third degree, the inheritance '*next* belongs, then on failure of *sapindas* and of 'their issue, the *samánódaca*, or distant kinsman, 'shall be the heir; or the spiritual preceptor, or 'the pupil, *or the fellow student of the deceased:*

188. 'On failure of all those, the lawful heirs 'are such *Bráhmens* as have read the three *Védas*, 'as are pure *in body and mind*, as have subdued 'their passions; *and they must consequently offer the* '*cake:* thus the rites of obsequies cannot fail.

189. 'The property of a *Bráhmen* shall never 'be taken *as an escheat* by the king; this is a 'fixed law: but the wealth of the other classes, 'on failure of all heirs, the king may take.

190. 'If the widow of a man, who died without a son, raise up a son to him by one of his 'kinsmen, let her deliver to that son, *at his full* '*age*, the collected estate of the deceased, whatever 'it be.

191. 'If two sons, begotten by two *successive* '*husbands, who are both dead*, contend for their 'property, then in the hands of their mother, 'let each take, exclusively of the other, his own 'father's estate.

192. 'On the death of the mother, let all the 'uterine brothers and the uterine sisters, *if unmarried*, equally divide the maternal estate: *each* '*married sister shall have a fourth part of a brother's* '*allotment*.

193. 'Even to the daughters of those daughters, it is fit that something should be given,

'from

'from the aſſets of their maternal grandmother, 'on the ſcore of natural affection.

194. 'WHAT was given before the nuptial 'fire, what was given on the bridal proceſſion, 'what was given in token of love, and what was 'received from a brother, a mother, or a father, 'are conſidered as the ſix-fold *ſeparate* property 'of a *married* woman:

195. 'What ſhe received after marriage from 'the family of her huſband, and what her affec-'tionate lord may have given her, ſhall be in-'herited, even if ſhe die in his life-time, by her 'children.

196. 'It is ordained, that the property of a 'woman, married by the ceremonies called *Bráh-'ma, Daiva, A'rſha, Gándharva,* or *Prájápatya,* 'ſhall go to her huſband, if ſhe die without iſſue;

197. 'But her wealth given on the marriage 'called *Aſura,* or on either of the *two* others, is 'ordained, on her death without iſſue, to become 'the property of her father and mother.

198. 'If a widow, *whoſe huſband had other 'wives of different claſſes,* ſhall have received 'wealth at any time, *as a gift* from her father, '*and ſhall die without iſſue,* it ſhall go to the daugh-'ter of the *Bráhmanì* wife, or to the iſſue of that 'daughter.

199. 'A woman ſhould never make a hoard 'from the goods of her kindred, *which are* com-'mon to *her and* many; or even from the pro-'perty of her lord, without his aſſent.

200. 'Such ornamental apparel, as women 'wear during the lives of their huſbands, the 'heirs of thoſe huſbands ſhall not divide among 'themſelves: they, who divide it among them-'ſelves, fall deep *into ſin.*

201. 'Eunuchs, and outcasts, persons born 'blind or deaf, madmen, idiots, the dumb, and 'such as have lost the use of a limb, are excluded 'from a share of the heritage;

202. 'But it is just, that the heir, who knows 'his duty, should give all of them food and rai-'ment *for life* without stint, according to the best 'of his power: he, who gives them nothing, sinks 'assuredly *to a region of punishment*.

203. 'If the eunuch and the rest should at any 'time desire to marry, *and if the wife of the eunuch* '*should raise up a son to him by a man legally ap-*'*pointed, that son and* the issue of such, as have 'children, shall be capable of inheriting.

204. 'After the death of the father, if the 'eldest brother acquire *wealth by his own efforts* '*before partition*, a share of that *acquisition* shall 'go to the younger brothers, if they have made 'a due progress in learning;

205. 'And if all of them, being unlearned, 'acquire property *before partition* by their own 'labour, there shall be an equal division of that 'property *without regard to the first born*; for it 'was not the wealth of their father: this rule is 'clearly settled.

206. 'Wealth, however, acquired by learning, 'belongs exclusively to any one *of them, who ac-*'*quired it*; so does any thing given by a friend, 'received on account of marriage, or presented 'as a mark of respect to a guest.

207. 'If any one of the brethren has a com-'petence from his own occupation, and wants not 'the property *of his father*, he may debar himself 'from his own share, some trifle being given him 'as a consideration, *to prevent future strife*.

208. 'What

208. 'What a brother has acquired by labour 'or ſkill, without uſing the patrimony, he ſhall 'not give up without his aſſent; for it was gained 'by his own exertion:

209. 'And if a ſon, by his own efforts, recover '*a debt or property unjuſtly detained*, which could 'not be recovered before *by his father*, he ſhall 'not, unleſs by his free will, put it into parcenary 'with his brethren, ſince in fact it was acquired 'by himſelf.

210. 'If brethren, once divided and living 'again together as parceners, make a ſecond par-'tition, the ſhares muſt in that caſe be equal; 'and the firſt born ſhall have no right of deduc-'tion.

211. 'Should the eldeſt or youngeſt of ſeveral 'brothers be deprived of his ſhare *by a civil death* '*on his entrance into the fourth order*, or ſhould any 'one of them die, his *veſted intereſt in a* ſhare ſhall 'not wholly be loſt;

212. 'But, *if he leave neither ſon, nor wife,* '*nor daughter, nor father, nor mother*, his uterine 'brothers and ſiſters, and ſuch brothers as were 're-united after a ſeparation, ſhall aſſemble and 'divide his ſhare equally.

213. 'Any eldeſt brother, who, from avarice, 'ſhall defraud his younger brother, ſhall forfeit '*the honours of* his primogeniture, be deprived 'of his own ſhare, and pay a fine to the king.

214. 'All thoſe brothers who are addicted to 'any vice, loſe their title to the inheritance: the 'firſt born ſhall not appropriate it to himſelf, but 'ſhall give ſhares to the youngeſt, *if they be not* '*vitious*.

215. 'If among undivided brethren *living* with 'their father, there be a common exertion for

'common gain, the father shall never make an 'unequal division among them, *when they divide* '*their families.*

216. 'A son, born after a division *in the life-* '*time of his father*, shall alone inherit the pa- 'trimony, or shall have a share of it with the 'divided brethren, if they return and unite them- 'selves with him.

217. 'OF a son, dying childless *and leaving no* '*widow*, the *father and* mother shall take the 'estate; and the mother also being dead, the pa- 'ternal *grandfather and* grandmother shall take 'the heritage, *on failure of brothers and nephews.*

218. 'When all the debts and wealth have 'been justly distributed according to law, any 'property, that may afterwards be discovered, 'shall be subject to a similar distribution.

219. 'Apparel, carriages, or riding horses, 'and ornaments *of ordinary value, which any of* '*the heirs had used by consent before partition,* 'dressed rice, water *in a well or cistern*, female 'slaves, family priests, or spiritual counsellors, 'and pasture ground for cattle, the wise have 'declared indivisible, *and still to be used as be-* '*fore.*

220. 'Thus have the laws of inheritance, and 'the rule for the conduct of sons (whether 'the son of the wife or others) been expounded 'to you in order: learn at present the law con- 'cerning games of chance.

221. 'GAMING, either with inanimate or with 'animated things, let the king exclude wholly 'from his realm: both those modes of play cause 'destruction to princes.

222. 'Such play with dice *and the like*, or by 'matches *between rams and cocks*, amounts to open

'theft;

'theft; and the king must ever be vigilant in 'suppressing both *modes of play*:

223. 'Gaming with lifeless things is known 'among men by the name of *dy'ta*; but *samáhwaya* signifies a match between living creatures.

224. 'Let the king punish corporally at discretion both the gamester and the keeper of a 'gaming-house, whether they play with inanimate 'or animated things; and men of the servile class, 'who wear the *string and other* marks of the 'twice born.

225. 'Gamesters, publick dancers, and singers, 'revilers of scripture, open hereticks, men who 'perform not the duties of their several classes, 'and sellers of spirituous liquors, let him instantly 'banish from the town:

226. 'Those wretches, lurking like unseen 'thieves in the dominion of a prince, continually 'harass his good subjects with their vitious conduct.

227. 'Even in a former creation was this *vice* '*of* gaming found a great provoker of enmity: 'let no sensible man, therefore, addict himself to 'play even for his amusement:

228. 'On the man addicted to it, either pri'vately or openly, let punishment be inflicted at 'the discretion of the king.

229. 'A MAN of the military, commercial, or 'servile class, who cannot pay a fine, shall dis'charge the debt by his labour: a priest shall dis'charge it by little and little.

230. 'For women, children, persons of crazy 'intellect, the old, the poor, and the infirm, the 'king shall order punishment with a small whip, 'a twig, or a rope.

231. 'THOSE ministers who are employed in 'publick affairs, and, inflamed by the blaze of

'wealth, mar the busineſs of any perſon con-
'cerned, let the king ſtrip of all their property.

232. 'Such as forge royal edicts, cauſe diſſen-
'ſions among the great miniſters, or kill women,
'prieſts, or children, let the king put to death;
'and ſuch as adhere to his enemies.

233. 'Whatever buſineſs has at any time been
'tranſacted conformably to law, let him conſider
'as finally ſettled, and refuſe to unravel;

234. 'But whatever buſineſs has been con-
'cluded illegally by his miniſters or by a judge,
'let the king himſelf re-examine; and let him
'fine them each a thouſand *panas*.

235. 'The ſlayer of a prieſt, a ſoldier, or
'merchant drinking arak, or a prieſt drinking
'arak, mead, or rum, he who ſteals the gold of
'a prieſt, and he who violates the bed of his *na-
'tural or ſpiritual* father, are all to be conſidered
'reſpectively as offenders in the higheſt degree,
'*except thoſe whoſe crimes are not fit to be named:*

236. 'On ſuch of thoſe four, as have not actual-
'ly performed an expiation, let the king legally
'inflict corporal puniſhment, together with a fine.

237. 'For violating the paternal bed, let *the
'mark of* a female part be impreſſed *on the fore-
'head with hot iron*; for drinking ſpirits a vint-
'ner's flag; for ſtealing ſacred gold, a dog's foot;
'for murdering a prieſt, *the figure of* a headleſs
'corpſe:

238. 'With none to eat with them, with none
'to ſacrifice with them, with none to read with
'them, with none to be allied by marriage to
'them, abject and excluded from all ſocial duties,
'let them wander over this earth:

239. 'Branded with *indelible* marks, they ſhall
'be deſerted by their paternal and maternal re-
lations,

'lations, treated by none with affection, received 'by none with respect: such is the ordinance of 'MENU.

240. '*Criminals of* all the classes, having per-'formed an expiation, as ordained by law, shall 'not be marked on the forehead, but condemned 'to pay the highest fine:

241. 'For crimes by a priest, *who had a good 'character before his offence,* the middle fine shall 'be set on him; or, *if his crime was premeditated,* 'he shall be banished from the realm, *taking* with '*him* his effects and his family;

242. 'But men of the other classes, who have 'committed those crimes, *though without preme-'ditation,* shall be stripped of all their possessions; 'and, if their offence was premeditated, shall be 'corporally, or even capitally punished, *according 'to circumstances.*

243. 'LET no virtuous prince appropriate the 'wealth of a criminal in the highest degree, for 'he who appropriates it through covetousness, 'is contaminated with the same guilt:

244. 'Having thrown such a fine into the 'waters, let him offer it to VARUNA; or let him 'bestow it on some priest of eminent learning in 'the scriptures:

245. 'VARUNA is the lord of punishment; he 'holds a rod even over kings; and a priest who 'has gone through the whole *Véda,* is *equal to* a 'sovereign of all the world.

246. 'Where the king abstains from receiving '*to his own use* the wealth of such offenders, there 'children are born in due season and enjoy long 'lives;

247. '*There* the grain of husbandmen rises 'abundantly, as it was respectively sown; there

'no younglings die, nor is one deformed animal
'born.

248. 'Should a man of the baſeſt claſs, with
'preconceived malice, give pain to *Bráhmens,* let
'the prince corporally puniſh him by various
'modes, that may raiſe terrour.

249. 'A king is pronounced equally unjuſt in
'releaſing the man who deſerves puniſhment, and
'in puniſhing the man who deſerves it not: he
'is juſt who always inflicts the puniſhment or-
'dained by law.

250. 'Theſe eſtabliſhed rules for adminiſtering
'juſtice between two litigant parties, have been
'propounded at length under eighteen heads.

251. 'Thus fully performing all duties re-
'quired by law, let a king ſeek, *with juſtice,* to
'poſſeſs regions yet unpoſſeſſed, and, when they are
'in his poſſeſſion, let him govern them well.

252. 'His realm being completely arranged
'and his fortreſſes amply provided, let him ever
'apply the moſt diligent care to eradicate *bad men,*
'*reſembling* thorny weeds, as the law directs.

253. 'By protecting ſuch as live virtuouſly,
'and by rooting up ſuch as live wickedly, thoſe
'kings, whoſe hearts are intent on the ſecurity of
'their people, ſhall riſe to heaven.

254. 'Of that prince, who takes a revenue with-
'out reſtraining rogues, the dominions are thrown
'into diſorder, and himſelf ſhall be precluded
'from a celeſtial abode;

255. 'But of him, whoſe realm, by the ſtrength
'of his arm, is defended and free from terrour,
'the dominions continually flouriſh, like trees
'duly watered.

256. 'Let the king, whoſe emiſſaries are his
'eyes, diſcern well the two ſorts of rogues, the

'open and the concealed, who deprive other men
'of their wealth:

2 7. 'Open rogues are they who ſubſiſt by
'cheating in various marketable commodities;
'and concealed rogues are they who ſteal and
'rob in foreſts and the like ſecret places.

258. 'Receivers of bribes, extorters of money
'by threats, debaſers of metals, gameſters. fortune-
'tellers, impoſters, and profeſſors of palmiſtry;

259. 'Elephant brakers, and quacks, not per-
'forming what they engage to perform, pretended
'artiſts, and ſubtil harlots;

260. 'Theſe and the like thorny weeds, over-
'ſpreading the world, let the king diſcover with a
'quick ſight, and others who act ill in ſecret;
'worthleſs men, yet bearing the outward ſigns of
'the worthy.

261. 'Having detected them by the means of
'truſty perſons diſguiſed, who *pretend to* have the
'ſame occupation with them, and of ſpies placed
'in ſeveral ſtations, let him bring them by ar-
'tifice into his power:

262. 'Then, having fully proclaimed their re-
'ſpective criminal acts, let the king inflict puniſh-
'ment legally, according to the crimes proved;

263. 'Since, without certain puniſhment, it is
'impoſſible to reſtrain the delinquency of ſcoun-
'drels with depraved ſouls, who ſecretly prowl
'over this earth.

264. 'Much frequented places, ciſterns of
'water, bake-houſes, the lodgings of harlots,
'taverns and victualling ſhops, ſquares where four
'ways meet, large well known trees, aſſemblies,
'and publick ſpectacles;

265. 'Old court yards, thickets, the houſes of
'artiſts, empty manſions, groves, and gardens;

 266. 'Theſe

266. ‘ Theſe and the like places let the king ‘ guard, for the prevention of robberies, with ‘ ſoldiers both ſtationary and patrolling, as well as ‘ with ſecret watchmen.

267. ‘ By the means of able ſpies, once thieves, ‘ *but reformed*, who well knowing the various ‘ machinations of rogues, aſſociate with them and ‘ follow them, let the king detect and draw them ‘ forth:

268. ‘ On pretexts of dainty food and gratifica- ‘ tions, or of ſeeing ſome wiſe prieſt, *who could en-* ‘ *ſure their ſucceſs*, or on pretence of *mock battles* ‘ *and the like* feats of ſtrength, let the ſpies procure ‘ an aſſembly of thoſe men.

269. ‘ Such as refuſe to go forth on thoſe occa- ‘ ſions, deterred by *former puniſhments, which* the ‘ king *had inflicted*, let him *ſeize* by force, *and* put ‘ to death, *on proof of their guilt*, with their friends ‘ and kinſmen, paternal and maternal, *if proved to* ‘ *be their confederates*.

270. ‘ Let not a juſt prince kill a man con- ‘ victed of ſimple theft, unleſs taken with the ‘ mainer or with implements of robbery; but any ‘ thief, taken with the mainer or with ſuch im- ‘ plements, let him deſtroy without heſitation;

271. ‘ And let him ſlay all thoſe, who give rob- ‘ bers food in towns, or ſupply them with imple- ‘ ments, or afford them ſhelter.

272. ‘ Should thoſe men, who were appointed ‘ to guard any diſtricts, or thoſe of the vicinity, ‘ who were employed for that purpoſe, be neutral ‘ in attacks by robbers *and inactive in ſeizing them*, ‘ let him inſtantly puniſh them as thieves.

273. ‘ Him, who lives *apparently* by the rules ‘ of his claſs, but *really* departs from thoſe rules,

‘ let

'let the king ſeverely puniſh by fine, as a wretch 'who violates his duty.

274. 'They who give no aſſiſtance on the 'plundering of a town, on the forcible breaking of 'a dike, or on ſeeing a robbery on the highway, 'ſhall be baniſhed with their cattle and utenſils.

275. 'Men, who rob the king's treaſure, or ob- 'ſtinately oppoſe his commands, let him deſtroy 'by various modes of juſt puniſhment; and thoſe 'who encourage his enemies.

276. 'Of robbers who break a wall or partition, 'and commit theft in the night, let the prince or- 'der the hands to be lopped off, and themſelves 'to be fixed on a ſharp ſtake.

277. 'Two fingers of a cutpurſe, *the thumb and* '*the index*, let him cauſe to be amputated on his 'firſt conviction; on the ſecond, one hand and 'one foot; on the third, he ſhall ſuffer death.

278. 'Such as give thieves fire, ſuch as give 'them food, ſuch as give them arms and apart- 'ments, and ſuch as knowingly receive a thing 'ſtolen, let the king puniſh as *he would puniſh* a 'thief.

279. 'The breaker of a *dam to ſecure a* pool, 'let him puniſh by long immerſion under water, 'or by keen corporal ſuffering; or the offender 'ſhall repair it, but muſt pay the higheſt mulct.

280. 'Thoſe, who break open the treaſury, or 'the arſenal, or the temple of a deity, and thoſe 'who carry off royal elephants, horſes, or cars, let 'him, without heſitation, deſtroy.

281. 'He, who ſhall take away the water of 'an ancient pool, or ſhall obſtruct a watercourſe, 'muſt be condemned to pay the loweſt uſual 'amercement.

282. 'He,

282. 'He, who shall drop his ordure on the 'king's highway, except in case of necessity, shall 'pay two *panas* and immediately remove the filth;

283. 'But a person in urgent necessity, a very 'old man, a pregnant woman, and a child, only 'deserves reproof, and shall clean the place them'selves: this is a settled rule.

284. 'All physicians and surgeons acting 'unskilfully in their several professions, must 'pay for *injury to* brute animals the lowest, but 'for *injury to* human creatures the middle amerce'ment.

285. 'The breaker of a foot bridge, of a pub'lick flag, of a palisade, and of idols *made of clay*, 'shall repair what he has broken, and pay a mulct 'of five hundred *panas*.

286. 'For mixing impure with pure commo'dities, for piercing fine gems, *as diamonds or* '*rubies*, and for boring *pearls or inferiour gems* 'improperly, the fine is the lowest of the three; '*but damages must always be paid.*

287. 'The man, who shall deal unjustly 'with purchasers at a fair price *by delivering goods* '*of less value*, or shall sell, at a high price, *goods of* '*ordinary value*, shall pay, *according to circumstances*, 'the lowest or the middle amercement.

288. 'Let the king place all prisons near a 'publick road, where offenders may be seen 'wretched or disfigured.

289. 'Him who breaks down a *publick* wall, 'him who fills up a *publick* ditch, him who 'throws down a *publick* gate, the king shall speedily 'banish.

290. 'For all sacrifices to destroy innocent 'men, the punishment is a fine of two hundred '*panas*; and for machinations with *poisonous* roots, 'and

'let the king ſeverely puniſh by fine, as a wretch 'who violates his duty.

274. 'They who give no aſſiſtance on the 'plundering of a town, on the forcible breaking of 'a dike, or on ſeeing a robbery on the highway, 'ſhall be baniſhed with their cattle and utenſils.

275. 'Men, who rob the king's treaſure, or ob-'ſtinately oppoſe his commands, let him deſtroy 'by various modes of juſt puniſhment; and thoſe 'who encourage his enemies.

276. 'Of robbers who break a wall or partition, 'and commit theft in the night, let the prince or-'der the hands to be lopped off, and themſelves 'to be fixed on a ſharp ſtake.

277. 'Two fingers of a cutpurſe, *the thumb and* '*the index*, let him cauſe to be amputated on his 'firſt conviction; on the ſecond, one hand and 'one foot; on the third, he ſhall ſuffer death.

278. 'Such as give thieves fire, ſuch as give 'them food, ſuch as give them arms and apart-'ments, and ſuch as knowingly receive a thing 'ſtolen, let the king puniſh as *he would puniſh* a 'thief.

279. 'The breaker of a *dam to ſecure a* pool, 'let him puniſh by long immerſion under water, 'or by keen corporal ſuffering; or the offender 'ſhall repair it, but muſt pay the higheſt mulct.

280. 'Thoſe, who break open the treaſury, or 'the arſenal, or the temple of a deity, and thoſe 'who carry off royal elephants, horſes, or cars, let 'him, without heſitation, deſtroy.

281. 'He, who ſhall take away the water of 'an ancient pool, or ſhall obſtruct a watercourſe, 'muſt be condemned to pay the loweſt uſual 'amercement.

282. 'He,

282. 'He, who ſhall drop his ordure on the 'king's highway, except in caſe of neceſſity, ſhall 'pay two *panas* and immediately remove the filth;

283. 'But a perſon in urgent neceſſity, a very 'old man, a pregnant woman, and a child, only 'deſerves reproof, and ſhall clean the place them-'ſelves: this is a ſettled rule.

284. 'All phyſicians and ſurgeons acting 'unſkilfully in their ſeveral profeſſions, muſt 'pay for *injury to* brute animals the loweſt, but 'for *injury to* human creatures the middle amerce-'ment.

285. 'The breaker of a foot bridge, of a pub-'lick flag, of a paliſade, and of idols *made of clay*, 'ſhall repair what he has broken, and pay a mulct 'of five hundred *panas*.

286. 'For mixing impure with pure commo-'dities, for piercing fine gems, *as diamonds or* '*rubies*, and for boring *pearls or inferiour gems* 'improperly, the fine is the loweſt of the three; '*but damages muſt always be paid.*

287. 'The man, who ſhall deal unjuſtly 'with purchaſers at a fair price *by delivering goods* '*of leſs value*, or ſhall ſell, at a high price, *goods of* '*ordinary value*, ſhall pay, *according to circumſtances*, 'the loweſt or the middle amercement.

288. 'Let the king place all priſons near a 'publick road, where offenders may be ſeen 'wretched or disfigured.

289. 'Him who breaks down a *publick* wall, 'him who fills up a *publick* ditch, him who 'throws down a *publick* gate, the king ſhall ſpeedily 'baniſh.

290. 'For all ſacrifices to deſtroy innocent 'men, the puniſhment is a fine of two hundred '*panas*; and for machinations with *poiſonous* roots,

'and

'and for the various *charms and* witcheries *in-*
'*tended* to kill, by perſons not effecting their
'purpoſe.

291. 'THE ſeller of bad grain for good, or of
'good ſeed placed at the top *of the bag, to conceal*
'*the bad below*, and the deſtroyer of known land-
'marks, muſt ſuffer ſuch corporal puniſhment as
'will diſfigure them;

292. 'But the moſt pernicious of all deceivers
'is a goldſmith, who commits frauds: the king
'ſhall order him to be cut piecemeal with razors.

293. 'FOR ſtealing implements of huſbandry,
'weapons, and prepared medicines, let the king
'award puniſhment according to the time and ac-
'cording to their uſe.

294. 'THE king, and his council, his metro-
'polis, his realm, his treaſure, and his army,
'together with his ally, are the ſeven members
'of his kingdom, *whence* it is called *Septánga:*

295. 'Among thoſe ſeven members of a king-
'dom, let him conſider the ruin of the firſt, and
'ſo forth in order, as the greateſt calamity;

296. 'Yet, in a ſeven-parted kingdom here
'below, there is no ſupremacy among the ſeveral
'parts, from any pre-eminence in uſeful qualities:
'but all the parts muſt reciprocally ſupport each
'other, like the three ſtaves of a holy mendicant:

297. 'In theſe and thoſe acts, *indeed*, this and
'that member may be diſtinguiſhed; *and* the
'member by which any affair is tranſacted, has
'the pre-eminence in that particular affair.

298. 'WHEN the king employs emiſſaries,
'when he exerts power, when he regulates pub-
'lic buſineſs, let him invariably know both his
'own ſtrength and that of his enemy,

299. 'With

299. 'With all *their several* distresses and vices: 'let him then begin his operations, having maturely 'considered the greater and less importance *of* '*particular acts:*

300. 'Let him, *though frequently disappointed,* 'renew his operations, how fatigued soever, again 'and again; since fortune always attends the man, 'who, *having begun well,* strenuously renews his 'efforts.

301. 'All the ages, called *Satya, Trétá, Dwápara,* 'and *Cali,* depend on the conduct of the king; 'who is declared *in turn* to represent each of 'those ages:

302. 'Sleeping, he is the *Cali* age; waking, 'the *Dwápara*; exerting himself in action, the '*Trétá*; living virtuously, the *Satya.*

303. 'Of Indra, of Su'rya, of Pavana, of 'Yama, of Varuna, of Chandra, of Agni, 'and of Prĭt'hivì, let the king emulate the 'power and attributes.

304. 'As Indra sheds plentiful showers during 'the four rainy months, thus let him, acting like 'the regent of clouds, rain just gratifications over 'his kingdom:

305. 'As Su'rya with strong rays draws up 'the water during eight months, thus let him, 'performing the function of the sun, gradually 'draw from his realm the legal revenue:

306. 'As Pavana, when he moves, pervades 'all creatures, thus let him, imitating the regent 'of wind, pervade *all places* by his concealed 'emissaries:

307. 'As Yama, at the appointed time, pu-'nishes friends and foes, *or those who revere, and* '*those who contemn him,* thus let the king, resem-

'bling

'bling the judge of departed spirits, punish offending subjects:

308. 'As VARUNA most assuredly binds the 'guilty in fatal cords, thus let him, representing 'the genius of water, keep offenders in close 'confinement:

309. 'When the people are no less delighted 'on seeing the king, than on seeing the full moon, 'he appears in the character of CHANDRA:

310. 'Against criminals let him ever be ardent 'in wrath, let him be splendid in glory, let him 'consume wicked ministers, thus emulating the 'functions of AGNI, regent of fire.

311. 'As PRĬT'HIVÍ supports all creatures 'equally, thus a king, sustaining all subjects, re-'sembles in his office the goddess of earth.

312. 'Engaged in these duties and in others, 'with continual activity, let the king, *above all* '*things*, restrain robbers, both in his own territories 'and in those of other princes, *from which they* '*come, or in which they seek refuge.*

313. 'LET him not, although in the greatest 'distress *for money*, provoke *Bráhmens* to anger '*by taking their property*; for they, once enraged, 'could immediately *by sacrifices and imprecations* 'destroy him with his troops, elephants, horses 'and cars.

314. 'Who without perishing could provoke 'those holy men, by whom, *that is, by whose an-*'*cestors, under* BRAHMÁ, the all-devouring fire 'was created, the sea with waters not drinkable, 'and the moon with its wane and increase?

315. 'What prince could gain wealth by op-'pressing those, who, if angry, could frame other 'worlds and regents of worlds, could give being 'to new gods and mortals?

316. 'What

316. 'What man desirous of life, would injure 'those, by the aid of whom, *that is, by whose oblations*, worlds and gods perpetually subsist; 'those who are rich in the learning of the *Véda*?

317. 'A *Bráhmen*, whether learned or ignorant, 'is a powerful divinity; even as fire is a powerful 'divinity, whether consecrated or popular.

318. 'Even in places for burning the dead, 'the bright fire is undefiled; and, when presented 'with clarified butter at *subsequent* sacrifices, blazes 'again with extreme splendour:

319. 'Thus though *Bráhmens* employ themselves 'in all sorts of mean occupation, they must in'variably be honoured; for they are something 'transcendently divine.

320. 'Of a military man, who raises his arm 'violently on all occasions against the priestly 'class, the priest himself shall be the chastiser; 'since the soldier originally proceeded from the '*Bráhmen*.

321. 'From the waters arose fire; from the 'priest, the soldier; from stone, iron: their all-'penetrating force is ineffectual in the places 'whence they respectively sprang.

322. 'The military class cannot prosper with'out the sacerdotal, nor can the sacerdotal be 'raised without the military: both classes by 'cordial union, are exalted in this world and in 'the next.

323. 'Should the king *be near his end through* '*some incurable disease, he* must bestow on the 'priests all his riches accumulated from legal fines; 'and, having duly committed his kingdom to his 'son, let him seek death in battle, *or, if there be* '*no war, by abstaining from food*.

324. 'Thus conducting himself, *and* ever firm

'in

'in difcharging his royal duties, let the king employ all his minifters in acts beneficial to his 'people.

325. 'Thefe rules for the conduct of a military 'man having been propounded, let mankind next 'hear the rules for the commercial and fervile 'claffes in due order.

326. 'LET the *Vaifya*, having been girt with 'his proper facrificial thread, and having married 'an equal wife, be always attentive to his bufinefs *of agriculture and trade*, and to that of keeping 'cattle;

327. 'Since the Lord of created beings, having 'formed herds, and flocks, intrufted them to the care of the *Vaifya*, while he intrufted the whole 'human fpecies to the *Bráhmen* and the *Cfhatriya*:

328. 'Never muft a *Vaifya* be difpofed to fay, "I keep no cattle;" nor, he being willing to keep 'them, muft they by any means be kept by men 'of another clafs.

329. 'Of gems, pearls, and coral, of iron, 'of woven cloth, of perfumes and of liquids, let 'him well know the prices both high and low:

330. 'Let him be fkilled likewife in *the time* '*and manner of* fowing feeds, and in the bad 'or good qualities of land; let him alfo perfectly 'know the correct modes of meafuring and 'weighing,

331. 'The excellence or defects of commodi-'ties, the advantages and difadvantages of differ-'ent regions, the probable gain or lofs on vendi-'ble goods, and the means of breeding cattle 'with large augmentation:

332. 'Let him know the juft wages of fervants, 'the various dialects of men, the beft way of

'keeping

'keeping goods, and *whatever elſe belongs to* pur-
'chaſe and ſale.

333. 'Let him apply the moſt vigilant care to 'augment his wealth by *performing* his duty; and, 'with great ſolicitude, let him give nouriſhment 'to all ſentient creatures.

334. 'Servile attendance on *Bráhmens* learned 'in the *Véda*, chiefly on ſuch as keep houſe and 'are famed for virtue, is of itſelf the higheſt duty 'of a *Súdra*, and leads him to future beatitude:

335. 'Pure *in body and mind*, humbly ſerving 'the three higher claſſes, mild in ſpeech, never 'arrogant, ever ſeeking refuge in *Bráhmens* prin-'cipally, he may attain the moſt eminent claſs *in* '*another tranſmigration.*

336. 'This clear ſyſtem of duties has been 'promulgated for the four claſſes; when they are 'not in diſtreſs for ſubſiſtence; now learn in 'order their ſeveral duties in times of neceſſity.'

CHAPTER THE TENTH.

On the mixed Classes; and on Times of Distress.

1. ' Let the three twice born classes, remaining
' ing firm in their several duties, carefully read
' the *Véda*; but a *Bráhmen* must explain it to
' them, not *a man of* the other two *classes*: this
' is an established rule.

2. ' The *Bráhmen* must know the means of
' subsistence ordained by law for all the classes,
' and must declare them to the rest: let him
' likewise act in conformity *to law*.

3. ' From priority of birth, from superiority of
' origin, from a more exact knowledge of scrip-
' ture, and from a distinction in the sacrificial
' thread, the *Bráhmen* is the lord of all classes.

4. ' The three twice born classes are the sacer-
' dotal, the military, and the commercial; but
' the fourth, or servile, is once born, *that is, has*
' *no second birth from the* gáyatrì, *and wears no*
' *thread*: nor is there a fifth pure class.

5. ' In all classes they, and they only, who are
' born, in a direct order, of wives equal in class,

'and virgins at the time of marriage, are
'to be considered as the same in class *with their*
'*fathers:*

6. 'Sons, begotten by twice born men, on wo-
'men of the class next immediately below them,
'wise legislators call similar, *not the same,* in class
'*with their parents,* because they are degraded
'*to a middle rank between both,* by the lowness of
'their mothers: *they are named in order* Múrdháb-
'hishicta, Máhishya, *and* Carana, *or* Cáyast'ha;
'*and their several employments are teaching military*
'*exercises; musick, astronomy, and keeping herds; and*
'*attendance on princes.*

7. 'Such is the primeval rule for the sons of
'women one degree lower *than their husbands:*
'for the sons of women two or three degrees
'lower, let this rule of law be known.

8. 'From a *Bráhmen,* on a wife of the *Vaisya*
'class, is born a son called *Ambasht'ha,* or
'*Vaidya,* on a *Súdrá* wife a *Nishpáda,* named also
'*Párasava:*

9. 'From a *Cshatriya,* on a wife of the *Súdra*
'class, springs a creature called *Ugra,* with a na-
'ture partly warlike and partly servile, ferocious
'in his manners, cruel in his acts.

10. 'The sons of a *Bráhmen* by *women of* three
'*lower* classes, of a *Cshatriya* by *women of* two,
'and of a *Vaisya* by one *lower* class, are called
'*Apasadáh,* or degraded *below their fathers.*

11. 'From a *Cshatriya,* by a *Bráhmenì* wife,
'springs a *Súta* by birth; from a *Vaisya,* by a
'military or sacerdotal wife, spring a *Mágadha* and
'a *Vaidéha.*

12. 'From a *Súdra,* on women of the com-
'mercial, military, and priestly classes, are born
'sons

'sons of a mixed breed, called *A'yógava*, *Cshattrĭ*, 'and *Chandála*, the lowest of mortals.

13. 'As the *Ambasht'ha* and *Ugra*, born in a 'direct order, with one class between *those of their* '*parents*, are considered in law, so are the *Cshattrĭ*, 'and the *Vaidéha*, born in an inverse order *with one* '*intermediate class*; *and all four may be touched* '*without impurity*.

14. 'Those sons of the twice born, who are 'begotten on women without an interval (*Antara*) between the classes mentioned in order, 'the wise call *Anantaras*, giving them a *distinct* name from the lower degree of their 'mothers.

15. 'From a *Bráhmen*, by a girl of the *Ugra* 'tribe, is born an *A'vrĭta*; by one of the *Ambast'ha* 'tribe, an *A'bhíra*; by one of the *A'yógava* tribe, 'a *Dhigvana*.

16. 'The *A'yógava*, the *Cshattrĭ*, and the *Chandála*, the lowest of men, spring from a *Súdra* in 'an inverse order *of the classes*, and are *therefore* 'all three excluded *from the performance of obsequies* '*to their ancestors*:

17. 'From a *Vaisya* the *Mágadha* and *Vaidéha*, 'from a *Cshatriya* the *Súta* only, are born in an 'inverse order; and they are three other sons excluded *from funeral rites to their fathers*.

18. 'The son of a *Nishádа* by a woman of the '*Súdra* class, is by tribe a *Puccasa*; but the son 'of a *Súdra* by a *Nishádì* woman, is named *Cuccutaca*.

19. 'One born of a *Cshattrĭ* by an *Ugrá*, is 'called *Swapáca*; and one begotten by a *Vaidéha* 'on an *Ambashthì* wife is called *Véna*.

20. 'Those, whom the twice born beget on 'women of equal classes, but who perform not

'the proper ceremonies *of assuming the thread, and* 'the like, people denominate *Vrátyas*, or excluded 'from the *gáyatrì*.

21. 'From such an outcast *Bráhmen* springs a 'son of a sinful nature, *who in different countries* 'is named a *Bhúrjacantaca*, an *A'vantya*, a *Vátad-* '*hána*, a *Pushpadha* and a *Saic'ha*:

22. 'From such an outcast *Cshatriya* comes a 'son called a *J'halla*, a *Malla*, a *Nich'hivi*, a *Nata*, 'a *Carana*, a *C'hasa*, and a *Dravira*:

23. 'From such an outcast *Vaisya* is born a son 'called *Sudhanwan*, *Chárya*, *Carusha*, *Vijanman*, '*Maitra*, and *Satwata*.

24 'By intermixtures of the classes, by their 'marriages with women who ought not to be 'married, and by their omission of prescribed 'duties, impure classes have been formed.

25. 'Those men of mingled births, who were 'born in the inverse order of classes, and who 'intermarry among themselves, I will now com- 'pendiously describe.

26. 'The *Súta*, the *Vaidéha*, and the *Chandála*, 'that lowest of mortals, the *Mágadha*, the *Cshattrì* 'by tribe, and the *A'yógava*.

27. 'These six beget similar sons on women of 'their own classes, or on women of the same class 'with their mothers; and they produce the like 'from women of the two highest classes, *and of* '*the lowest*:

28 'As a twice born son may spring from a '*Bráhmen*, by women of two classes out of 'three, *a similar son*, when there is no interval, 'and *an equal son* from a woman of his own 'class, it is thus in the case of the low tribes in 'order.

29. 'Those

29. ‘ Thoſe ſix beget, on women of their own ‘ tribes, reciprocally, very many deſpicable and ‘ abject races even more foul than their begetters.

30. ‘ Even as a *Súdra* begets, on a *Bráhmenì* ‘ woman, a ſon more vile than himſelf, thus any ‘ other low man begets, on *women of* the four ‘ claſſes, a ſon yet lower.

31. ‘ The ſix low claſſes, marrying inverſely, ‘ beget fifteen yet lower tribes, the baſe producing ‘ ſtill baſer; *and in a direct order they produce fifteen* ‘ *more.*

32. ‘ A *Daſyu*, or outcaſt of any pure claſs, ‘ begets, on an *A'yógavì* woman, a *Sairindhra*, who ‘ ſhould know how to attend and to dreſs his ‘ maſter; though not a ſlave, he muſt live by ‘ ſlaviſh work, and may alſo gain ſubſiſtence by ‘ catching wild beaſts in toils:

33. ‘ A *Vaidéha* begets on her a ſweet-voiced ‘ *Maitréyaca*, who, ringing a bell at the appear- ‘ ance of dawn, continually praiſes great men:

34. ‘ A *Niſháda* begets on her a *Márgava* or ‘ *Dáſa*, who ſubſiſts by his labour in boats, and ‘ is named *Caiverta* by thoſe who dwell in *A'ryá-* ‘ *verta*, or the land of the venerable.

35. ‘ Thoſe three of a baſe tribe are ſeverally ‘ begotten on *A'yógavì* women, who wear the ‘ clothes of the deceaſed and eat reprehenſible food.

36. ‘ From a *Niſháda* ſprings, *by a woman of the* ‘ Vaidéha *tribe*, a *Cáràvara*, who cuts leather, and ‘ from a *Vaidéha* ſpring, *by women of* the Cáràvara ‘ *and* Niſháda *caſts*, an *Andhra* and a *Méda*, who ‘ muſt live without the town

37. ‘ From a *Chandála*, by a *Vaidéhì* woman, ‘ comes a *Pánduſópáca*, who works with cane and ‘ reeds; and from a *Niſháda*, an *Ahindica*, who ‘ acts as a jailor.

38. ‘ From a *Chandála*, by a *Puccasì* woman, ‘ is born a *Sópáca*, who lives by puniſhing cri- ‘ minals condemned by the king, a ſinful wretch ‘ ever deſpiſed by the virtuous.

39. ‘ A *Niſhádì* woman, by a *Chandála*, pro- ‘ duces a ſon called *Antyavaſáyin*, employed in ‘ places for burning the dead, contemned even ‘ by the contemptible.

40. ‘ Theſe, among various mixed claſſes, ‘ have been deſcribed by their ſeveral fathers and ‘ mothers; and, whether concealed or open, they ‘ may be known by their occupations.

41. ‘ Six ſons, *three* begotten on women of the ‘ ſame claſs, and *three* on women of lower claſſes, ‘ muſt perform the duties of twice born men; ‘ but thoſe who are *born in an inverſe order, and* ‘ called low born, are equal, in reſpect of duty, to ‘ mere *Súdras*.

42. ‘ By the force of extreme devotion and of ‘ exalted fathers, all of them may riſe *in time* to ‘ high birth, as, *by the reverſe*, they may ſink to a ‘ lower ſtate, in every age among mortals in this ‘ inferiour world.

43. ‘ The following races of *Cſhatriyas*, by ‘ their omiſſion of holy rites, and by ſeeing no ‘ *Bráhmens*, have gradually ſunk among men, to ‘ the loweſt of the four claſſes:

44. ‘ *Paund'racas*, *Odras*, and *Draviras*; *Cám-* ‘ *bójas*, *Yavanas*, and *Sacas*; *Páradas*, *Pahlavas*, ‘ *Chínas*, *Cirátas*, *Deradas*, and *C'haſas*.

45. ‘ All thoſe tribes of men, who ſprang from ‘ the mouth, the arm, the thigh, and the foot of ‘ Brahma', *but* who became outcaſts *by having* ‘ *neglected their duties*, are called *Daſyus*, or *plun-* ‘ *derers*, whether they ſpeak the language of ‘ *Mléchch'has*, or that of *A'ryas*.

46. ‘ Those

46. 'THOSE ſons of the twice born who are 'ſaid to be degraded, and who are conſidered as 'low born, ſhall ſubſiſt only by ſuch employments, 'as the twice born deſpiſe.

47. '*Sútas* muſt live by managing horſes and 'by driving cars; *Ambaſht'has*, by curing diſ-'orders; *Vaidéhas*, by waiting on women; *Má-'gadhas*, by travelling with merchandize;

48. '*Niſhádas*, by catching fiſh; an *A'yógava*, 'by the work of a carpenter; a *Méda*, an *Andhra*, 'and (the ſons of a *Bráhmen* by wives of the *Vai-'déha* and *Ugra* claſſes, reſpectively called) a *Chun-'chu* and a *Madgu*, by ſlaying beaſts of the foreſt;

49. 'A *Cſhattrí*, an *Ugra*, and a *Puccaſa*, by 'killing or confining ſuch animals as live in holes: '*Dhigvanas*, by ſelling leather; *Vénas*, by ſtriking 'muſical inſtruments:

50. 'Near large publick trees, in places for 'burning the dead, on mountains, and in groves, 'let thoſe tribes dwell, generally known, and en-'gaged in their ſeveral works.

51. 'THE abode of a *Chandála* and a *Swapáca* 'muſt be out of the town; they muſt not have 'the uſe of entire veſſels; their ſole wealth muſt 'be dogs and aſſes:

52. 'Their clothes muſt be the mantles of the 'deceaſed; their diſhes for food, broken pots; 'their ornaments, ruſty iron; continually muſt 'they roam from place to place:

53. 'Let no man, who regards his duty reli-'gious and civil, hold any intercourſe with them; 'let their tranſactions be confined to themſelves, 'and their marriages only between equals:

54. 'Let food be given to them in potſherds, 'but not by the hands of the giver; and let them 'not walk by night in cities or towns:

55. 'By day they may walk about for the 'purpose of work, distinguished by the king's 'badges; and they shall carry out the corpse of 'every one who dies without kindred: such is 'the fixed rule.

56. 'They shall always kill those who are to 'be slain by the sentence of the law, and by the 'royal warrant; and let them take the clothes of 'the slain, their beds, and their ornaments.

57. 'Him, who was born of a sinful mother, '*and consequently* in a low class, but is not openly 'known, who, though worthless in truth, bears 'the semblance of a worthy man, let people dis-'cover by his acts:

58. 'Want of virtuous dignity, harshness of 'speech, cruelty, and habitual neglect of pre-'scribed duties, betray, in this world, the son of a 'criminal mother.

59. 'Whether a man of debased birth assume 'the character of his father or of his mother, he 'can at no time conceal his origin:

60. 'He, whose family had been exalted, but 'whose parents were criminal in marrying, has a 'base nature, according as the offence *of his mother* 'was great or small.

61. 'In whatever country such men are born, 'as destroy the purity of the four classes, that 'country soon perishes, together with the natives 'of it.

62. 'Desertion of life, without reward, for the 'sake of preserving a priest or a cow, a woman 'or a child, may cause the beatitude of those base-'born tribes.

63. 'Avoiding all injury *to animated beings*, 'veracity, abstinence from theft, *and from unjust* '*seizure of property*, cleanliness, and command

'over

'over the bodily organs, form the compendious
'system of duty which MENU has ordained for
'the four classes.

64. SHOULD the tribe sprung from a *Bráhmen*
'by a *Súdra* woman, produce *a succession of children*
'by the marriages of its women with other *Brá-*
'*mens*, the low tribe shall be raised to the highest
'in the seventh generation.

65. 'As the son of a *Súdra* may *thus* attain the
'rank of a *Bráhmen*, and as the son of a *Bráhmen*
'may sink to a level with *Súdras*, even so must it
'be with him who springs from a *Cshatriya*; even
'so with him who was born of a *Vaisya*.

66. 'IF there be a doubt, as to the preference
'between him who was begotten by a *Bráhmen*
'for his pleasure, *but not in wedlock*, on a *Súdra*
'woman, and him who was begotten by a *Súdra*
'on a *Bráhmenì*,

67. 'Thus is it removed: he, who was be-
'gotten by an exalted man on a base woman,
'may, by his good acts, become respectable; but
'he, who was begotten on an exalted woman by
'a base man, must himself continue base:

68. 'Neither of the two (as the law is fixed)
'shall be girt with a sacred string; not the former,
'because his mother was low; nor the second,
'because the order of the classes was inverted.

69. 'As good grain, springing from good soil,
'is in all respects excellent, thus a man, springing
'from a respectable father by a respectable mo-
'ther, has a claim to the whole institution of the
'twice born.

70. 'Some sages give a preference to the
'grain; others to the field; and others consider
'both field and grain; on this point the decision
'follows:

71. 'Grain,

71. 'Grain, cast into bad ground, wholly 'perishes, and a good field, with no grain sown in 'it, is a mere heap of clods;

72. 'But since, by the virtue of eminent fathers, even the sons of wild animals, *as* Rĭshyasringa, *and others*, have been transformed into 'holy men revered and extolled, the paternal side, 'therefore, prevails.

73. 'BRAHMA' himself, having compared a '*Súdra*, who performs the duties of the twice-born, with a twice born man, who does the acts 'of a *Súdra*, said: "Those two are neither equal "nor unequal," *that is, they are neither equal in* '*rank, nor unequal in bad conduct.*

74. 'LET such *Bráhmens* as are intent on the 'means of attaining the supreme godhead, and 'firm in their own duties, completely perform, in 'order, the six following acts:

75. 'Reading the *Védas*, and teaching *others* 'to read them, sacrificing, and assisting *others* to 'sacrifice, giving *to the poor, if themselves have* '*enough*, and accepting *gifts from the virtuous, if* '*themselves are poor*, are the six prescribed acts of 'the first born class;

76. 'But, among those six acts of a *Bráhmen*, 'three are his *means of* subsistence; assisting to 'sacrifice, teaching the *Védas*, and receiving gifts 'from a pure-handed giver.

77. 'Three acts of duty cease with the *Bráhmen*, and belong not to the *Cshatriya*; teaching 'the *Védas*, officiating at a sacrifice, and, thirdly, 'receiving presents:

78. 'Those *three* are also, by the fixed rule of 'law, forbidden to the *Vaisya*; since MENU, the 'lord of all men, prescribed not those acts to the 'two *classes, military and commercial.*

79. 'The

79. 'The means of ſubſiſtence, peculiar to the 'Cſhatriya, are bearing arms, either held for ſtriking or miſſile, to the *Vaiſya*, merchandize, attending on cattle, and agriculture: but, *with a view to the next life*, the duties of both are alms-giving, reading, ſacrificing.

80. 'Among the ſeveral occupations *for gaining a livelihood*; the moſt commendable reſpectively for the ſacerdotal, military, and mercantile claſſes, are teaching the *Véda*, defending the people, and commerce, or keeping herds and flocks.

81. 'Yet a *Bráhmen*, unable to ſubſiſt by his duties juſt mentioned, may live by the duty of a ſoldier; for that is the next in rank.

82. 'If it be aſked, how he muſt live, ſhould he be unable to get a ſubſiſtence by either of thoſe employments; *the anſwer is*, he may ſubſiſt as a mercantile man, applying himſelf *in perſon* to tillage and attendance on cattle:

83. 'But a *Bráhmen* and a *Cſhatriya*, obliged to ſubſiſt by the acts of a *Vaiſya*, muſt avoid with care, *if they can live by keeping herds*, the buſineſs of tillage, which gives great pain *to ſentient creatures*, and is dependant on *the labour of* others, *as bulls and ſo forth*.

84. 'Some are of opinion, that agriculture is excellent; but it is a mode of ſubſiſtence which the benevolent greatly blame; for the iron-mouthed pieces of wood not only wound the earth, but the creatures dwelling in it.

85 'If, through want of a virtuous livelihood, they cannot follow laudable occupations, they may then gain a competence of wealth by ſelling commodities uſually ſold by merchants, avoiding what ought to be avoided.

86. 'They muſt avoid ſelling liquids of all
'ſorts, dreſſed grain, ſeeds of *tila*, ſtones, ſalt,
'cattle, and human creatures;

87. 'All woven cloth dyed red, cloth made of
'*ſana*, of *cſhumá* bark, and of wool, even though
'not red; fruit, roots, and medicinal plants;

88. 'Water, iron, poiſon, fleſh-meat, the
'moon-plant, and perfumes of any ſort; milk,
'honey, butter-milk, clarified butter, oil of *tila*,
'wax, ſugar, and blades of *cuſa*-graſs;

89. 'All beaſts of the foreſt, *as deer and the*
'*like*; ravenous beaſts, birds, *and fiſh*; ſpirituous
'liquors, *níli*, or indigo, and *lácſhá*, or lac; and
'all beaſts with uncloven hoofs.

90. 'But the *Bráhmen* huſbandman may at
'pleaſure ſell pure *tila*-ſeeds for the purpoſe of
'holy rites, if he keep them not long *with a hope*
'*of more gain*, and ſhall have produced them by
'his own culture:

91. 'If he apply ſeeds of *tila* to any purpoſe
'but food, anointing, and ſacred oblations, he
'ſhall be plunged, in the ſhape of a worm, to-
'gether with his parents, into the ordure of
'dogs.

92. 'By ſelling fleſh-meat, *lácſhá*, or ſalt,
'a *Bráhmen* immediately ſinks low, by ſelling
'milk three days, he falls to a level with a *Súdra*;

93. 'And by ſelling the other forbidden com-
'modities with his own free will, he aſſumes in
'this world, after ſeven nights, the nature of a
'mere *Vaiſya*.

94. 'Fluid things may, however, be bartered
'for other fluids, but not ſalt for any thing liquid;
'ſo may dreſſed grain for grain undreſſed, and *tila*-
'ſeeds for grain in the huſk, equal weights or
'meaſures being given and taken.

95. 'A

95. ‘A MILITARY man, in diſtreſs, may ſub-
‘ſiſt by all theſe means, but at no time muſt
‘he have recourſe to the higheſt, *or ſacerdotal*
‘function.

96. ‘A man of the loweſt claſs, who, through
‘covetouſneſs, lives by the acts of the higheſt, let
‘the king ſtrip of all his wealth and inſtantly
‘baniſh:

97. ‘His own office, though defectively per-
‘formed, is preferable to that of another, though
‘performed completely; for he, who *without ne-
‘ceſſity* diſcharges the duties of another claſs,
‘immediately forfeits his own.

98. ‘A MERCANTILE man, unable to ſubſiſt
‘by his own duties, may deſcend even to the
‘ſervile acts of a *Súdra*, taking care never to do
‘what ought never to be done: but, when he has
‘gained a competence, let him depart from
‘ſervice.

99. ‘A MAN of the fourth claſs, not finding
‘employment by waiting on the twice born, while
‘his wife and ſon are tormented with hunger,
‘may ſubſiſt by handicrafts:

100. ‘Let him principally follow thoſe mecha-
‘nical occupations, *as joinery and maſonry*, or thoſe
‘various practical arts, *as painting and writing*, by
‘following of which he may ſerve the twice born.

101. ‘SHOULD a *Bráhmen*, afflicted and pining
‘through want of food, chooſe rather to remain fix-
‘ed in the path of his own duty, than to adopt the
‘practice of *Vaiſyas*, let him act in this manner:

102. ‘The *Bráhmen*, having fallen into diſtreſs,
‘may receive gifts from any perſon whatever,
‘for by no ſacred rule can it be ſhown, that ab-
‘ſolute purity can be ſullied.

103. ‘From

103. ‘ From interpreting the *Véda*, from officiating at sacrifices, or from taking presents, though in modes generally disapproved, no sin is committed by priests *in distress*; for they are as pure as fire or water.

104. ‘ He who receives food, when his life could not otherwise be sustained, from any man whatever, is no more tainted by sin than the subtil ether by mud:

105. ‘ AJI′GARTA, dying with hunger, was going to destroy his own son (*named* SU′NAHS′E′P′HA) *by selling him for some cattle*, yet he was guilty of no crime, since he only sought a remedy against famishing:

106. ‘ VA′MADE′VA who well knew right and wrong, was by no means rendered impure, though desirous, when oppressed *with hunger*, of eating the flesh of dogs for the preservation of his life:

107. ‘ BHARADWA′JA, eminent in devotion, when he and his son were almost starved in a dreary forest, accepted several cows from the carpenter VRĬDHU:

108. ‘ VISWA′MITRA too, than whom none better knew the distinctions between virtue and vice, resolved, when he was perishing with hunger, to eat the haunch of a dog, which he had received from a CHANDA′LA.

109. ‘ Among *the* acts *generally disapproved*, *namely*, accepting presents *from low men*, assisting *them* to sacrifice, and explaining the scripture *to them*, the receipt of presents is the meanest *in this world*, and the most blamed in a *Bráhmen* after his present life;

110. ‘ Because assisting to sacrifice and explaining

'ing the ſcripture, are two acts always performed
'for thoſe, whoſe minds have been improved *by
'the ſacred initiation*; but gifts are alſo received
'from a ſervile man of the loweſt claſs.

111. 'The guilt incurred by aſſiſting *low men*
'to ſacrifice, and by teaching *them* the ſcripture,
'is removed by repetitions of the *gáyatrì* and ob-
'lations to fire; but that, incurred by accepting
'gifts *from them*, is expiated only by abandoning
'the gifts and by rigorous devotion.

112. 'It were better for a *Bráhmen*, who could
'not maintain himſelf, to glean ears and grains,
'after harveſt, from *the field of* any perſon what-
'ever: gleaning whole ears would be better than
'accepting a preſent, and picking up ſingle grains
'would be ſtill more laudable.

113. '*Bráhmens*, who keep houſe, and are in
'want of any metals, *except gold and ſilver*, or of
'articles *for good uſes*, may aſk the king for them,
'if he be of the military claſs; but a king, *known
'to be avaricious and* unwilling to give, muſt not
'be ſolicited.

114. 'The foremoſt, *in order*, of theſe things
'may be received more innocently than that which
'follows it: a field untilled, a tilled field, cows,
'goats, ſheep, precious metals or gems, new grain,
'dreſſed grain.

115. 'There are ſeven virtuous means of ac-
'quiring property; ſucceſſion, occupancy or dona-
'tion, and purchaſe or exchange, *which are al-
'lowed to all claſſes*; conqueſts, *which is peculiar
'to the military claſs*; lending at intereſt, huſban-
'dry or commerce, *which belong to the mercantile
'claſs*; and acceptance of preſents, *by the ſacer-
'dotal claſs*, from reſpectable men.

116. 'Learning,

116. 'Learning, *except that contained in the* '*scriptures*, art, *as mixing perfumes and the like*, 'work for wages, menial ſervice, attendance on 'cattle, traffick, agriculture, content with little, 'alms, and receiving high intereſt on money, are 'ten modes of ſubſiſtence *in times of diſtreſs*.

117. 'Neither a prieſt nor a military man, '*though diſtreſſed*, muſt receive intereſt on loans, 'but each of them, if he pleaſe, may pay *the* ſmall 'intereſt *permitted by law, on borrowing* for ſome 'pious uſe, to the ſinful man *who demands it*.

118. 'A MILITARY king, who takes even a 'fourth part *of the crops of his realm* at a time of 'urgent neceſſity, *as of war or invaſion*, and pro- 'tects his people to the utmoſt of his power, 'commits no ſin:

119. 'His peculiar duty is conqueſt, and he 'muſt not recede from battle; ſo that while he 'defends by his arms the merchant and huſband- 'man, he may levy the legal tax *as the price of* '*protection*.

120. 'The tax on the mercantile claſs, *which* '*in times of proſperity muſt be only a twelfth part of* '*their crops, and a fiftieth of their perſonal profits*, 'may be an eighth of their crops *in a time of diſtreſs*, '*or a ſixth, which is the medium, or even a fourth* '*in great publick adverſity*; but a twentieth of 'their *gains on* money, and other moveables, is 'the higheſt *tax*: ſerving men, artiſans, and me- 'chanicks muſt aſſiſt by their labour, *but at no* '*time pay taxes*.

121. 'IF a *Súdra* want a ſubſiſtence, *and cannot* '*attend a prieſt*, he may ſerve a *Cſhatriya*; or, *if* '*he cannot wait on a ſoldier by birth*, he may gain 'his livelihood by ſerving an opulent *Vaiſya*.

122. 'To

122. ‘ To him, who ſerves *Bráhmens* with a view to a heavenly reward, or even with a view to both *this life and the next*, the union of the word *Bráhmen* with his *name of ſervant* will aſſuredly bring ſucceſs.

123. ‘ Attendance on *Bráhmens* is pronounced the beſt work of a *Súdra:* whatever elſe he may perform will comparatively avail him nothing.

124. ‘ They muſt allot him a fit maintenance according to their own circumſtances, after conſidering his ability, his exertions, and the number of thoſe whom he muſt provide with nouriſhment:

125. ‘ What remains of their dreſſed rice muſt be given to him; and apparel which they have worn, and the refuſe of their grain, and their old houſehold furniture.

126. ‘ THERE is no guilt in a man of the ſervile claſs *who eats leeks and other forbidden vegetables:* he muſt not have the ſacred inveſtiture: he has no buſineſs with *the* duty *of making oblations to fire and the like*; but there is no prohibition againſt *his offering dreſſed grain as a ſacrifice, by way of diſcharging* his own duty.

127. ‘ Even *Súdras*, who are anxious to perform their entire duty, and, knowing what they ſhould perform, imitate the practice of good men *in the houſehold ſacraments*, but without any holy text, *except thoſe containing praiſe and ſalutation*, are ſo far from ſinning, that they acquire juſt applauſe:

128. ‘ As a *Súdra*, without injuring another man, performs the *lawful* acts of the twice born, even thus, without being cenſured, he gains exaltation in this world and in the next.

129. ‘ No *ſuperflucus* collection of wealth muſt ‘ be made by a *Súdra,* even though he has power ‘ *to make it,* ſince a ſervile man, who has amaſſed ‘ riches, *becomes proud, and, by his inſolence or ne-* ‘ *glect,* gives pain even to *Bráhmens.*

130. ‘ SUCH, as have been fully declared, are ‘ the ſeveral duties of the four claſſes in diſtreſs ‘ for ſubſiſtence ; and, if they perform them ex- ‘ actly, they ſhall attain the higheſt beatitude.

131. ‘ Thus has been propounded the ſyſtem ‘ of duties, religious and civil, ordained for all ‘ claſſes : I next will declare the pure law of ex- ‘ piation for ſin.’

122. 'To him, who serves *Bráhmens* with a 'view to a heavenly reward, or even with a view 'to both *this life and the next,* the union of the 'word *Bráhmen* with his *name of servant* will as'suredly bring success.

123. 'Attendance on *Bráhmens* is pronounced 'the best work of a *Súdra:* whatever else 'he may perform will comparatively avail him 'nothing.

124. 'They must allot him a fit maintenance 'according to their own circumstances, after con'sidering his ability, his exertions, and the 'number of those whom he must provide with 'nourishment:

125. 'What remains of their dressed rice must 'be given to him; and apparel which they have 'worn, and the refuse of their grain, and their 'old household furniture.

126. 'THERE is no guilt in a man of the ser'vile class *who eats leeks and other forbidden vege'tables:* he must not have the sacred investiture: 'he has no business with *the* duty *of making obla'tions to fire and the like*; but there is no prohibi'tion against *his offering dressed grain as a sacrifice,* '*by way of discharging* his own duty.

127. 'Even *Súdras,* who are anxious to per'form their entire duty, and, knowing what they 'should perform, imitate the practice of good 'men *in the household sacraments,* but without any 'holy text, *except those containing praise and saluta'tion,* are so far from sinning, that they acquire 'just applause:

128. 'As a *Súdra,* without injuring another 'man, performs the *lawful* acts of the twice 'born, even thus, without being censured, he 'gains exaltation in this world and in the next.

129. ‘ No *superflucus* collection of wealth must ‘ be made by a *Súdra,* even though he has power ‘ *to make it,* since a servile man, who has amassed ‘ riches, *becomes proud, and, by his insolence or ne-* ‘ *glect,* gives pain even to *Bráhmens.*

130. ‘ Such, as have been fully declared, are ‘ the several duties of the four classes in distress ‘ for subsistence ; and, if they perform them ex- ‘ actly, they shall attain the highest beatitude.

131. ‘ Thus has been propounded the system ‘ of duties, religious and civil, ordained for all ‘ classes : I next will declare the pure law of ex- ‘ piation for sin.’

CHAPTER THE ELEVENTH.

On Penance and Expiation.

1. 'Him, who intends to marry for the ſake of 'having iſſue; him, who wiſhes to make a ſa'crifice; him, who travels; him, who has given 'all his wealth at a ſacred rite; him, who deſires 'to maintain his preceptor, his father, or his mo'ther; him, who needs a maintenance for him'ſelf, when he firſt reads the *Véda*; and him, 'who is afflicted with illneſs;

2. 'Theſe nine *Bráhmens* let mankind conſider 'as virtuous mendicants, called *ſnátacas*; and, 'to relieve their wants, let gifts *of cattle or gold* 'be preſented to them, in proportion to their 'learning:

3. 'To theſe moſt excellent *Bráhmens* muſt 'rice alſo be given, with holy preſents *at oblations* '*to fire, and within the conſecrated circle*; but the 'dreſſed rice, which others are to receive, muſt be 'delivered on the outſide of the ſacred hearth: '*gold and the like may be given any where.*

4. 'On ſuch *Bráhmens* as well know the *Véda*, 'let the king beſtow, as it becomes him, jewels 'of all ſorts, and the ſolemn reward for officiating 'at the ſacrifice.

5. 'He,

5. ‘ He, who has a wife, and, having begged ‘ money *to defray his nuptial expences*, marries an- ‘ other woman, ſhall have no advantage but ſen- ‘ ſual enjoyment: the offspring belongs to the ‘ beſtower of the gift.

6. ‘ Let every man, according to his ability, ‘ give wealth to *Bráhmens* detached from the ‘ world and learned in ſcripture: ſuch a giver ‘ ſhall attain heaven after this life.

7. ‘ He alone is worthy to drink the juice of ‘ the moon-plant, who keeps a proviſion of grain ‘ ſufficient to ſupply thoſe, whom the law com- ‘ mands him to nouriſh, for the term of three ‘ years or more;

8. ‘ But a twice-born man, who keeps a leſs ‘ proviſion of grain, yet preſumes to taſte the ‘ juice of the moon-plant, ſhall gather no fruit ‘ from that ſacrament, even though he taſte it ‘ at the firſt, *or ſolemn, much leſs at any occaſional* ‘ ceremony.

9. ‘ He, who beſtows gifts on ſtrangers, *with a* ‘ *view to worldly fame*, while he ſuffers his family ‘ to live in diſtreſs, though he has power *to ſup-* ‘ *port them*, touches his lips with honey, but ‘ ſwallows poiſon; ſuch virtue is counterfeit:

10. ‘ Even what he does for the ſake of his ‘ future ſpiritual body, to the injury of thoſe ‘ whom he is bound to maintain, ſhall bring him ‘ ultimate miſery both in this life and in the next.

11. ‘ Should a ſacrifice, performed by any ‘ twice born ſacrificer, and by a *Bráhmen* eſpe- ‘ cially, be imperfect from the want of ſome ‘ ingredient, during the reign of a prince who ‘ knows the law,

12. ‘ Let him take that article, for the com- ‘ pletion

'pletion of the sacrifice, from the house of any 'Vaisya, who possesses considerable herds, but 'neither sacrifices, nor drinks the juice of the 'moon-plant:

13. 'If such a *Vaisya* be not near, he may take 'two or three such necessary articles, at pleasure, 'from the house of a *Súdra*; since a *Súdra* has 'no business with solemn rites.

14. 'Even from the house of a *Bráhmen* or a '*Cshatriya*, who possesses a hundred cows, but has 'no consecrated fire, or a thousand cows, but 'performs no sacrifice *with the moon-plant*, let a 'priest, without scruple, take *the articles wanted*.

15. 'From another *Bráhmen*, who continually 'receives presents but never gives, let him take 'such ingredients of the sacrifice, if not bestowed '*on request*: so shall his fame be spread abroad, 'and his habits of virtue increase.

16. 'Thus, likewise, may a *Bráhmen*, who has 'not eaten at the time of six meals, *or has fasted* '*three whole days*, take at the time of the seventh 'meal, *or on the fourth morning*, from the man 'who behaves basely *by not offering him food* 'enough to supply him till the morrow:

17. 'He may take it from the floor, where 'the grain is trodden out of the husk, or from 'the field, or from the house, or from any place 'whatever; but, if the owner ask *why he takes it*, 'the cause of the taking must be declared.

18. 'The wealth of a virtuous *Bráhmen* must 'at no time be seized by a *Cshatriya*; but, having 'no other means *to complete a sacrifice*, he may 'take the goods of any man who acts wickedly, 'and of any who performs not his religious duties:

19. 'He who takes property from the bad, *for* '*the purpose before-mentioned*, and bestows it on the

 'good,

'good, transforms himself into a boat, and car-
'ries both *the good and the bad* over *a sea of ca-*
'*lamities.*

20. 'Wealth, possessed by men for the performance of sacrifices, the wise call the property of the gods; but the wealth of men, who perform no sacrifice, they consider as the property of demons.

21. 'Let no pious king fine the man *who takes by stealth, or by force, what he wants to make a sacrifice perfect*; since it is the king's folly, that causes the hunger or wants of a *Bráhmen*:

22. 'Having reckoned up the persons, whom the *Bráhmen* is obliged to support, having ascertained his divine knowledge and moral conduct, let the king allow him a suitable maintenance from his own household;

23. 'And, having appointed him a maintenance, let the king protect him on all sides; for he gains from the *Bráhmen* whom he protects, a sixth part of *the reward for* his virtue.

24. 'Let no *Bráhmen* ever beg a gift from a *Súdra*; for, if he perform a sacrifice after such begging, he shall, in the next life, be born a *Chandála.*

25. 'The *Bráhmen* who begs any articles for a sacrifice, and disposes not of them all for that purpose, shall become a kite or a crow for a hundred years.

26. 'Any evil-hearted wretch, who, through covetousness, shall seize the property of the gods or of *Bráhmens*, shall feed in another world on the orts of vultures.

27. 'The sacrifice *Vaiswánari* must be constantly performed on the first day of the new year, or on the new moon of *Chaitra*, as an

'expiation

'expiation for having omitted, *through mere forgetfulneſs*, the appointed ſacrifices of cattle and 'the rites of the moon-plant:

28. 'But a twice born man, who, without 'neceſſity, does an act allowed only in a caſe of 'neceſſity, reaps no fruit from it hereafter: thus 'has it been decided.

29. 'By the *Viſwédévas*, by the *Sádhyas*, and 'by eminent *Riſhis* of the ſacerdotal claſs, the 'ſubſtitute was adopted for the principal act, 'when they were apprehenſive of dying in times 'of imminent peril;

30. 'But no reward is prepared in a future 'ſtate for that ill-minded man, who, when able 'to perform the principal ſacrifice, has recourſe 'to the ſubſtitute.

31. 'A Priest, who well knows the law, 'needs not complain to the king of any grievous 'injury; ſince, even by his own power, he may 'chaſtiſe thoſe who injure him:

32. 'His own power, *which depends on himſelf 'alone*, is mightier than the royal power, *which 'depends on other men:* by his own might, there'fore, may a *Bráhmen* coerce his foes.

33. 'He may uſe, without heſitation, the 'powerful charms revealed to At'harvan, and '*by him* to Angiras; for ſpeech is the weapon 'of a *Bráhmen*: with that he may deſtroy his 'oppreſſors.

34. 'A ſoldier may avert danger from himſelf 'by the ſtrength of his arm; a merchant and a 'mechanick, by their property; but the chief of 'the twice born, by holy texts and oblations 'to fire.

35. 'A prieſt, who performs his duties, who 'juſtly corrects *his children and pupils*, who adviſes

'expiations for ſin, and who loves all animated 'creatures, is truly called a *Bráhmen*: to him let 'no man ſay any thing unpropitious, nor uſe any 'offenſive language.

36. 'Let not a girl, nor a young woman, *married or unmarried*, nor a man with little learning, 'nor a dunce, perform an oblation to fire; nor a 'man diſeaſed, nor one uninveſted *with the ſacrificial ſtring*;

37. 'Since any of thoſe perſons, who make 'ſuch an oblation, ſhall fall into a region of torture, together with him who ſuffers his hearth 'to be uſed: he alone, who perfectly knows the 'ſacred ordinances, and has read all the *Védas*, 'muſt officiate at an oblation to holy fire.

38. 'A *Bráhmen* with abundant wealth, who 'preſents not the prieſt that hallows his fire, with 'a horſe conſecrated to PRAJA'PATI, becomes 'equal to one who has no fire hallowed.

39. 'Let him, who believes the ſcripture, and 'keeps his organs in ſubjection, perform all other 'pious acts; but never in this world let him offer 'a ſacrifice with trifling gifts to the officiating 'prieſt:

40. 'The organs of ſenſe and action, reputation *in this life*, a heavenly manſion *in the next*, 'life *itſelf*, a great name *after death*, children *and* 'cattle, are all deſtroyed by a ſacrifice offered 'with trifling preſents: let no man, therefore, 'ſacrifice without liberal gifts.

41. 'THE prieſt who keeps a ſacred hearth, 'but voluntarily neglects *the morning and evening* '*oblations to* his fires, muſt perform, *in the manner* '*to be deſcribed*, the penance *chándráyana* for one 'month; ſince that *neglect* is equally ſinful with 'the ſlaughter of a ſon.

42. 'They

42. ‘ They who receive property from a *Súdra,*
‘ for the performance of rites to conſecrated fire,
‘ are contemned, as miniſters of the baſe, by all
‘ ſuch as pronounce texts of the *Véda* :

43. ‘ Of thoſe ignorant prieſts, who ſerve the
‘ holy fire for the wealth of a *Súdra,* the giver
‘ ſhall always tread on the foreheads, and thus
‘ paſs over miſeries *in the gloom of death.*

44. ‘ Every man, who does not an act pre-
‘ ſcribed, or does an act forbidden, or is guilty
‘ of exceſs, *even* in *legal* gratifications of the ſenſes,
‘ muſt perform an expiatory penance.

45. ‘ Some of the learned conſider an expiation
‘ as confined to involuntary ſin; but others, from
‘ the evidence of the *Véda,* hold it effectual even
‘ in the caſe of a voluntary offence :

46. ‘ A ſin, involuntarily committed, is re-
‘ moved by repeating certain texts of the ſcrip-
‘ ture; but a ſin committed intentionally, through
‘ ſtrange infatuation, by harſh penances of dif-
‘ ferent ſorts.

47. ‘ If a twice born man, by the will of God
‘ in this world, or from his natural birth, have
‘ any corporeal mark of an expiable ſin committed
‘ in this or a former ſtate, he muſt hold no in-
‘ tercourſe with the virtuous, while his penance
‘ remains unperformed.

48. ‘ Some evil-minded perſons, for ſins com-
‘ mitted in this life, and ſome for bad actions in
‘ a preceding ſtate, ſuffer a morbid change in
‘ their bodies :

49. ‘ A ſtealer of gold from a *Bráhmen* has
‘ whitlows on his nails; a drinker of ſpirits, black
‘ teeth; the ſlayer of a *Bráhmen,* a maraſmus; the
‘ violator of his *guru's* bed, a deformity in the
‘ generative organs;

50. ‘ A

50. 'A malignant informer, fetid ulcers in his 'nostrils; a false detractor, stinking breath; a 'stealer of grain, the defect of some limb; a 'mixer *of bad wares with good*, some redundant 'member;

51. 'A stealer of dressed grain, dyspepsia; a 'stealer of holy words, *or an unauthorized reader 'of the scriptures*, dumbness; a stealer of clothes, 'leprosy; a horse-stealer, lameness;

52. 'The stealer of a lamp, total blindness; 'the mischievous extinguisher of it, blindness in 'one eye; a delighter in hurting sentient crea-'tures, perpetual illness; an adulterer, windy 'swellings in his limbs:

53. 'Thus, according to the diversity of ac-'tions, are born men despised by the good, 'stupid, dumb, blind, deaf, and deformed.

54. 'Penance, therefore, must invariably be 'performed for the sake of expiation; since they, 'who have not expiated their sins, will again 'spring to birth with disgraceful marks.

55. 'KILLING a *Bráhmen*, drinking forbidden 'liquor, stealing gold from a priest, adultery 'with the wife of a father, natural or spiritual, 'and associating with such as commit those of-'fences, wise legislators must declare to be crimes 'in the highest degree, *in respect of those after men-'tioned, but less than incest in a direct line, and some 'others.*

56. 'FALSE boasting of a high tribe, malignant 'information, before the king, of a criminal *who 'must suffer death*, and falsely accusing a spiritual 'preceptor, are crimes *in the second degree, and* 'nearly equal to killing a *Bráhmen*.

57. 'Forgetting the texts of scripture, showing 'contempt of the *Véda*, giving false evidence

'*with-*

'*without a bad motive*, killing a friend *without malice*, 'eating things prohibited, or, *from their manifeſt* '*impurity*, unfit to be taſted, are ſix crimes nearly 'equal to drinking ſpirits; *but perjury and homi-* '*cide require, in atrocious caſes, the harſheſt expiation.*

58. 'To appropriate a thing depoſited *or lent* '*for a time*, a human creature, a horſe, precious 'metals, a field, a diamond, or any other gem, 'is nearly equal to ſtealing the gold of a *Bráhmen*.

59. 'Carnal commerce with ſiſters by the ſame 'mother, with little girls, with women of the 'loweſt mixed claſs, or with the wives of a friend, 'or of a ſon, the wiſe muſt conſider as nearly 'equal to a violation of the paternal bed.

60. 'SLAYING a bull or cow, ſacrificing what 'ought not to be ſacrificed, adultery, ſelling 'oneſelf, deſerting a preceptor, a mother, a fa- 'ther, or a ſon, omitting to read the ſcripture, 'and neglect of the fires *preſcribed by the* Dher- 'maſáſtra *only*,

61. 'The marriage of a younger brother be- 'fore the elder, and that elder's omiſſion to marry 'before the younger, giving a daughter to either 'of them, and officiating at their nuptial ſacrifice,

62 'Defiling a damſel, uſury, want of perfect 'chaſtity in a ſtudent, ſelling a holy pool or 'garden, a wife, or a child,

63. 'Omitting the ſacred inveſtiture, abandon- 'ing a kinſman, teaching the *Véda* for hire, learn- 'ing it from a hired teacher, ſelling commodities 'that ought not to be ſold,

64. 'Working in mines of any ſort, engaging 'in *dykes, bridges, or other* great mechanical works, 'ſpoiling medicinal plants *repeatedly*, ſubſiſting by '*the harlotry of* a wife, offering ſacrifices and 'preparing charms to deſtroy *the innocent*,

65. 'Cutting

65. ‘ Cutting down green trees for firewood, ‘ performing holy rites with a ſelfiſh view merely, ‘ and eating prohibited food *once without a previous* ‘ *deſign*,

66. ‘ Neglecting to keep up the conſecrated ‘ fire, ſtealing *any valuable thing beſides gold*, non- ‘ payment of *the three* debts, application to the ‘ books of a falſe religion, and exceſſive attention ‘ to muſick or dancing,

67. ‘ Stealing grain, baſe metals, or cattle, ‘ familiarity, *by the twice born*, with women who ‘ have drunk inebriating liquor, killing *without* ‘ *malice* a woman, *a Súdra*, *a Vaiſya*, or a *Cſhatriya*, ‘ and denying a future ſtate of rewards and pu- ‘ niſhments, are all crimes in the third degree, ‘ *but higher or lower according to circumſtances.*

68. ‘ Giving pain to a *Bráhmen*, ſmelling at ‘ any ſpirituous liquor or any thing *extremely fetid* ‘ *and* unfit to be ſmelt, cheating, and unnatural ‘ practices with a male, are conſidered as cauſing ‘ a loſs of claſs.

69. ‘ To kill an aſs, a horſe, a camel, a deer, ‘ an elephant, a goat, a ſheep, a fiſh, a ſnake, or ‘ a buffalo, is declared an offence which degrades ‘ the killer to a mixed tribe.

70. ‘ Accepting preſents from deſpicable ‘ men, illegal traffick, attendance on a *Súdra* ‘ maſter, and ſpeaking falſehood, muſt be con- ‘ ſidered as cauſes of excluſion from ſocial repaſts.

71. Killing an inſect, ſmall or large, a worm, ‘ or a bird, eating what has been brought *in the* ‘ *ſame baſket* with ſpirituous liquor, ſtealing fruit, ‘ wood, or flowers, and great perturbation of ‘ mind on trifling occaſions, are offences which ‘ cauſe defilement.

72. ‘ You

72. ‘ You ſhall now be completely inſtructed ‘ in thoſe penances, by which all the ſins juſt ‘ mentioned are expiable.

73. ‘ If a *Bráhmen* have killed a man of the ‘ ſacerdotal claſs, *without malice prepenſe, the ſlayer* ‘ *being far ſuperiour to the ſlain in good qualities,* he ‘ muſt himſelf make a hut in a foreſt and dwell in ‘ it twelve whole years, ſubſiſting on alms for the ‘ purification of his ſoul, placing near him, as a ‘ token *of his crime, the ſkull of the ſlain, if he can* ‘ *procure it, or, if not, any human ſkull. The time* ‘ *of penance for the three lower claſſes muſt be twenty-* ‘ *four, thirty-ſix, and forty-eight years.*

74. ‘ Or, *if the ſlayer be of the military claſs,* he ‘ may voluntarily expoſe himſelf as a mark to ‘ archers, who know *his intention*; or, *according to* ‘ *circumſtances,* may caſt himſelf head-long thrice, ‘ or even till he die, into blazing fire.

75. ‘ Or, *if he be a king, and ſlew a prieſt with-* ‘ *out malice or knowledge of his claſs,* he may per- ‘ form, *with preſents of great wealth,* one of the ‘ following ſacrifices; an *Aſwamédha*, or a *Swerjit*, ‘ or a *Goſava*, or an *Abhijit*, or a *Viſwajit*, or a ‘ *Trivrĭt*, or an *Agniſhtut*.

76. ‘ Or, to expiate the guilt of killing a prieſt ‘ *without knowing him and without deſign,* the killer ‘ may walk *on a pilgrimage* a hundred *yójanas*, re- ‘ peating any one of the *Védas*, eating barely ‘ enough to ſuſtain life, and keeping his organs in ‘ perfect ſubjection;

77. ‘ Or, *if in that caſe the ſlayer be unlearned,* ‘ *but rich,* he may give all his property to ſome ‘ *Bráhmen* learned in the *Véda*, or a ſufficiency of ‘ wealth for his life, or a houſe and furniture *to* ‘ *hold while he lives:*

78. ‘ Or,

78. 'Or, eating only ſuch wild grains as are 'offered to the gods, he may walk to *the head of* 'the river *Saraſwatì* againſt the courſe of the 'ſtream; or, ſubſiſting on very little food, he 'may thrice repeat the whole collection of *Védas*, 'or the *Rĭch*, *Yajuſh*, and *Sáman*.

79. 'Or, his hair being ſhorn, he may dwell 'near a town, or on paſture ground for cows, 'or in ſome holy place, or at the root of a ſacred 'tree, taking pleaſure in doing good to cows and 'to *Bráhmens*:

80. 'There, for the preſervation of a cow or 'a *Bráhmen*, let him inſtantly abandon life; ſince 'the preſerver of a cow or a *Bráhmen* atones for 'the crime of killing a prieſt:

81. 'Or, by attempting at leaſt three times 'forcibly to recover *from robbers* the property of a '*Bráhmen*, or by recovering it in one of its attacks, 'or even by loſing his life in the attempt, he 'atones for his crime.

82. 'Thus continually firm in religious auſte-'rity, chaſte as a ſtudent in the firſt order, with 'his mind intent on virtue, he may expiate the 'guilt of *undeſignedly* killing a *Bráhmen*, after the 'twelfth year has expired.

83. 'Or, *if a virtuous* Bráhmen *unintentionally kill* '*another, who had no good quality*, he may atone for 'his guilt by proclaiming it in an aſſembly of 'prieſts and military men, at the ſacrifice of a 'horſe, and by bathing with other *Bráhmens* at the 'cloſe of the ſacrifice:

84. '*Bráhmens* are declared to be the baſis, and '*Cſhatriyas* the ſummit of the legal ſyſtem: he, 'therefore, expiates his offence by fully proclaim-'ing it in ſuch an aſſembly.

85. 'From

85. 'From his high birth alone, a *Bráhmen* is 'an object of veneration even to deities; his de-'clarations to mankind are decisive evidence; 'and the *Véda* itself confers on him that character.

86. 'Three at least, who are learned in the '*Véda*, should be assembled to declare the proper 'expiation for the sin *of a priest*, *but*, *for the three 'other classes*, *the number must be doubled*, *tripled*, *and 'quadrupled:* what they declare shall be an atone-'ment for sinners, since the words of the learned 'give purity.

87. 'Thus a *Bráhmen*, who has performed one 'of the preceding expiations, *according to the cir-'cumstances of the homicide and the characters of the 'persons killed and killing*, with his whole mind fixed 'on GOD, purifies his soul, and removes the guilt 'of slaying a man of his own class:

88. 'He must perform the same penance for 'killing an embryo, *the sex of which was* unknown, 'but whose parents were *sacerdotal*, or a military 'or a commercial man employed in a sacrifice, or 'a *Bráhmení* woman, who has bathed after tem-'porary uncleanness;

89. 'And *the same* for giving false evidence *in 'a cause concerning land or gold*, *or precious commodi-'ties*, and for accusing his preceptor unjustly, and 'for appropriating a deposit, and for killing the 'wife of a priest, *who keeps a consecrated fire*, or 'for slaying a friend.

90. 'Such is the atonement ordained for killing 'a priest *without malice*; but for killing a *Bráh-'men* with malice prepense, this is no expia-'tion: *the term of twelve years must be doubled*, *or*, '*if the case was atrocious*, *the murderer must actually 'die in flames or in battle*.

91. 'Any twice born man, who has *intentionally* drunk spirit of rice, through perverse delusion of mind, may drink more spirit in flame, and atone for his offence by severely burning his body;

92. 'Or he may drink boiling hot, until he die, the urine of a cow, or pure water, or milk, or clarified butter, or juice expressed from cow dung:

93. 'Or, *if he tasted it unknowingly*, he may expiate the sin of drinking spirituous liquor, by eating only some broken rice or grains of *tila*, from which oil has been extracted, once every night for a whole year, wrapped in coarse vesture of hairs from a cow's tail, *or sitting unclothed in his house*, wearing his locks and beard uncut, and putting out the flag of a tavern-keeper.

94. 'Since the spirit of rice is *distilled from the* Mala, *or* filthy refuse of the grain, and since *Mala* is also a name for sin, let no *Bráhmen*, *Cshatriya* or *Vaisya* drink that spirit.

95. 'Inebriating liquor may be considered as of three *principal* sorts: that extracted from dregs of sugar, that extracted from bruised rice, and that extracted from the flowers of the *Madhúca*: as one, so *are* all; they shall not be tasted by the chief of the twice born.

96. 'Those liquors, and *eight* other sorts, with the flesh of animals, and *Asava*, the most pernicious beverage, *prepared with narcotick drugs*, are swallowed at the juncates of *Yacshas*, *Racshasas*, and *Pisachas*: they shall not, therefore, be tasted by a *Bráhmen* who feeds on clarified butter offered to gods.

97. 'A *Bráh-*

98. ‘ When the divine ſpirit, *or the light of holy* ‘ *knowledge*, which has been infuſed into his body, ‘ has once been ſprinkled with any intoxicating ‘ liquor, even his prieſtly character leaves him, ‘ and he ſinks to the low degree of a *Súdra*.

99. ‘ THUS have been promulgated the various ‘ modes of expiation for drinking ſpirits: I will ‘ next propound the atonement for ſtealing the ‘ gold of a prieſt *to the amount of a* ſuverna.

100. ‘ HE, who has purloined the gold of a ‘ *Bráhmen*, muſt haſten to the king, and proclaim ‘ his offence; adding, “ Inflict on me the puniſh-“ ment due to my crime.”

101. ‘ Then ſhall the king himſelf, taking ‘ from him an iron mace, *which the criminal muſt* ‘ *bear on his ſhoulder*, ſtrike him with it once; ‘ and by that ſtroke, *whether he die or be only left* ‘ *as dead*, the thief is releaſed from ſin: a *Bráh-* ‘ *men*, by rigid penance alone, *can expiate that of-* ‘ *fence*; *another twice born man may alſo perform* ‘ *ſuch a penance* at his election.

102. ‘ The twice born man, who deſires to ‘ remove, by auſtere devotion, the taint cauſed ‘ by ſtealing gold, muſt perform in a foreſt, co-‘ vered with a mantle of rough bark, the penance ‘ *before ordained* for him, who, *without malice per-* ‘ *penſe*, has killed a *Bráhmen*.

103. ‘ By theſe expiations may the twice ‘ born atone for the guilt of ſtealing gold from ‘ a prieſt; but the ſin of adultery with the wife ‘ of a father, *natural or ſpiritual*, they muſt expiate ‘ by the following penances.

104. ‘ HE, who *knowingly and actually* has ‘ defiled the wife of his father, *ſhe being of the* ‘ *ſame claſs*, muſt extend himſelf on a heated

'iron bed, loudly proclaiming his guilt; and, 'there embracing the red hot iron image of a 'woman, he ſhall atone for his crime by death:

105. 'Or, having himſelf amputated his penis 'and ſcrotum, and holding them in his fingers, 'he may walk in a direct path toward the ſouth-'weſt, or the region of NIRRĬTI, until he fall 'dead on the ground:

106. 'Or, *if he had miſtaken her for another 'woman*, he may perform, for a whole year, with 'intenſe application of mind, the penance *prá-'jápatya*, with part of a bed, *or a human bone*, 'in his hand, wrapped in veſture of coarſe bark, 'letting his hair and beard grow, and living in a 'deſerted foreſt:

107. 'Or, *if ſhe was of a lower claſs and a 'corrupt woman*, he may expiate the ſin of violat-'ing the bed of his father, by continuing the 'penance *chándráyana* for three months, always 'mortifying his body by eating only foreſt herbs, 'or wild grains boiled in water.

108. 'By the preceding penances, may ſinners 'of the two higher degrees atone for their guilt; 'and the leſs offenders may expiate theirs by the 'following auſterities.

109. 'HE, who has committed the ſmaller 'offence of killing a cow, *without malice*, muſt 'drink, for the firſt month, barley corns boiled 'ſoft in water; his head muſt be ſhaved en-'tirely; and, covered with the hide *of the ſlain 'cow*, he muſt fix his abode on her late paſture 'ground:

110. 'He may eat a moderate quantity *of 'wild grains*, but without any factitious ſalt, for 'the next two months at the time of each fourth 'repaſt,

'repast, *on the evening of every second day*; regularly bathing in the urine of cows, and keeping his members under controul:

111. 'All day he must wait on the herd, and stand quaffing the dust raised *by their hoofs*; at night, having servilely attended and stroked and saluted them, he must surround them with a fence, and sit near *to guard* them:

112. 'Pure and free from passion, he must stand, while they stand; follow them, when they move together; and lie down by them, when they lie down:

113. 'Should a cow be sick or terrified by tigers or thieves, or fall, or stick in mud, he must relieve her by all possible means:

114. 'In heat, in rain, or in cold, or while the blast furiously rages, let him not seek his own shelter, without first sheltering the cows to the utmost of his power:

115. 'Neither in his own house, or field, or floor for treading out grain, nor in those of any other person, let him say a word of a cow, who eats *corn or grass*, or of a calf who drinks *milk*:

116. 'By waiting on a herd, according to these rules, for three months, the slayer of a cow atones for his guilt;

117. '*But*, his penance being performed, he must give ten cows and a bull, or, his stock not being so large, must deliver all he possesses, to such as best know the *Véda*.

118. 'THE preceding penances, or that called *chándráyana*, must be performed for the absolution of all twice born men, who have committed sins of the lower *or third* degree; except those, who have incurred the guilt of an *avacírna*;

119. 'But he, who has become *Avacírni*, must 'sacrifice *a black or* a one-eyed ass, by way of a 'meat-offering to NIRRĬTI, *patroness of the south-west*, by night, in a place where four ways meet:

120. 'Let him daily offer to her, in fire, the 'fat of that ass, and, at the close *of the ceremony*, 'let him offer clarified butter, with the holy text '*Sem* and so forth, to PAVANA, to INDRA, to 'VRĬHASPATI, and to AGNI, *regents of wind*, '*clouds, a planet, and fire.*

121. 'A voluntary effusion, *naturally or other-wise*, of that which may produce a man, by a 'twice born youth, during the time of his student-ship, *or before marriage*, has been pronounced '*avacírna*, or a violation of the rule prescribed '*for the first order*, by sages who knew the whole 'system of duty, and uttered the words of the '*Véda*.

122. 'To the four *deities of purification*, MA'-'RUTA, INDRA, VRĬHASPATI, AGNI, goes all the 'divine light, which the *Véda* had imparted, from 'the student, who commits the foul sin *avacírna*;

123. 'But, this crime having actually been 'committed, he must go begging to seven houses, 'clothed only with the hide of the *sacrificed* ass, 'and openly proclaiming his act:

124. 'Eating a single meal begged from them, 'at the regular time of the day, *that is, in the* '*morning or evening*, and bathing *each day* at the 'three *savanas*, he shall be absolved from his guilt 'at the end of one year.

125. 'HE, who has voluntarily committed 'any sin, which causes a loss of class, must per-'form the *tormenting* penance, *thence* called *sánta-pana*; or the *prájápatya*, if he offended involun-'tarily.

126. 'For ſins, which degrade to a mixed 'claſs, or exclude from ſociety, the ſinner muſt 'have recourſe to the *lunar* expiation *chándráyana* 'for one month: to atone for acts which occa-'ſion defilement, he muſt ſwallow nothing for 'three days but hot barley cruel.

127. 'For killing *intentionally* a *virtuous* man 'of the military claſs, the penance muſt be a 'fourth part of that ordained for killing a prieſt; 'for killing a *Vaiſya*, only an eighth; for killing 'a *Súdra*, who had been conſtant in *diſcharging* his 'duties, a ſixteenth part:

128. 'But, if a *Bráhmen* kill a *Cſhatriya* with-'out malice, he muſt, after a full performance of 'his religious rites, give the prieſts one bull to-'gether with a thouſand cows;

129. 'Or he may perform for three years the 'penance for ſlaying a *Bráhmen*, mortifying his 'organs of ſenſation and action, letting his hair 'grow long, and living remote from the town, 'with the root of a tree for his manſion.

130. 'If he kill *without malice* a *Vaiſya*, who 'had a good moral character, he may perform 'the ſame penance for one year, or give the 'prieſts a hundred cows and a bull:

131. 'For ſix months muſt he perform this 'whole penance, if, *without intention*, he kill a '*Súdra*; or he may give ten white cows and a 'bull to the prieſts.

132. 'If he kill, *by deſign*, a cat, or an ichneu-'mon, the bird *cháſha*, or a frog, a dog, a lizard, 'an owl, or a crow, he muſt perform the *ordinary* 'penance required for the death of a *Súdra*, that 'is, the *chándráyana*:

133. 'Or, *if he kill one of them undeſignedly*, he 'may drink nothing but milk for three *days and*

'nights, or *each night* walk a *yógan*, or *thrice* 'bathe in a river, or silently repeat the text on 'the divinity of water; *that is, if he be disabled by* '*real infirmity from performing the first mentioned* '*penances, he may have recourse to the next in order.*

134. 'A *Bráhmen*, if he kill a snake, must give '*to some priest* a hoe, *or iron-headed stick*; if an 'eunuch, a load of rice straw, and a *másha* of 'lead;

135. 'If a boar, a pot of clarified butter; if 'the bird *tittiri*, a *drôna* of *tila*-seeds; if a parrot, 'a steer two years old, if the water-bird *craun*-'*cha*, a steer aged three years:

136. 'If he kill *a goose, or* a phenicopteros, a '*heron, or* cormorant, a bittern, a peacock, an 'ape, a hawk, or a kite, he must give a cow to 'some *Bráhmen*:

137. 'If he kill a horse, he must give a man-'tle; if an elephant, five black bulls; if a goat 'or a sheep, one bull; if an ass, a calf one year 'old:

138. 'If he kill a carnivorous wild beast, he 'must give a cow with abundance of milk; if a 'wild beast not carnivorous, a fine heifer; and 'a *ráctica* of gold, if he slay a camel:

139. 'If he kill a woman *of any class* caught 'in adultery, he must give, as an expiation, in the 'direct order of the four classes, a leathern pouch, 'a bow, a goat, and a sheep.

140. 'Should a *Bráhmen* be unable to expiate 'by gifts the sin of killing a snake and the rest, 'he must atone for his guilt by performing, on 'each occasion, the penance *prájápatya*.

141. 'For the slaughter of a thousand small 'animals which have bones, or for that of bone-'less animals enow to fill a cart, he must per-

'form

'form the *chándráyana,* or common penance for 'killing a *Súdra*;

142. 'But, for killing boned animals, he must 'also give some trifle, *as a* pana *of copper,* to a '*Bráhmen:* for killing those without bones, he 'may be absolved by holding his breath, *at the* '*close of his penance,* while he thrice repeats the *gá*-'*yatrì* with its *head,* the *pranava,* and the *vyáhritis.*

143. 'For cutting *once without malice* trees 'yielding fruit, shrubs with many crowded stems, 'creeping or climbing plants, or such as grow 'again when cut, if they were in blossom *when he* '*hurt them,* he must repeat a hundred texts of the '*Véda.*

144. 'For killing insects of any sort bred in 'rice or other grains, or those bred in honey *or* '*other* fluids, or those bred in fruit or flowers, 'eating clarified butter is a full expiation.

145. If a man cut, *wantonly and* for no good 'purpose, such grasses as are cultivated, or such 'as rise in the forest spontaneously, he must wait 'on a cow for one day, nourished by milk alone.

146. 'By these penances may mankind atone 'for the sin of injuring sentient creatures, whether 'committed by design or through inadvertence: 'hear now what penances are ordained for eating 'or drinking what ought not to be tasted.

147. 'He, who drinks undesignedly any spirit '*but that of rice,* may be absolved by a new in-'vestiture with the sacrificial string: even for 'drinking intentionally *the weaker sorts of spirit,* 'a penance extending to death must not (as the 'law is now fixed) be prescribed.

148. 'For drinking water which has stood in 'a vessel, where spirit of rice or any other spi-'rituous liquor had been kept, he must swallow

'nothing for five *days and* nights, but the plant '*sanc'hapushpi* boiled in milk:

149. 'If he touch any spirituous liquor, or 'give any away, or accept any in due form, *or* '*with thanks*, or drink water left by a *Súdra*, he 'must swallow nothing for three *days and* nights, 'but *cusa*-grass boiled in water.

150. 'Should a *Bráhmen*, who has once tasted 'the holy juice of the moon-plant, even smell 'the breath of a man who has been drinking 'spirits, he must remove the taint by thrice 'repeating the *gáyatrì*, while he suppresses his 'breath in water, and by eating clarified butter '*after that ceremony*.

151. 'If any of the three twice born classes 'have tasted unknowingly human ordure or urine, 'or any thing that has touched spirituous liquor, 'they must, *after a penance*, be girt anew with 'the sacrificial thread;

152. 'But, in such new investiture of the twice 'born, the partial tonsure, the zone, the staff, the 'petition of alms, and the strict rules of absti-'nence, need not be renewed.

153. 'Should one of them eat the food of 'those persons, with whom he ought never to 'eat, or food left by a woman or a *Súdra*, or any 'prohibited flesh, he must drink barley gruel only 'for seven *days and* nights.

154. 'If a *Bráhmen* drink sweet liquors turned 'acid, or astringent juices from impure fruits, he 'becomes unclean as long as those fluids remain 'undigested.

155. 'Any twice born man, who *by accident* 'has tasted the dung or urine of a tame boar, an 'ass, a camel, a shakal, an ape, or a crow, must 'perform the penance *chándráyana*.

156. 'If he taste dried flesh meat, or mushrooms rising from the ground, or any thing brought from a slaughter-house, though he knew not whence it came, he must perform the same penance.

157. 'For *knowingly* eating the flesh of carnivorous beasts, of town boars, of camels, of gallinaceous birds, of human creatures, of crows, or of asses, the penance *taptacrĭch'hra*, or *burning and severe*, is the only atonement.

158. 'A *Bráhmen*, who, before he has completed his theological studies, eats food at monthly obsequies *to one ancestor*, must fast three days *and nights*, and sit in water a day:

159. 'But a student in theology, who at any time *unknowingly* tastes honey or flesh, must perform the lowest penance, or the *prájápatya*, and proceed to finish his studentship.

160. 'Having eaten what has been left by a cat, a crow, a mouse, a dog, or an ichneumon, or what has even been touched by a louse, he must drink, *boiled in water*, the plant *brahmasuverchalá*.

161. 'By the man, who seeks purity of soul, no forbidden food must be tasted: what he has undesignedly swallowed, he must instantly vomit up, or must purify himself with speed by legal expiations.

162. 'Such, as have been declared, are the various penances for eating prohibited food: hear now the law of penance for an expiation of theft.

163. 'The chief of the twice born, having voluntarily stolen such property, as grain, raw or dressed, from the house of another *Bráhmen*,

'shall

'shall be absolved on performing the penance 'prájápatya for a whole year;

164. 'But the penance *chándráyana* must be 'performed for stealing a man, woman, or child, 'for seizing a field, or a house, or for taking the 'waters of an enclosed pool or well.

165. 'Having taken goods of little value from 'the house of another man, he must procure 'absolution by performing the penance *sántapana*; 'having first restored, *as the penitent thief always* '*must*, the goods that he stole.

166. 'For taking what may be eaten, or what 'may be sipped, a carriage, a bed, or a seat, 'roots, flowers, or fruit, an atonement may be 'made by swallowing the five pure things pro-'duced by a cow, *or milk, curds, butter, urine*, '*dung*:

167. 'For stealing grass, wood, or trees, rice 'in the husk, molasses, cloth or leather, fish, or 'other animal food, a strict fast must be kept 'three *days and three* nights.

168. 'For stealing gems, pearls, coral, copper, 'silver, iron, brass, or stone, nothing but broken 'rice must be swallowed for twelve days;

169. 'And nothing but milk for three days, 'if cotton or silk, or wool had been stolen, or a 'beast either with cloven or uncloven hoofs, or 'a bird, or perfumes, or medicinal herbs, or 'cordage.

170. 'By these penances may a twice born 'man atone for the guilt of theft; but the fol-'lowing austerities only can remove the sin of 'carnally approaching those, who must not be 'carnally approached.

171. 'He, who has wasted his manly strength 'with sisters by the same womb, with the wives 'of

156. 'If he taſte dried fleſh meat, or muſh-
'rooms riſing from the ground, or any thing
'brought from a ſlaughter-houſe, though he knew
'not whence it came, he muſt perform the ſame
'penance.

157. 'For *knowingly* eating the fleſh of carni-
'vorous beaſts, of town boars, of camels, of
'gallinaceous birds, of human creatures, of crows,
'or of aſſes, the penance *taptacrĭch'hra*, or *burning*
'*and ſevere*, is the only atonement.

158. 'A *Bráhmen*, who, before he has com-
'pleted his theological ſtudies, eats food at
'monthly obſequies *to one anceſtor*, muſt faſt three
'days *and nights*, and ſit in water a day:

159. 'But a ſtudent in theology, who at any
'time *unknowingly* taſtes honey or fleſh, muſt per-
'form the loweſt penance, or the *prájápatya*, and
'proceed to finiſh his ſtudentſhip.

160. 'Having eaten what has been left by a
'cat, a crow, a mouſe, a dog, or an ichneumon,
'or what has even been touched by a louſe, he
'muſt drink, *boiled in water*, the plant *brahmaſu-*
'*verchalá*.

161. 'By the man, who ſeeks purity of ſoul,
'no forbidden food muſt be taſted: what he
'has undeſignedly ſwallowed, he muſt inſtantly
'vomit up, or muſt purify himſelf with ſpeed by
'legal expiations.

162. 'Such, as have been declared, are the
'various penances for eating prohibited food:
'hear now the law of penance for an expiation
'of theft.

163. 'The chief of the twice born, having
'voluntarily ſtolen ſuch property, as grain, raw
'or dreſſed, from the houſe of another *Bráhmen*,

'ſhall

'shall be absolved on performing the penance 'prájápatya for a whole year;

164. 'But the penance *chándráyana* must be 'performed for stealing a man, woman, or child, 'for seizing a field, or a house, or for taking the 'waters of an enclosed pool or well.

165. 'Having taken goods of little value from 'the house of another man, he must procure 'absolution by performing the penance *sántapana*; 'having first restored, *as the penitent thief always 'must*, the goods that he stole.

166. 'For taking what may be eaten, or what 'may be sipped, a carriage, a bed, or a seat, 'roots, flowers, or fruit, an atonement may be 'made by swallowing the five pure things pro-'duced by a cow, *or milk, curds, butter, urine, 'dung*:

167. 'For stealing grass, wood, or trees, rice 'in the husk, molasses, cloth or leather, fish, or 'other animal food, a strict fast must be kept 'three *days and three* nights.

168. 'For stealing gems, pearls, coral, copper, 'silver, iron, brass, or stone, nothing but broken 'rice must be swallowed for twelve days;

169. 'And nothing but milk for three days, 'if cotton or silk, or wool had been stolen, or a 'beast either with cloven or uncloven hoofs, or 'a bird, or perfumes, or medicinal herbs, or 'cordage.

170. 'By these penances may a twice born 'man atone for the guilt of theft; but the fol-'lowing austerities only can remove the sin of 'carnally approaching those, who must not be 'carnally approached.

171. 'He, who has wasted his manly strength 'with sisters by the same womb, with the wives

'of

'of his friend or of his son, with girls under the 'age of puberty, or with women of the lowest 'classes, must perform the penance ordained for 'defiling the bed of a preceptor:

172. 'He, who has carnally known the daughter of his paternal aunt, *who is almost equal to* a 'sister, or the daughter of his maternal aunt, or 'the daughter of his maternal uncle, *who is* a near 'kinsman, must perform the *chándráyana*, or *lunar* '*penance*;

173. 'No man of sense would take one of 'those three as his wife: they shall not be taken 'in marriage by reason of their consanguinity; 'and he, who marries any one of them, falls 'deep *into sin*.

174. 'He, who has wasted what might have 'produced a man, with female brute animals, 'with a woman during her courses, or in any 'but the natural part, or in water, must perform 'the penance *sántapana*: *for a beastial act with a* '*cow the penance must be far more severe.*

175. 'A twice born man, dallying lasciviously 'with a male *in any place or at any time*, or with 'a female in a carriage drawn by bullocks, or in 'water, or by day, *shall be degraded, and* must 'bathe himself *publickly* with his apparel.

176. 'Should a *Bráhmen* carnally know a wo'man of the *Chandála* or *Mléch'ha* tribes, or taste 'their food, or accept a gift from them, he loses 'his own class; *if he acted unknowingly*, or, *if* '*knowingly*, sinks to a level *with them*.

177. 'A wife, excessively corrupt, let her 'husband confine to one apartment, and compel 'her to perform the penance ordained for a man 'who has committed adultery:

178. 'If,

178. ‘ If, having been ſolicited by a man of
‘ her own claſs, ſhe again be defiled, her expiation
‘ muſt be the penance *prájápatya* added to the
‘ *chándráyana*.

179. ‘ The guilt of a *Bráhmen*, who has dallied
‘ a whole night with a *Chándalì* woman, he may
‘ remove in three years by ſubſiſting on alms,
‘ and inceſſantly repeating the *gáyatrì* with other
‘ myſterious texts.

180. ‘ Theſe penances have been declared for
‘ ſinners of four ſorts, *thoſe who hurt ſentient crea-*
‘ *tures, thoſe who eat prohibited food, thoſe who*
‘ *commit theft, and thoſe who are guilty of laſcivi-*
‘ *ouſneſs*: hear now the preſcribed expiation for
‘ ſuch as hold any intercourſe with degraded
‘ offenders.

181. ‘ He, who aſſociates himſelf for one year
‘ with a fallen ſinner, falls like him; not by ſa-
‘ crificing, reading the *Véda*, or contracting af-
‘ finity with him, *ſince by thoſe acts he loſes his*
‘ *claſs immediately*, but even by uſing the ſame
‘ carriage or ſeat, or by taking his food at the
‘ ſame board:

182. ‘ That man who holds an intercourſe
‘ with any one of thoſe degraded offenders, muſt
‘ perform, as an atonement for ſuch intercourſe,
‘ the penance ordained for that ſinner himſelf.

183. ‘ The *ſapindas* and *ſamánódacas* of a man
‘ degraded, *for a crime in the firſt degree*, muſt
‘ offer a libation of water to his manes, *as if*
‘ *he were naturally dead*, out of the town, in
‘ the evening of ſome inauſpicious day, *as the*
‘ *ninth of the moon*, his paternal kinſman, his
‘ officiating prieſt, and his ſpiritual guide being
‘ preſent.

184. ‘ A female ſlave muſt kick down with
‘ her

'her foot an old pot filled with wate r, *which had* '*for that purpose been placed toward the south*, as 'if it were an oblation for the dead; and all the 'kinsmen, in the nearer and remoter degrees, 'must remain impure for a day and a night:

185. 'They must thenceforth desist from speak-'ing to him, from sitting in his company, from 'delivering to him any inherited or other pro-'perty, and from every civil or usual attention, '*as inviting him on the first day of the year, and the* '*like.*

186. 'His right of primogeniture, *if he was* '*an elder brother*, must be with-holden from him, 'and whatever perquisites arise from priority of 'birth: a younger brother, excelling him in vir-'tue, must appropriate the share of the first-born.

187. 'But, when he has performed his due 'penance, his kinsmen and he must throw down 'a new vessel full of water, after having bathed 'together in a pure pool:

188. 'Then must he cast that vessel into the 'water; and, having entered his house, he may 'perform, as before, all the acts incident to his 'relation by blood.

189. 'The same ceremony must be performed 'by the kindred even of women degraded, for 'whom clothes, dressed rice, and water must be 'provided; and they must dwell *in huts* near the 'family house.

190. 'With sinners, whose expiations are un-'performed, let not a man transact business of 'any kind; but those, who have performed their 'expiations, let him at no time reproach:

191. 'Let him not, however, live with those 'who have slain children, or injured their bene-'factors, or killed suppliants for protection, or

'put

'put women to death, even though ſuch offenders
'have been legally purified.

192. 'THOSE men of the twice born claſſes, 'to whom the *gáyatrì* has not been repeated and 'explained, according to law, the aſſembly muſt 'cauſe to perform three *prájápatya* penances, and '*afterwards* to be girt with the ſacrificial ſtring;

193. 'And the ſame penance they muſt preſcribe to ſuch twice born men, as are anxious to 'atone for ſome illegal act, or a neglect of the *Véda*.

194. 'IF prieſts have accepted any property 'from baſe hands, they may be abſolved by re'linquiſhing the preſents, by repeating myſterious 'texts, and by acts of devotion:

195 'By three thouſand repetitions of the '*gáyatrì* with intenſe application of mind, and by 'ſubſiſting on milk only for a whole month in 'the paſture of cows, a *Bráhmen*, who has re'ceived any gift from a bad man, *or a bad gift* '*from any man*, may be cleared from ſin.

196. 'When he has been mortified by ab'ſtinence, and has returned from the paſturage, 'let him bend low to the other *Bráhmens*, who 'muſt thus interrogate him: "Art thou really "deſirous, good man, of re-admiſſion to an equa"lity with us?"

197. 'If he anſwer in the affirmative, let him 'give ſome graſs to the cows, and in the place, 'made pure by their having eaten on it, let the 'men of his claſs give their aſſent to his re'admiſſion.

198. 'HE, who has officiated at a ſacrifice for 'outcaſts, or burned the corpſe of a ſtranger, or 'performed rites to deſtroy the innocent, or 'made the impure ſacrifice, called *Ahína*, may 'expiate his guilt by three *prájápatya* penances.

199. 'A TWICE BORN man, who has rejected 'a ſuppliant for his protection, or taught the *Véda* 'on a forbidden day, may atone for his offence by 'ſubſiſting a whole year on barley alone.

200. 'HE, who has been bitten by a dog, a 'ſhakal, or an aſs, by any carnivorous animal fre- 'quenting a town, by a man, a horſe, a camel, or 'a boar, may be purified by ſtopping his breath 'during one repetition of the *gáyatrì*.

201. 'To eat only at the time of the ſixth 'meal, *or on the evening of every third day*, for a 'month, to repeat a *Sanhità* of the *Védas*, and to 'make *eight* oblations to fire, accompanied with '*eight* holy texts, are always an expiation for 'thoſe, who are excluded from ſociety at repaſts.

202. 'SHOULD a *Bráhmen* voluntarily aſcend a 'carriage borne by camels or drawn by aſſes, or 'deſignedly bathe quite naked, he may be ab- 'ſolved by one ſuppreſſion of breath, while he re- 'peats, in his mind, the moſt holy text.

203. 'HE, who has made any excretion, be- 'ing greatly preſſed, either without water *near* '*him*, or in water, may be purified by bathing 'in his clothes out of town, and by touching a 'cow.

204. 'FOR an omiſſion of the acts, which the '*Véda* commands to be conſtantly performed, 'and for a violation of the duties preſcribed to a 'houſekeeper, the atonement is faſting *one day*.

205. 'HE, who ſays huſh or piſh to a *Bráh*- '*men*, or thou *to a ſuperiour*, muſt *immediately* 'bathe, eat nothing for the reſt of the day, and 'appeaſe him by claſping his feet with reſpectful 'ſalutation.

206. 'For ſtriking a *Bráhmen* even with a 'blade of graſs, or tying him by the neck with a 'cloth,

'cloth, or overpowering him in argument, and 'adding contemptuous words, the offender muſt 'ſoothe him by falling proſtrate.

207. 'An aſſaulter of a *Bráhmen*, with intent 'to kill, ſhall remain in hell a hundred years; 'for actually ſtriking him *with the like intent*, a 'thouſand:

208. 'As many ſmall pellets of duſt as the 'blood of a *Bráhmen* collects on the ground, for 'ſo many thouſand years muſt the ſhedder of that 'blood be tormented in hell.

209. 'For a ſimple aſſault, the firſt *or common* 'penance muſt be performed; for a battery, the '*third or* very ſevere penance; but for ſhedding 'blood, *without killing*, both of thoſe penances.

210. 'To remove the ſins, for which no par'ticular penance has been ordained, the aſſembly 'muſt award a fit expiation, conſidering the ability 'of the ſinner *to perform it*, and the *nature of* '*the* ſin.

211. 'Those penances, by which a man may 'atone for his crimes, I now will deſcribe to you; 'penances, which have been performed by deities, 'by holy ſages, and by forefathers *of the human* '*race*.

212. 'When a twice born man performs the '*common* penance, *or that* of Praja'pati, he muſt, 'for three days, eat only in the morning; for 'three days, only in the evening; for three days, 'food unaſked *but preſented to him*; and for three 'more days, nothing.

213. 'Eating *for a whole day* the dung and 'urine of cows mixed with curds, milk, clarified 'butter, and water boiled with *cuſa*-graſs, and 'then faſting entirely for a *day and a* night, is the 'penance

'penance called *Sántapana*, either from the de-'vout man SANTAPANA, or from *tormenting*.

214. 'A twice born man performing the pe-'nance, called very ſevere, *in reſpect of the common*, 'muſt eat, as before, a ſingle mouthful, *or a ball 'of rice as large as a hen's egg* for three times 'three days; and for the laſt three days, muſt 'wholly abſtain from food.

215. 'A *Bráhmen*, performing the ardent pe-'nance, muſt ſwallow nothing but hot water, hot 'milk, hot clarified butter, and hot ſteam, each 'of them for three days ſucceſſively, performing 'an ablution and mortifying all his members.

216. 'A total faſt for twelve days *and nights*, 'by a penitent with his organs controlled and his 'mind attentive, is the penance named *parâca*, 'which expiates all *degrees of* guilt.

217. 'If he diminiſh his food by one mouthful '*each day*, during the dark fortnight, *eating fifteen 'mouthfuls on the day of the oppoſition*, and increaſe 'it, *in the ſame proportion*, during the bright fort-'night, *faſting entirely on the day of the conjunction*, 'and perform an ablution regularly at ſunriſe, 'noon, and ſunſet, this is the *chándráyana*, or the 'lunar penance:

218. 'Such is the *penance* called ant-ſhaped *or 'narrow in the middle*; but, if he perform the 'barley-ſhaped *or broad in the middle*, he muſt 'obſerve the ſame rule, beginning with the bright 'half month, and keeping under command his 'organs of action and ſenſe.

219. 'To perform the lunar penance of an 'anchoret, he muſt eat only eight mouthfuls of 'foreſt grains at noon, *for a whole month*, taking 'care to ſubdue his mind.

220. 'If a *Bráhmen* eat only four mouthfuls at

'sunrise, and four at sunset, *for a month*, keeping 'his organs controlled, he performs the lunar 'penance of children.

221. 'He, who, for a whole month, eats no 'more than thrice eighty mouthfuls of wild 'grains, *as he happens* by any means *to meet with them*, keeping his organs in subjection, shall attain the same abode with the regent of the moon:

222. 'The eleven *Rudras*, the twelve *A'dityas*, 'the eight *Vasus*, the *Maruts*, or genii of the 'winds, and the seven great *Rishis*, have performed this lunar penance as a security from 'all evil.

223. 'The oblation *of clarified butter* to fire 'must every day be made by *the penitent* himself, 'accompanied with the mighty words, *earth*, *sky*, '*heaven*; he must perfectly abstain from injury 'to sentient creatures, from falsehood, from wrath, 'and from all crooked ways.

224. 'Or, thrice each day and thrice each 'night for a month, the penitent may plunge into 'water, clothed in his mantle, and at no time conversing with a woman, a *Súdra*, or an outcast.

225. 'Let him be always in motion, sitting 'and rising alternately; or, if unable *to be thus restless*, let him sleep low *on the bare ground*; 'chaste as a student of the *Véda*, bearing the sacred zone and staff, showing reverence to his 'preceptor, to the gods, and to priests;

226. 'Perpetually must he repeat the *gáyatrí*, 'and other pure texts to the best of his knowledge: thus in all penances for absolution from 'sin, must he vigilantly employ himself.

227. 'By these expiations are twice born men 'absolved, whose offences are publickly known, '*and are mischievous by their example*; but for

'sins not publick, the assembly of priests must 'award them penances, with holy texts and ob- 'lations to fire.

228. 'By open confession, by repentance, by 'devotion, and by reading the scripture, a sinner 'may be released from his guilt; or by alms- 'giving, in case of his inability *to perform the other 'acts of religion.*

229. 'In proportion as a man, who has com- 'mitted a sin, shall truly and voluntarily confess 'it, so far he is disengaged from that offence, like 'a snake from his slough;

230. 'And, in proportion as his heart sincerely 'loathes his evil deed, so far shall his vital spirit 'be freed from the taint of it.

231. 'If he commit sin, and actually repent, 'that sin shall be removed from him; but if he 'merely say, "I will sin thus no more," he can 'only be released by an actual abstinence from 'guilt.

232. 'Thus revolving in his mind the cer- 'tainty of retribution in a future state, let him 'be constantly good in thoughts, words, and 'action.

233. 'If he desire complete remission of any 'foul act which he has committed, either ig- 'norantly or knowingly, let him beware of com- 'mitting it again: *for the second fault his penance 'must be doubled.*

234. 'If, having performed any expiation, he 'feel not a perfect satisfaction of conscience, let 'him repeat the same devout act, until his con- 'science be perfectly satisfied.

235. 'All the bliss of deities and of men is 'declared by sages, who discern the sense of the

'*Véda,* to have in devotion its cause, in devotion 'its continuance, in devotion its fullness.

236. 'Devotion is *equal to the performance of 'all duties; it is* divine knowledge in a *Bráhmen*; 'it is defence of the people in a *Cshatriya*; de-'votion is *the* business *of trade and agriculture* in 'a *Vaisya*; devotion is dutiful service in a *Súdra.*

237. 'Holy sages, with subdued passions, feed-'ing only on food, roots, and air, by devotion 'alone are enabled to survey the three worlds, '*terrestrial, ethereal, and celestial,* peopled with 'animal creatures, locomotive and fixed.

238. 'Perfect health, or unfailing medicines, 'divine learning, and the various mansions of 'deities, are acquired by devotion alone: their 'efficient cause is devotion.

239. 'Whatever is hard to be traversed, what-'ever is hard to be acquired, whatever is hard to 'be visited, whatever is hard to be performed, all 'this may be accomplished by true devotion; 'for the difficulty of devotion is the greatest 'of all.

240. 'Even sinners in the highest degree, and 'of course the other offenders, are absolved from 'guilt by austere devotion well practised.

241. '*Souls, that animate* worms, and insects, 'serpents, moths, beasts, birds, and vegetables, 'attain heaven by the power of devotion.

242. 'Whatever sin has been conceived in the 'hearts of men, uttered in their speech, or com-'mitted in their bodily acts, they speedily burn 'it all away by devotion, if they preserve devo-'tion as their best wealth.

243. 'Of a priest, whom devotion has purified, 'the divine spirits accept the sacrifices, and grant 'the desires with ample increase.

 244. 'Even

244. 'Even BRAHMA', lord of creatures, by 'devotion enacted this code of laws; and the 'sages by devotion acquired a knowledge of the '*Védas*.

245. 'Thus the gods themselves, observing 'in this universe the incomparable power of de-'votion, have proclaimed aloud the transcendent 'excellence of pious austerity.

246. 'By reading each day as much as possible 'of the *Véda*, by performing the *five* great sa-'craments, and by forgiving all injuries, even sins 'of the highest degree shall be soon effaced:

247. 'As fire consumes in an instant, with his 'bright flame, the wood that has been placed on 'it, thus, with the flame of knowledge, a *Bráh-'men*, who understands the *Véda*, consumes all sin.

248. 'Thus has been declared, according to 'law, the mode of atoning for open sins: now 'learn the mode of obtaining absolution for secret 'offences.

249. 'SIXTEEN suppressions of the breath, '*while the holiest of texts is repeated* with the three 'mighty words, and the triliteral syllable, con-'tinued each day for a month, absolve even the 'slayer of a *Bráhmen* from his hidden faults.

250. 'Even a drinker of spirituous liquor is 'absolved by repeating each day the text *apa* used 'by the sage CAUTSA, or that beginning with '*preti* used by VASISHT'HA, or that called *má-'hitra*, or that, of which the first word is *suddha-'vatyah*.

251. 'By repeating *each day*, *for a month*, the 'text *ásyavámiya*, or the hymn *Sivasancalpa*, the 'stealer of gold from a priest becomes instantly 'pure.

252. 'He, who has violated the bed of his

'preceptor, is cleared *from ſecret faults* by repeat-
'ing *ſixteen times a day* the text *haviſhyantíya*, or
'that beginning with *na tamanhah*, or by revolv-
'ing in his mind the *ſixteen* holy verſes, called
'*Pauruſha*.

253. 'The man, who deſires to expiate *his*
'*hidden* ſins, great and ſmall, muſt repeat *once a*
'*day*, for a year, the text *ava*, or the text *yat-*
'*cinchida*.

254. 'He, who has accepted an illegal preſent,
'or eaten prohibited food, may be cleanſed in
'three days by repeating the text *taratſamandíya*.

255. 'Though he have committed many ſecret
'ſins, he ſhall be purified by repeating, for a
'month, the text *ſómáraudra*, or the three texts
'*áryamna*, while he bathes in a ſacred ſtream.

256. 'A grievous offender muſt repeat the
'ſeven verſes, beginning with INDRA, for half a
'year; and he, who has defiled water with any
'impurity, muſt ſit a whole year ſubſiſting by
'alms.

257. 'A twice born man, who ſhall offer
'clarified butter for a year, with *eight* texts ap-
'propriated to *eight* ſeveral oblations, or with the
'text *na mé*, ſhall efface a ſin even of an extreme-
'ly high degree.

258. 'He, who had committed a crime of the
'firſt degree, ſhall be abſolved, if he attend a
'herd of kine for a year, mortify his organs, and
'continually repeat the texts beginning with *pá-*
'*vamánī*, living ſolely on food given in charity:

259. 'Or, if he thrice repeat a *Sanhitá* of the
'*Védas*, or *a large portion of them with all the*
'mantras *and* bráhmanas, dwelling in a foreſt with
'ſubdued organs, and purified by three *parácas*,

'he

'he ſhall be ſet free from all ſins how heinous 'ſoever.

260. 'Or he ſhall be releaſed from all deadly 'ſins, if he faſt three days, with his members 'mortified, and twice a day plunge into water, 'thrice repeating the text *aghamarſhana:*

261. 'As the ſacrifice of a horſe, the king of 'ſacrifices, removes all ſin, thus the text *agha*-'*marſhana* deſtroys all offences.

262. 'A prieſt, who ſhould retain in his me-'mory the whole *Rigvéda,* would be abſolved 'from guilt, even if he had ſlain the inhabitants 'of the three worlds, and had eaten food from the 'fouleſt hands.

263. 'By thrice repeating the *mantras* and '*bráhmanas* of the *Rich,* or thoſe of the *Yajuſh,* 'or thoſe of the *Sáman,* with the *upaniſhads,* he 'ſhall perfectly be cleanſed from every poſſible 'taint:

264. 'As a clod of earth, caſt into a great lake, 'ſinks in it, thus is every ſinful act ſubmerged in 'the triple *Véda.*

265. 'The diviſions of the *Rich,* the ſeveral 'branches of the *Yajuſh,* and the manifold ſtrains 'of the *Sáman,* muſt be conſidered as forming the 'triple *Véda:* he knows the *Véda,* who knows 'them collectively.

266. 'The primary triliteral ſyllable, in which 'the three *Védas* themſelves are compriſed, muſt 'be kept ſecret, as another triple *Véda:* he knows 'the *Véda,* who *diſtinctly* knows *the myſtick ſenſe of* 'that word.'

CHAPTER THE TWELFTH.

On Transmigration and Final Beatitude.

1. 'O THOU, who art free from sin,' *said the devout sages,* 'thou hast declared the whole system 'of duties ordained for the four classes of men: 'explain to us now, from the first principles, the 'ultimate retribution for their deeds.'

2. BHRIGU, whose heart was the pure essence of virtue, who proceeded from MENU himself, thus addressed the great sages: 'Hear the in-'fallible rules for *the fruit of* deeds in this uni-'verse.

3. 'ACTION, either mental, verbal, or cor-'poreal, bears good or evil fruit, *as itself is good 'or evil*; and from the actions of men proceed 'their various transmigrations in the highest, the 'mean, and the lowest degree:

4. 'Of that three-fold action, connected with 'bodily functions, disposed in three classes, and 'consisting of ten orders, be it known in this 'world, that the heart is the instigator.

5. 'Devising means to appropriate the wealth 'of other men, resolving on any forbidden deed, 'and

'and conceiving notions of atheiſm or mate-
'rialiſm, are the three bad acts of the mind:

6. 'Scurrilous language, falſehood, indiſcri-
'minate backbiting, and uſeleſs tattle, are the
'four bad acts of the tongue:

7. 'Taking effects not given, hurting ſentient
'creatures without the ſanction of law, and cri-
'minal intercourſe with the wife of another, are
'the three bad acts of the body; *and all the ten*
'*have their oppoſites, which are good in an equal*
'*degree.*

8. 'A rational creature has a reward or a
'puniſhment for mental acts, in his mind; for
'verbal acts, in his organs of ſpeech; for corpo-
'real acts, in his bodily frame.

9. 'For ſinful acts moſtly corporeal, a man
'ſhall aſſume *after death* a vegetable or mineral
'form; for ſuch acts moſtly verbal, the form of
'a bird or a beaſt; for acts moſtly mental, the
'loweſt of human conditions:

10. 'He, whoſe firm underſtanding obtains a
'command over his words, a command over his
'thoughts, and a command over his whole body,
'may juſtly be called a *tridandi*, or *triple com-*
'*mander*; *not a mere anchoret, who bears three*
'*viſible ſtaves.*

11. 'The man, who exerts this triple ſelf-
'command with reſpect to all animated creatures,
'wholly ſubduing both luſt and wrath, ſhall by
'thoſe means attain beatitude.

12. 'THAT ſubſtance, which gives a power of
'motion to the body, the wiſe call *cſhétrajnya*, or
'*jívátman*, the vital ſpirit; and that body, which
'thence derives active functions, they name *bhú-*
'*tátman*, or *compoſed of elements*:

13. 'Another internal ſpirit, called *mahat*, or
'*the*

'*the great ſoul*, attends the birth of all creatures
'imbodied, and thence, in all mortal forms, is
'conveyed a perception either pleaſing or painful.

14. 'Thoſe two, the vital ſpirit and reaſonable
'ſoul, are cloſely united with *five* elements, but
'connected with the ſupreme ſpirit, or divine
'eſſence, which pervades all beings high and low:

15. 'From the ſubſtance of that *ſupreme ſpirit*,
'are diffuſed, *like ſparks from fire*, innumerable
'vital ſpirits, which perpetually give motion to
'creatures exalted and baſe.

16. 'By the vital ſouls of thoſe men, who
'have committed ſins *in the body reduced to aſhes*,
'another body, compoſed of *nerves with* five
'ſenſations, in order to be ſuſceptible of torment,
'ſhall certainly be aſſumed after death;

17. 'And, being intimately united with thoſe
'minute nervous particles, according to their diſ-
'tribution, they ſhall feel, in that new body,
'the pangs inflicted in each caſe by the ſentence
'of YAMA.

18. 'When the vital ſoul has gathered the
'fruit of ſins, which ariſe from a love of ſenſual
'pleaſure, but muſt produce miſery, and, when
'its taint has thus been removed, it approaches
'again thoſe two moſt effulgent eſſences, *the in-*
'*tellectual ſoul and the divine ſpirit*:

19. 'They two, cloſely conjoined, examine
'without remiſſion the virtues and vices of that
'ſenſitive ſoul, according to its union with which
'it acquires pleaſure or pain in the preſent and
'future worlds.

20. 'If the vital ſpirit had practiſed virtue
'for the moſt part, and vice in a ſmall degree,
'it enjoys delight in celeſtial abodes, clothed
'with

'with a body formed of pure elementary particles;

21. 'But, if it had generally been addicted to 'vice, and seldom attended to virtue, then shall 'it be deserted by those pure elements, and, *having a coarser body of sensible nerves*, it feels the 'pains to which YAMA shall doom it:

22. 'Having endured those torments according 'to the sentence of YAMA, and its taint being 'almost removed, it again reaches those five pure 'elements in the order of their natural distribution.

23. 'Let each man, considering with his intellectual powers these migrations of the soul, 'according to its virtue or vice, *into a region of bliss or pain*, continually fix his heart on virtue.

24. 'BE it known, that the three qualities of 'the rational soul are a tendency to goodness, to 'passion, and to darkness; and, endued with one 'or more of them, it remains incessantly attached 'to all these created substances:

25. 'When any one of the *three* qualities predominates in a mortal frame, it renders the 'imbodied spirit eminently distinguished for that 'quality.

26. 'Goodness is declared to be true knowledge; darkness, gross ignorance; passion, an 'emotion of desire or aversion: such is the compendious description of those qualities, which 'attend all souls.

27. 'When a man perceives, in the reasonable 'soul, a disposition tending to virtuous love, unclouded with any malignant passion, clear as the 'purest light, let him recognise it as the quality 'of goodness:

28. 'A temper of mind, which gives uneasiness

'and

'and produces disaffection, let him consider as 'the adverse quality of passion, ever agitating 'imbodied spirits:

29. 'That indistinct, inconceivable, unaccountable disposition of a mind naturally sensual, and 'clouded with infatuation, let him know to be 'the quality of darkness.

30. 'Now will I declare at large the various 'acts, in the highest, middle, and lowest degrees, 'which proceed from those three dispositions of 'mind.

31. 'Study of scripture, austere devotion, sacred knowledge, corporeal purity, command 'over the organs, performance of duties, and 'meditation on the divine spirit, accompany the 'good quality of the soul:

32. 'Interested motives for acts *of religion or morality*, perturbation of mind on slight occasions, commission of acts forbidden by law, and 'habitual indulgence in selfish gratifications, are 'attendant on the quality of passion:

33. 'Covetousness, indolence, avarice, detraction, atheism, omission of prescribed acts, a 'habit of soliciting favours, and inattention to 'necessary business, belong to the dark quality.

34. 'Of those three qualities, as they appear 'in the three times, *past, present, and future*, the 'following in order *from the lowest* may be considered as a short *but certain* criterion.

35. 'Let the wise consider, as belonging to 'the quality of darkness, every act, which a man 'is ashamed of having done, of doing, or of 'going to do:

36. 'Let them consider, as proceeding from 'the quality of passion, every act, by which a 'man seeks exaltation and celebrity in this world,

'though

'though he may not be much afflicted, if he fail 'of attaining his object:

37. 'To the quality of goodneſs belongs every 'act, by which he hopes to acquire divine know-'ledge, which he is never aſhamed of doing, and 'which brings placid joy to his conſcience.

38. 'Of the dark quality, as deſcribed, the 'principal object is pleaſure; of the paſſionate, 'worldly proſperity; but of the good quality, 'the chief object is virtue: the laſt mentioned '*objects* are ſuperiour in dignity.

39. 'Such tranſmigrations, as the ſoul procures 'in this univerſe by each of thoſe qualities, I now 'will declare in order ſuccinctly.

40. 'Souls, endued with goodneſs, attain al-'ways the ſtate of deities; thoſe filled with am-'bitious paſſions, the condition of men; and 'thoſe immerſed in darkneſs, the nature of beaſts: 'this is the triple order of tranſmigration.

41. 'Each of thoſe three tranſmigrations, cauſed 'by the ſeveral qualities, muſt alſo be conſidered 'as three-fold, the loweſt, the mean, and the 'higheſt, according to as many diſtinctions of 'acts and of knowledge.

42. 'Vegetable and mineral ſubſtances, worms, 'inſects, and reptiles, ſome very minute, ſome 'rather larger, fiſh, ſnakes, tortoiſes, cattle, 'ſhakals, are the loweſt forms, to which the dark 'quality leads:

43. 'Elephants, horſes, men of the ſervile claſs, 'and contemptible *Mléch'has*, or *barbarians*, lions, 'tigers, and boars, are the mean ſtates procured 'by the quality of darkneſs:

44. 'Dancers and ſingers, birds, and deceitful 'men, giants and blood-thirſty ſavages, are the 'higheſt conditions, to which the dark quality can 'aſcend.

45. '*Jhallas*,

45. '*J'hallas*, or cudgel players, *Mallas*, or 'boxers and wrestlers, *Natas*, or actors, those 'who teach the use of weapons, and those who are 'addicted to gaming or drinking, are the lowest 'forms occasioned by the passionate quality:

46. 'Kings, men of the fighting class, domestick 'priests of kings, and men skilled in the war of 'controversy, are the middle states caused by the 'quality of passion:

47. '*Gandharvas*, or aerial musicians, *Guhyacas* 'and *Yacshas*, or servants and companions of 'CUVE'RA, genii attending superiour gods, as the '*Vidyádharas* and others, together with various 'companies of *Apsarases* or nymphs, are the 'highest of those forms, which the quality of 'passion attains.

48. 'Hermits, religious mendicants, other '*Bráhmens*, such orders of demigods as are wafted 'in airy cars, genii of the signs and lunar mansions, and *Daityas*, or the offspring of DITI, 'are the lowest of states procured by the quality 'of goodness:

49. 'Sacrificers, holy sages, deities of the 'lower heaven, genii of the *Védas*, regents of stars '*not in the paths of the sun and moon*, divinities of 'years, *Pitrĭs* or progenitors of mankind, and the 'demigods named *Sádhyas*, are the middle forms, 'to which the good quality conveys *all spirits* '*moderately endued with it*:

50. 'BRAHMA' with four faces, creators of 'worlds *under him, as* MARÍCHI *and others*, the 'genius of virtue, the divinities presiding over (*two* '*principles of nature in the philosophy of* CAPILA) '*mahat*, or the *mighty*, and *avyacta*, or *unperceived*; 'are the highest conditions, to which, by the 'good quality, souls are exalted.

51. 'This

51. 'This triple ſyſtem of tranſmigrations, in 'which each claſs has three orders, according to 'actions of three kinds, and which compriſes all 'animated beings, has been revealed in its full 'extent:

52. 'Thus, by indulging the ſenſual appetites, 'and by neglecting the performance of duties, 'the baſeſt of men, ignorant of ſacred expiations, 'aſſume the baſeſt forms.

53. 'WHAT particular bodies the vital ſpirit 'enters in this world, and in conſequence of what 'ſins here committed, now hear at large and in 'order.

54. 'Sinners, in the firſt degree, having paſſed 'through terrible regions of torture for a great 'number of years, are condemned to the following 'births, at the cloſe of that period, *to efface all re-'mains of their ſin.*

55. 'The ſlayer of a *Bráhmen* muſt enter *ac-'cording to the circumſtances of his crime* the body 'of a dog, a boar, an aſs, a camel, a bull, a goat, 'a ſheep, a ſtag, a bird, a *Chandála*, or a *Puccaſa.*

56. 'A prieſt, who has drunk ſpirituous liquor, 'ſhall migrate into the form of a ſmaller or larger 'worm or inſect, of a moth, of a fly feeding on 'ordure, or of ſome ravenous animal.

57. 'He, who ſteals the gold of a prieſt, ſhall 'paſs a thouſand times into the bodies of ſpiders, 'of ſnakes and cameleons, of *crocodiles and other* 'aquatick monſters, or of miſchievous blood-'ſucking demons.

58. 'He, who violates the bed of his *natural* '*or ſpiritual* father, migrates a hundred times into 'the form of graſſes, of ſhrubs with crowded 'ſtems, or of creeping and twining plants, of '*vultures and other* carnivorous animals, of *lions*

'*and*

'*and other* beasts with sharp teeth, or of *tigers and* '*other* cruel brutes.

59. 'They who hurt any sentient beings, are 'born *cats and other* eaters of raw flesh; they who 'taste what ought not to be tasted, maggots or 'small flies; they who steal *ordinary things*, de-'vourers of each other: they who embrace very 'low women, become restless ghosts.

60. 'He who has held intercourse with de-'graded men, or been criminally connected with 'the wife of another, or stolen *common things* from 'a priest, shall be changed into a spirit called '*Brahmarácshasa*.

61. 'The wretch, who through covetousness 'has stolen *rubies or other* gems, pearls, or coral, 'or precious things, of which there are many sorts, 'shall be born *in the tribe of goldsmiths, or* among '*birds called* hémacáras, *or gold makers*.

62. 'If a man steal grain in the husk, he shall 'be born a rat; if a yellow mixed metal, a gan-'der; if water, a *plava*, or diver; if honey, a 'great stinging gnat; if milk, a crow; if ex-'pressed juice, a dog; if clarified butter, an ich-'neumon weasel;

63. 'If he steal flesh meat, a vulture; if any 'sort of fat, the water-bird *madgu*; if oil, a blatta, 'or oil-drinking beetle; if salt, a cicada or cricket; 'if curds, the bird *valáca*;

64. 'If silken clothes, the bird *tittiri*; if wo-'ven flax, a frog; if cotton cloth, the water bird '*crauncha*; if a cow, the lizard *gódhá*; if molasses, 'the bird *vágguda*;

65. If exquisite perfumes, a musk-rat; if pot-'herbs, a peacock; if dressed grain in any of its 'various forms, a porcupine; if raw grain, a 'hedge-hog;

66. ‘ If he ſteal fire, the bird *vaca* ; if a houſe-
‘ hold utenſil, an ichneumon fly ; if dyed cloth, the
‘ bird *chacora* ;

67. ‘ If a deer or an elephant, he ſhall be born
‘ a wolf; if a horſe, a tiger ; if roots or fruit, an ape ;
‘ if a woman, a bear ; if water from a jar, the bird
‘ *chátaca* ; if carriages, a camel ; if ſmall cattle, a
‘ goat.

68. ‘ That man, who deſignedly takes away the
‘ property of another, or eats any holy cakes not
‘ firſt preſented *to the deity* at a ſolemn rite, ſhall
‘ inevitably ſink to the condition of a brute.

69. ‘ Women, who have committed ſimilar
‘ thefts, incur a ſimilar taint, and ſhall be paired
‘ with thoſe male beaſts in the form of their
‘ females.

70. ‘ If any of the four claſſes omit, without
‘ urgent neceſſity, the performance of their ſeveral
‘ duties, they ſhall migrate into ſinful bodies, and
‘ become ſlaves to their foes.

71. ‘ Should a *Bráhmen* omit his peculiar duty,
‘ he ſhall be changed into a demon called *Ulcá-*
‘ *muc'ha* or *with a mouth like a firebrand*, who de-
‘ vours what has been vomited ; a *Cſhatriya* into
‘ a demon called *Catapútana*, who feeds on ordure
‘ and carrion ;

72. ‘ A *Vaiſya*, into an evil being called *Mai-*
‘ *trácſhajyótica*, who eats purulent carcaſſes ; and
‘ a *Súdra*, who neglects his occupations, becomes
‘ a foul imbodied ſpirit called *Chailáſaca*, who
‘ feeds on lice.

73. ‘ As far as vital ſouls, addicted to ſenſu-
‘ ality, indulge themſelves in forbidden pleaſures,
‘ even to the ſame degree ſhall the acuteneſs of
‘ their ſenſes be raiſed *in their future bodies, that*
‘ *they may endure analogous pains* ;

74. 'And, in consequence of their folly, they 'shall be doomed, as often as they repeat their cri- 'minal acts, to pains more and more intense in 'despicable forms on this earth.

75. 'They shall first have a sensation of agony 'in *Tamisra* or *utter darkness*, and in other seats 'of horrour; in *Asipatravana*, or *the sword-leaved 'forest*, and in different places of binding fast and 'of rending:

76. 'Multifarious tortures await them: they 'shall be mangled by ravens and owls, shall swal- 'low cakes boiling hot; shall walk over inflamed 'sands, and shall feel the pangs of being baked 'like the vessels of a potter:

77. 'They shall assume the forms of beasts con- 'tinually miserable, and suffer alternate afflictions 'from extremities of cold and of heat, surrounded 'with terrours of various kinds:

78. 'More than once shall they lie in different 'wombs; and, after agonizing births, be con- 'demned to severe captivity, and to servile atten- 'dance on creatures like themselves:

79. 'Then shall follow separations from kindred 'and friends, forced residence with the wicked, 'painful gains and ruinous losses of wealth; 'friendships hardly acquired, and at length 'changed into enmities,

80. 'Old age without resource, diseases at- 'tended with anguish, pangs of innumerable sorts, 'and, lastly, unconquerable death.

81. 'With whatever disposition of mind a 'man shall perform in this life any act *religious 'or moral*, in a future body endued with the same 'quality, shall he receive his retribution.

82. 'Thus has been revealed to you the system

‘ of punishments for evil deeds: next learn those ‘ acts of a *Bráhmen* which lead to eternal bliss.

83. ‘ Studying and comprehending the *Véda*, ‘ practising pious austerities, acquiring divine ‘ knowledge *of law and philosophy*, command over ‘ the organs of sense and action, avoiding all injury ‘ to sentient creatures, and showing reverence to ‘ a *natural and spiritual* father, are the chief ‘ branches of duty which ensure final happiness.’

84. ‘ Among all those good acts performed in ‘ this world, *said the sages*, is no single act held ‘ more powerful than the rest in leading men to ‘ beatitude?’

85. ‘ Of all those duties, *answered* Bhrĭgu, the ‘ principal is to acquire from the *Upanishads* a ‘ true knowledge of one supreme GOD; that is ‘ the most exalted of all sciences, because it en- ‘ sures immortality:

86. ‘ In this life, indeed, as well as the next, ‘ the study of the *Véda*, to acquire a knowledge of ‘ GOD, is held the most efficacious of those six ‘ duties in procuring felicity to man;

87. ‘ For in the knowledge and adoration of ‘ one GOD, which the *Véda* teaches, all the rules ‘ of good conduct, *before-mentioned* in order, are ‘ fully comprised.

88. ‘ The ceremonial duty, prescribed by the ‘ *Véda*, is of two kinds; *one* connected with this ‘ world, and causing prosperity on earth; *the* ‘ *other* abstracted from it, and procuring bliss in ‘ heaven.

89. ‘ A religious act, proceeding from selfish ‘ views in this world, *as a sacrifice for rain*, or in ‘ the next, *as a pious oblation in hope of a future* ‘ *reward*, is declared to be concrete and interested; ‘ but

'but an act performed with a knowledge of God, 'and without self-love, is called abstract and dis-'interested.

90. 'He, who frequently performs interested 'rites, attains an equal station with the regents of 'the lower heaven: but he, who frequently per-'forms disinterested acts of religion, becomes for 'ever exempt from *a body composed of* the five ele-'ments:

91. 'Equally perceiving the supreme soul in 'all beings, and all beings in the supreme soul, he 'sacrifices his own spirit by fixing it on the spirit 'of GOD, and approaches the nature of that sole 'divinity who shines by his own effulgence.

92. 'Thus must the chief of the twice born, 'though he neglect the ceremonial rites mentioned 'in the *Sástras*, be diligent alike in attaining 'a knowledge of God, and in repeating the '*Véda*:

93. 'Such is the advantageous privilege of 'those, who have a double birth *from their natu-'ral mothers and from the* gáyatrì *their spiritual 'mother*, especially of a *Bráhmen*; since the twice 'born man, by performing this duty, but not 'otherwise, may soon acquire endless felicity.

94. 'To patriarchs, to deities, and to man-'kind, the scripture is an eye giving constant 'light; nor could the *Véda Sástra* have been made 'by human faculties; nor can it be measured by 'human reason *unassisted by revealed glosses and com-'ments*: this is a sure proposition.

95. 'Such codes of law as are not grounded 'on the *Véda*, and the various heterodox theories 'of men, produce no good fruit after death; 'for they all are declared to have their basis on 'darkness.

96. ‘ All ſyſtems which are repugnant to the *Véda*, muſt bave been compoſed by mortals, and ſhall ſoon periſh: their modern date proves them vain and falſe.

97. ‘ The three worlds, the four claſſes of men, and their four diſtinct orders, with all that has been, all that is, and all that will be, are made known by the *Véda*:

98. ‘ The nature of ſound, of tangible and viſible ſhape, of taſte, and of odour, the fifth object of ſenſe, is clearly explained in the *Véda* alone, together with the three qualities of mind, the births attended with them, and the acts which they occaſion.

99. ‘ All creatures are ſuſtained by the primeval *Véda Sáſtra*, which the wiſe therefore hold ſupreme, becauſe it is the ſupreme ſource of proſperity to this creature, man.

100. ‘ Command of armies, royal authority, power of inflicting puniſhment, and ſovereign dominion over all nations, he only well deſerves, who perfectly underſtands the *Véda Sáſtra*.

101. ‘ As fire with augmented force burns up even humid trees, thus he, who well knows the *Véda*, burns out the taint of ſin, which has infected his ſoul.

102. ‘ He who completely knows the ſenſe of the *Véda Sáſtra*, while he remains in any one of the four orders, approaches the divine nature, even though he ſojourn in this low world.

103. ‘ They who have read many books, are more exalted than ſuch as have ſeldom ſtudied they who retain what they have read, than forgetful readers; they who fully underſtand, than ſuch as only remember; and they who

‘ perform

'perform their known duty, than ſuch men as 'barely know it.

104. 'Devotion and ſacred knowledge are the 'beſt means by which a *Bráhmen* can arrive at 'beatitude: by devotion he may deſtroy guilt; 'by ſacred knowledge he may acquire immortal 'glory.

105. 'Three modes of proof, ocular demon-'ſtration, logical inference, and the authority of 'thoſe various books, which are deduced from the '*Véda*, muſt be well underſtood by that man who 'ſeeks a diſtinct knowledge of all his duties.

106. 'He alone comprehends the ſyſtem of 'duties, religious and civil, who can reaſon, by 'rules of logic agreeable to the *Véda*, on the 'general heads of that ſyſtem, as revealed by the 'holy ſages.

107. 'Theſe rules of conduct, which lead to 'ſupreme bliſs, have been exactly and compre-'henſively declared: the more ſecret learning of 'this *Mánava Sáſtra* ſhall now be diſcloſed.

108. 'If it be aſked, how the law ſhall be aſ-'certained, when particular caſes are not com-'priſed *under any of the general rules, the an-'ſwer is this:* "That, which well inſtructed "*Bráhmens* propound, ſhall be held inconteſtable "law."

109. 'Well inſtructed *Bráhmens* are they who 'can adduce ocular proof from the ſcripture it-'ſelf, having ſtudied, as the law ordains, the *Vé-'das* and their extended branches, or *Védangas*, '*Mímánſá*, *Nyáya*, *Dherma ſáſtra*, *Puránas*:

110 'A point of law, *before not expreſsly re-'vealed*, which ſhall be decided by an aſſembly of 'ten ſuch virtuous *Bráhmens* under one chief, or, '*if ten be not procurable*, of three ſuch, under one 'preſident, let no man controvert.

111. 'The

111. 'The assembly of ten under a chief, ' *either the king himself, or a judge appointed by him,* ' must consist of three, each of them peculiarly ' conversant with one of the three *Védas*; of a ' fourth, skilled in the *Nyáya*, and a fifth in the *Mímánsà* philosophy; of a sixth, who has particularly ' studied the *Niructa*; a seventh, who has applied ' himself most assiduously to the *Dhermasástra*; ' and of three *universal scholars*, who are in the ' three first orders.

112. 'One, who has chiefly studied the *Rĭg-véda*, a second who principally knows the *Yajush*, and a third best acquainted with the *Saman*, ' are the assembly of three under a head, who may ' remove all doubts, both in law and casuistry.

113. 'Even the decision of one priest, *if more cannot be assembled*, who perfectly knows the principles of the *Védas*, must be considered as law of ' the highest authority; not the opinion of myriads, who have no sacred knowledge.

114. 'Many thousands of *Bráhmens* cannot ' form a legal assembly for the decision of contests, ' if they have not performed the duties of a regular studentship, are unacquainted with scriptural ' texts, and subsist only by *the name of* their sacerdotal class.

115. 'The sin of that man, to whom dunces, ' pervaded by the quality of darkness, propound ' the law, of which they are themselves ignorant, ' shall pass, increased a hundred-fold, to the wretches ' who propound it.

116. 'This comprehensive system of duties, ' the chief cause of ultimate felicity, has been declared to you; and the *Bráhmen*, who never departs from it, shall attain a superiour state above.

117. 'Thus did the all-wise Menu, who pos-

'sesses extensive dominion, and blazes with heavenly splendour, disclose to me, from his benevolence to mankind, this transcendent system of law, which must be kept devoutly concealed *from persons unfit to receive it*.

118. 'LET every *Bráhmen* with fixed attention consider all nature, both visible and invisible, as existing in the divine spirit; for, when he contemplates the boundless universe existing in the divine spirit, he cannot give his heart to iniquity:

119. 'The divine spirit alone is the whole assemblage of gods; all worlds are seated in the divine spirit; and the divine spirit, no doubt, produces, *by a chain of causes and effects consistent with free-will*, the connected series of acts performed by imbodied souls.

120. 'We may contemplate the subtil ether in the cavities of his body; the air in his muscular motion and sensitive nerves; the supreme *solar and igneous* light, in his digestive heat and his visual organs; in his corporeal fluids, water; in the terrene parts of his fabric, earth;

121. 'In his heart, the moon; in his auditory nerves, the guardians of eight regions; in his progressive motion, VISHNU; in his muscular force, HARA; in his organs of speech, AGNI; in excretion, MITRA; in procreation, BRAHMÁ:

122. 'But he must consider the supreme omnipresent intelligence as the sovereign lord of them all, *by whose energy alone they exist*; a spirit, *by no means the object of any sense*, which can only be conceived by a mind *wholly abstracted from matter, and as it were* slumbering; but which, *for the purpose of assisting his meditation*, he may imagine more subtil than the finest conceivable essence, and more bright than the purest gold.

123. 'Him some adore as transcendently pre-

'sent

'sent in elementary fire; others, in MENU, lord of 'creatures, *or an immediate agent in the creation*; 'some, as more distinctly present in INDRA, *regent of the clouds and the atmosphere*; others, in pure 'air; others, as the most High Eternal Spirit.

124. 'It is He, who, pervading all beings in 'five elemental forms, causes them, by the gra-'dations of birth, growth, and dissolution, to re-'volve in this world *until they deserve beatitude*, 'like the wheels of a car.

125. 'Thus the man, who perceives in his 'own soul the supreme soul present in all creatures, 'acquires equanimity toward them all, and shall 'be absolved at last in the highest essence, even 'that of the Almighty himself.'

126. HERE ended the sacred instructor; and every twice born man, who, attentively reading this *Mánava Sástra*, promulgated by BHRĬGU, shall become habitually virtuous, will attain the beatitude which he seeks.

GENERAL NOTE.

The learned *Hindus* are unanimoufly of opinion, that many laws enacted by Menu, their oldeft reputed legiflator, were confined to the three firft ages of the world, and have no force in the prefent age, in which a few of them are certainly obfolete; and they ground their opinion on the following texts, which are collected in a work entitled, *Madana ratna pradípa.*

I. Cratu: In the *Cali* age a fon muft not be begotten *on a widow* by the brother *of the deceafed hufband*; nor muft a damfel, *once* given away *in marriage*, be given a *fecond time*; nor muft a bull be offered in a facrifice; nor muft a water-pot be carried *by a ftudent in theology.*

II. Vrĭhaspati: 1. Appointments *of kinfmen to beget children on widows, or married women, when the hufbands are deceafed or impotent*, are mentioned by the fage Menu, but forbidden by himfelf, with a view to the order of the four ages; no fuch act can be legally done in this age by any others *than the hufband.*

2. In the firft and fecond ages men were endued with true piety and found knowledge; fo *they were* in the third age; but in the fourth, a diminution of their *moral and intellectual* powers was ordained *by their Creator:*

3. Thus

to the three first ages; that of the *Smrĭti*, or sacred code, is quoted without the name of the legislator; and that the prohibition, in any age, of *self-defence*, even against *Bráhmens*, is repugnant to a text of SUMANTU, to the precept and example of CRISHNA himself, according to the *Mahábhárat*, and even to a sentence in the *Véda*, by which every man is commanded *to defend his own life from all* violent aggressors.

THE END.

CONTENTS.